The Dancing Woman

This is a picture of a person for whom the Lord has turned mourning into dancing. Only the Lord can turn sorrow into joy for you. Can you see yourself in her freedom from care? If you can, give Him praise! If you cannot, know He has this joy for you; you're not alone, and read on!

> Psalm 30:11-12: *You have turned for me my mourning into dancing; You have loosed my sackcloth and girded me with gladness, that my soul may sing praise to You and not be silent. O Lord my God, I will give thanks to You forever!*

The Lily of the Valley

In the Song of Songs, the Shulamite says of herself:

> *"I am the rose of Sharon, The lily of the valleys"* (Song of Songs 2:1)

The lily of the valley is a delicate, cupped white flower which hangs down its head. When we see many together, they look like tiny white wedding bells or wedding dresses. These flowers have a sweet aroma that can be detected from a long distance. They are one of God's magnificent yet humble flowers, bowing low. Can these flowers represent us as we are Yeshua's Bride? Through His atonement, He gives us His pure white linen robes and the privilege of knowing Him as our Beloved. He brings us through our thorn-filled situations clothed in His righteousness. In response, we humbly worship Him and praise Him for His eternal love.

In the next verse, Solomon responds:

> *Like a lily among the thorns, so is my darling among the maidens"* (Song of Songs 2:2).

Solomon's love for his Shulamite is a picture of Yeshua's love for His Bride. This statement speaks of His value for each of us in His exquisite creation. Can you characterize yourself as a beautiful flower, part of the purified bridal company who is awaiting His return?

> Matthew 6:25–34 (emphasis added): *"For this reason I say to you, do not be worried about your life, as to what you will eat or what you will drink; nor for your body, as to what you will put on. Is not life more than food, and the body more than clothing? 26 Look at the birds of the air, that they do not sow, nor reap nor gather into barns, and yet your heavenly Father feeds them. Are you not worth much more than they? 27 And who of you by being worried can add a single hour to his life? 28 And why are you worried about clothing?* **Observe how the lilies of the field grow**; *they do not toil nor do they spin, 29 yet I say to you that not even Solomon in all his glory clothed himself like one of these. 30 But if God so clothes the grass of the field, which is alive today and tomorrow is thrown into the furnace, will He not much more clothe you? You of little faith! 31 Do not worry then, saying, 'What will we eat?' or 'What will we drink?' or 'What will we wear for clothing?' 32 For the [pagans] eagerly seek all these things; for your heavenly Father knows that you need all these things. 33 But seek first His kingdom and His righteousness, and all these things will be added to you. 34 So do not worry about tomorrow; for tomorrow will care for itself. Each day has enough trouble of its own."*

Acknowledgements:

For the writing of this book, I give all praise to Yeshua, my Redeemer, my Healer, and my Lord, because all honor belongs to Him. I am eternally thankful for His many promises:

1 Thessalonians 5:24: *Faithful is He who calls you, and He also will bring it to pass.*

2 Corinthians 12:9: *[Yeshua said,] "My grace is sufficient for you, for power is perfected in weakness."*

I memorized these promises in my early twenties, when I entered ministry in New York City. However, it wasn't until I was in my sixties that He called me to minister to women as an author. And yes, Yeshua's power continues to be my strength in my weaknesses.

Special appreciation and love to my husband, Sam, who suggested the theme: Messiah: The Healer of Women. Sam encouraged me to understand God's healing power for women and consider how God included women in His loving redemptive program, which culminated in Yeshua, our Healer. With some hesitation and trepidation, I began in Genesis with the first woman mentioned in scripture, Eve. As our studies progressed, I was increasingly thankful for Sam's inspiration and Biblical wisdom.

By the Lord's amazing grace, this book is the fifth book that I have been privileged to write. My studies and teaching at the Hope of Israel Sisterhood have contributed greatly to the fulfilment of this project. Each week, our Tuesday night Sisterhood class read through the chapters of *Messiah: The Healer of Women*, adding helpful comments and corrections. The material resonated in our hearts and minds as we realized God's redemptive plan for the world was inextricably tied to the women Yeshua called and healed.

Those who faithfully came to the study added valuable feedback for one and a half years. Special thanks to Yuliana, who would take the edits and incorporate them into the chapters each week. And special thanks to Sherry who worked on a number of chapters, breathing new life and grammar into the "rough parts." Much gratitude to Madelyn, who worked through the completed manuscript with Alyssa in the editing process, and Tracy and Devorah who test-read the final product. This book would not have happened without our fellowship of women encouraging each other. I love and appreciate these amazing women who attended for the year and a half period! So, thank you Stacy, Laurie, Rachel, Donna, Tami, Elaine, Susie, Sherry, Yuliana, and Yelena! I also praise the Lord for Alyssa Rinehart who designed the cover and layout of this book!

We all pray that this book will bless you and draw you closer to Yeshua the Messiah as you consider His great love for you!

Volume One covers the women of the Old Testament Scriptures. Volume Two, encompassing the women of the New Covenant, which will be published in a few months!

Table of Contents

Rejoice in the Lord always;
again I will say, rejoice! Let
your gentle spirit be known to
all men. The Lord is near. Be
anxious for nothing, but in
everything by prayer and
supplication with thanksgiving
let your requests be made known
to God. And the peace of God,
which surpasses all
comprehension, will guard your
hearts and your minds in
Messiah Yeshua.

Philippians 4:4—7

Introduction

What is the foundation of your identity? To put this question another way, what or who do you base your perception of yourself upon? Would it surprise you to discover that in God's plan for you, He had already chosen you before the foundation of His world? God is outside of this time-space continuum, but in His grace and love, He puts certain truths in the context of time to be understood by His creation. Some of these truths are that God predestined *you* to be in His kingdom; He chose you to be adopted as His daughter because God desired for you to be in His presence. He did this all before the foundation of the world.

Does this give you assurance of your value and a firm, unshakeable basis for who you are in Messiah? I would hope to join you in a resounding YES! However I think, like many of us, my perception of myself is flawed. I struggle to realize my true identity in Messiah Yeshua. In her book *Captivating*, Stasi Eldredge says this:

> I know I am not alone in this nagging sense of failing to measure up, a feeling of not being good enough as a woman. Every woman I've ever met feels it—something deeper than just the sense of failing at what she does. An underlying, gut

feeling of failing at who she is. I am not enough, and I am too much at the same time. Not pretty enough, not thin enough, not kind enough, not gracious enough, not disciplined enough. But too emotional, too needy, too sensitive, too strong, too opinionated, too messy. The result is shame ... [which] haunts us, nipping at our heels, feeding on our deepest fear that we will end up abandoned and alone. After all, if we were better women—whatever that means—life wouldn't be so hard. Right? We wouldn't have so many struggles; there would be less sorrow in our hearts. Why is it so hard to create meaningful friendships and sustain them? Why do our days seem so unimportant, filled not with romance and adventure but with duties and demands? We feel unseen, even by those who are closest to us. We feel unsought—that no one has the passion or the courage to pursue us, to get past our messiness to find the woman deep inside. And we feel uncertain—uncertain of what it truly means to be a woman ... (pp. 6–7).

These feelings arise when a person has become self-oriented and lacks God's perspective. When I stop focusing on Yeshua, I definitely lose the value and purpose that God has established for me. This book will help our focus be on God's Word and God's truth about who we really are. He gives us His value and His purpose, anchored in His amazing love and grace that He pours out to each of us.

To reiterate, God's redemptive plan began for you before He laid the *foundation of this world*. This phrase appears in Ephesians 1:4, where Paul describes us as chosen to be adopted as His daughters *"before the foundation of the world."* This chapter is one of my favorite portions of God's Word, one to commit to memory to help you understand these amazing promises.

Ephesians 1:3–6: *Blessed be the God and Father of our Lord Yeshua the Messiah, who has blessed us with every spiritual blessing in the heavenly places in Messiah, just as*

*He chose us in Him before the foundation of the world,
that we should be holy and blameless before Him. In love
He predestined us to adoption as [daughters] through
Yeshua the Messiah to Himself, according to the kind
intention of His will to the praise of the glory of His grace,
which He freely bestowed on us in the Beloved.*

Remember, God predestined you to be in His kingdom, chose you to be adopted as His daughter, and desired for you to be in His presence—all *before the foundation of the world.* As we move through the Scriptures, beginning in Genesis, we will see God's redemptive plan unfolding. We will understand more clearly that God's intention was always to restore and heal the world back to Himself. This message is what John the Baptizer proclaimed when he first saw Yeshua, *"Behold, the Lamb of God who takes away the sin of the world"* (John 1:29)!

THE PURPOSE OF THIS BOOK

Let me be clear from the outset as to why I wanted to write this book. My desire is to speak to women and in so doing highlight God's vital purpose for us. As you read, you will discover that in Yeshua's redemptive plan for the world, women take center stage. I'm so thankful that this teaching has been life-affirming for myself and others. I am beginning to understand how valuable and essential we women are in God's redemptive program. Consequently, my prayer is that this teaching will build you up in your faith as you grasp His love and gracious purpose for your life.

THE CONCLUSION OF ALL THINGS

Before we begin in Genesis—the book of beginnings—I want to go to the final book of the Bible and take a closer look at Revelation 22, the last chapter of the Bible. This is the conclusion of God's redemption program, where Yeshua declares, *"Behold, I am coming quickly, and My reward is with*

Me, to render to every man according to what he has done. I am the Alpha and the Omega, the first and the last, the beginning and the end" (Rev 22:12–13).

In this present age, it often seems that evil is certainly overcoming what is true and good. Therefore, it is important to begin with the truth of Scripture and note that Yeshua has already secured the victory for each of us individually as well as for this world. As we begin, I want us to read the end of the plan of Redemption first. Why? Because we win! When the new heaven and new earth are established, we are not only victorious here on earth, but we also have a glorious future ahead of us. These verses, Revelation 22:12 and 13, are foundational as we anticipate His return and desire to live for Him today.

Who Is the Content of Your Life?

When Yeshua declares that He is *the Alpha and Omega,* He is referring to the first and final letters of the Greek alphabet. In Hebrew, it would be the *Alef and the Tav;* and in English the A and Z. There is a similar concept in every written language. What does this mean for us? Think of how you teach your two-year-old to read. Do you give him the complete volumes of *The Chronicles of Narnia* and say, "You'll figure it out, good luck?" No, you get alphabet books and letter games that will familiarize your small child with the shapes and sounds of each letter. There is much repetition required— and there may be some trial and error! Eventually, when he's ready, these letters will form words and sentences.

Consider how, as God's daughters, we learn His Scriptures. We grow *"precept upon precept, line by line"* (Isa 28:10, 13), and this powerful and living Word is always teaching us how to live. The fact that Yeshua is the Alpha and Omega tells us that the **content** of our lives should be filled with Him. Our daily lives should be overflowing with His words and teachings because He is the Living Word. John 1:1–3 says,

> *In the beginning was the Word, and the Word was with God, and the Word was God. He was in the beginning with God. All things came into being through Him, and apart from Him nothing came into being that has come into being.*

In John 1:14 we read,

> *And the Word became flesh, and dwelt among us, and we saw His glory, glory as of the only begotten from the Father, full of grace and truth.*

Are we filling our lives with His living and written Word—His Sacred Scriptures?

Are You Living in the Context of Yeshua's Plan for You?

The next phrase Yeshua uses to describe Himself in Revelation 22:12–13 is *the First and the Last*. In Hebrew, this phrase is *rishon* and *acharon*. In teaching the Word of God, I've learned that if I take a verse out of its intended context, it can become a pretext or excuse for anything I want to teach. This principle rings true for our lives. The word "first" is *rishon* which parallels the word *protos* in Greek. Yeshua used this word in Matthew 6:33–34 when He taught us:

> *But seek **first** His kingdom and His righteousness, and all these things will be added to you. So do not worry about tomorrow; for tomorrow will care for itself. Each day has enough trouble of its own* (emphasis added).

If our lives are to make sense, we must put ourselves in the **context** of His plan for us. He sees the overview of our lives and knows the end from the beginning (Isa 46:10). You can trust Him as the Master Weaver who is weaving your life into

21

His tapestry. His context for our lives is found in Romans 8:28–31:

> *And we know that God causes all things to work together for good to those who love God, to those who are called according to His purpose. For those whom He foreknew, He also predestined to become conformed to the image of His Son, so that He would be the firstborn among many brethren; and these whom He predestined, He also called; and these whom He called, He also justified; and these whom He justified, He also glorified. What then shall we say to these things? If God is for us, who is against us?*

MESSIAH YESHUA'S FINISHED WORK OF REDEMPTION

The Beginning and the End (*arche* and *telos* in Greek) tells us that Yeshua **completes** our redemption. We can rest in His finished work. When Yeshua was dying for our sins as the spotless Lamb of God, His final words from the cross were, "It is finished" (John 19:30)! The word "finished" that Yeshua declared is from this root *telos*, meaning He accomplished and completed our salvation. As a new believer many years ago, Philippians 1:6 was a verse that I memorized to remind me that God is the One who not only saved me but by His grace will bring me to my eternal home.

> Philippians 1:6: *For I am confident of this very thing, that He who began a good work in you will perfect it until the day of Messiah Yeshua.*

Are you resting in Messiah Yeshua's finished work of salvation for you? Sometimes as women, we are prone to fill our lives with "to-do lists" and take on the burden of caring for everyone around us in our own puny strength. Remember to rest in His grace and His finished work of redemption for you.

To Sum Up All Things

God's redemptive plan is summed up in Messiah, as it states in Ephesians 1:7–10:

> *In Him we have redemption through His blood, the forgiveness of our trespasses, according to the riches of His grace, which He lavished upon us. In all wisdom and insight He made known to us the mystery of His will, according to His kind intention which He purposed in Him with a view to an administration suitable to the fullness of the times, that is, the summing up of all things in Messiah, things in the heavens and things on the earth* (Luke 24:25–27; John 5:39–47).

In other words, God's redemptive plan was always in His choosing, in His way, and in His timing; just as Paul taught us in Galatians 4:4: *But when the fullness of the time came, God sent forth His Son, born of a woman, born under the Law.*

I hope this introductory chapter, which focused on Yeshua's teaching about Himself from Revelation, will give us a sure anchor and foundation for this study. In our next chapter, we will meet the mother of all the living: Eve. *Now the man called his wife's name Eve, because she was the mother of all the living* (Genesis 3:20).

For further consideration, take time to think about the context of Revelation 13:8 and how this impacts your life as you are assured that your name is written in the Lamb's Book of Life.

According to Revelation 13:8, God's plan of redemption was put in place before the fall of Adam and Eve, "And all that dwell upon the earth shall worship him (the antichrist), whose names are not written in the book of life of the Lamb slain from the foundation of the world" (KJV).

QUESTIONS FOR FURTHER APPLICATION:

1. How does the description that Yeshua gives of Himself in Revelation 22:12–13 encourage your heart?

2. In what ways do you see Yeshua—the Alpha and Omega, Alef and Tav—as the *content* of your life?

3. In what ways do you see Yeshua— First and the Last— as the *context* of your life?

4. In what ways do you see Yeshua—the Beginning and the End—completing the good work He began in You?

Consider memorizing these Scriptures to grow deeper in your understanding of who Yeshua is!

- John 1:1-3, 14: *In the beginning was the Word, and the Word was with God, and the Word was God. ²He was in the beginning with God. ³All things came into being through Him, and apart from Him nothing came into being that has come into being. … ¹⁴And the Word became flesh, and dwelt among us, and we saw His glory, glory as of the only begotten from the Father, full of grace and truth.*

- Matthew 6:33: *But seek first His kingdom and His righteousness, and all these things will be added to you.*

- Romans 8:28-31: *And we know that God causes all things to work together for good to those who love God, to those who are called according to His purpose. ²⁹For those whom He foreknew, He also predestined to become conformed to the image of His Son, so that He would be the firstborn among many brethren; ³⁰and these whom He predestined, He also called; and these whom He called, He also justified; and these whom He justified, He also glorified.* *31What then shall we say to these things? If God is for us, who is against us?*

- Philippians 1:6: *For I am confident of this very thing, that He who began a good work in you will perfect it until the day of Messiah Yeshua.*

In the beginning was the
Word, and the Word was
with God, and the Word was
God. He was in the beginning
with God.
All things came into being
through Him, and apart from
Him nothing came into being
that has come into being.
In Him was life, and the life
was the Light of men. The
Light shines in the darkness,
and the darkness did not
comprehend it.

John 1:1-5

One

In the Beginning: Eve

In this exploration of healing through the Messiah, we will start at the beginning—in the book of Genesis. As we travel through the Word of God, we will see that what was destroyed when sin broke our relationship with God is redeemed, restored, rebuilt, and repaired through His redemptive plan for all humanity. God redeems and heals women, as we are a central part of His redemptive program. What does this healing look like? It involves the restoration of every aspect of a person's life to the condition He intended for it. Everything God does is for the purpose of His redemptive program, including the healing and restoring that we are here to discuss. Yeshua the Messiah makes this possible for He is the Great Physician. He came to restore each of us to a whole person and new creation who can enter the presence of the living God.

THE PROMISE

B'Resheet: Restoring, Redeeming, Rebuilding

God's communication with us begins in Genesis. It states in Genesis 1:1:

In the beginning God created the heavens and the earth.

In the beginning is the Hebrew phrase *B'resheet*. The *b'* means "in" and *resheet* means "beginning." In our introductory chapter, we noted that Yeshua is the *"first and the last"* (Revelation 22:12) The word "beginning," *resheet*, is a synonym to "first," *reshon*, from Revelation 22:12. As we said, this points to the fact that Yeshua is the context of our lives—the First and the Last.

Tov: Good!

But before we get to the need for restoration, let's take a quick look at the world in God's Garden. It's all good! Here in the creation account, we learn about the good things God made. This reflects God's character. His being good (or *tov* in Hebrew) resonates throughout all of Scriptures. Many of our favorite verses speak about the goodness of God. Paul taught us in Romans 8:28:

And we know that God causes all things to work together for good to those who love God, to those who are called according to His purpose.

King David's chief worship leader, Asaph, wrote this in Psalm 73:25–26, 28:

Whom have I in heaven but You? And besides You, I desire nothing on earth. My flesh and my heart may fail, but God is the strength of my heart and my portion forever... the nearness of God is my good; I have made the Lord God my refuge, that I may tell of all Your works.

Asaph wrote this as he was struggling with evil men, who seemed to be getting away with sin and seemed to be going unpunished. His conclusion was that regardless of outside circumstances, *"the nearness of God is my good."*

In the final chapter of Genesis, Joseph spoke to his brothers about the goodness of God.

> Genesis 50:19–20: *But Joseph said to them, "Do not be afraid, for am I in God's place? And as for you, you meant evil against me, but God meant it for good in order to bring about this present result, to preserve many people alive."*

We are exhorted in many verses to give thanks to the Lord for He is good!

> Psalm 136:1: *Give thanks to the LORD, for He is good; For His lovingkindness is everlasting.*

Lo Tov: It's Not Good for Man to Live Alone

How Did the Woman Come To Be Created?

Until Genesis 2:18, God's creation has been described as good; but in verse eighteen God Himself declared that something was *lo tov*—not good. God described the circumstance that was not good:

> Genesis 2:18: *Then the LORD God said, "It is not good for the man to be alone; I will make him a helper suitable* (ezer kenegdo) *for him."*

God regarded Adam as incomplete and deficient as he lived without the benefit of a proper counterpart. The benefit of not being alone is echoed in Ecclesiastes 4:9–11:

> *Two are better than one because they have a good return for their labor. For if either of them falls, the one will lift up his companion. But woe to the one who falls when there is not another to lift him up. Furthermore, if two lie down*

together they keep warm, but how can one be warm alone?

In order to end man's loneliness, God formed for Adam a suitable helper. The phrase *helper suitable* is meant to encourage us. God did not make us to be like Hamburger Helper™ to spice up an otherwise boring hamburger meal. On the contrary, my study of various translations confirms the interpretation of many noted Hebrew scholars who say this is an accurate reflection of the Hebrew Scripture: *"I will make the woman a power or strength* (ezer) *corresponding to and equal to* (kenegdo) *the man."*

Though frequently translated into English as "help," *power* and *strength* are both essential qualities indicated in the Hebrew word *ezer,* which usually is used in the Scripture to refer to the power and strength of God. One example is found in Deuteronomy 33:29:

> *Happy art thou, O Israel: who is like unto thee, O people saved by the Lord, the shield of thy help (ezer)* (KJV).

The shield or *magen* of God's help (*ezer*) would be a shield of His strength and power.

Saving the Best for Last!

The context of the creation of woman is found in Genesis 2:19–25. Genesis 2:19 teaches us that all the living creatures were formed from the ground (*adamah*) including Adam. When God formed every living creature, He fashioned each animal and had Adam name it. After this, we come to the end of verse twenty, which reiterates there was not found a *helper suitable (ezer kenegdo)* for him.

> Genesis 2:19–22: *Out of the ground the Lord God formed every beast of the field and every bird of the sky, and brought them to the man to see what he would call them; and whatever the man called a living creature, that was its name. The man gave names to all the cattle, and to the*

birds of the sky, and to every beast of the field, but for Adam there was not found a helper suitable for him. So the Lord God caused a deep sleep to fall upon the man, and he slept; then He took one of his ribs and closed up the flesh at that place. The Lord God fashioned (banah) *into a woman the rib which He had taken from the man, and brought her to the man.*

In verse twenty-two, the word *fashioned* is from the Hebrew word *banah,* which means "build."

God built or fashioned the first woman from Adam's rib. This brings to mind another Scripture where the word *build* is used. In Psalm 127:1 it says,

Unless the Lord builds (banah) *the house, they labor in vain who build it.*

The Lord Himself designed Eve to bring His plan of redemption to the world. She was not made of dust like Adam, rather she was carefully designed from living flesh and bone. We could say that Adam was refined dirt and Eve was a glorious refinement of humanity itself. She was a special gift to Adam. She was a necessary partner who finally made his existence complete. The astounding fact is that God *built* the first woman and that signaled the completion of all creation. She was utterly unique—the only being ever directly created by God from the living tissue of another creature.

Personal Application: You Are Fearfully and Wonderfully Made!

God's creation of women was not an afterthought, as though it had just occurred to Him: "Oops, I need someone to put on the arm of Adam! Let me create a woman for him." Not at all. In God's infinite wisdom, we women are created with His strength and power to complement what man needs. We are not diminished by the "helpmeet" or "helper suitable" description, but rather God created and built us to be a source of strength and power corresponding to what man lacked.

God built us with wombs which can give birth and bodies that can nourish as God weaves our children together and has plans for each one of them.

> Psalm 139:13–17: *For You formed my inward parts; You wove me in my mother's womb. I will give thanks to You, for I am fearfully and wonderfully made; wonderful are Your works, and my soul knows it very well. My frame was not hidden from You, when I was made in secret, and skillfully wrought in the depths of the earth; Your eyes have seen my unformed substance; and in Your book were all written the days that were ordained for me, when as yet there was not one of them. How precious also are Your thoughts to me, O God! How vast is the sum of them!*

What an affirming, tremendous truth for us to keep and cherish in our hearts! Though these truths of our creation as women must never be a cause for pride but rather always lead us to humble ourselves before our Creator and express, like David, that we will give thanks to our Creator God who has awesomely and wondrously formed us.

THE PROBLEM:

Genesis 3: Where It All Goes Wrong

Despite all that she had been created with, all the advantages Eve had as the pinnacle of God's creation, chapter three happened. It all went wrong. How was the woman so deceived? Where was Adam?

Adam and His Two Responsibilities

Let's back up to Genesis 2:15, where the Lord gave Adam a twofold job description:

> *Then the Lord God took the man and put him into the garden of Eden to cultivate* (avad) *it and keep* (shomer) *it.*

According to verse fifteen, the first part of Adam's job was to cultivate the Garden. But what does it mean to *cultivate*? Cultivate is *avad* in Hebrew, which is the root word for both "serve" and "worship" (*avodah*). Can you imagine serving in the perfect Garden created by God Himself? I think we can safely suggest that his serving in the garden of God would entail honoring and worshipping his Creator.

The second part of his job was to *keep* the Garden. Keep is from the Hebrew root word *shomer,* which means "to guard." The question could be raised, "What would he need to guard against if it is a perfect Garden?" Well, somehow a serpent gained access to Eve. If we understand that some way Adam failed to guard Eve against the serpent's crafty ways, it becomes clear how important it was for him to be the guardian of the Garden.

All women have heard statements like, "If only Eve had not listened to the serpent!" The fall of humanity and ruin of everything has been blamed on women since Eve. Consider with me that Adam may not have been doing his job for the Lord to guard (*shomer*) the Garden. If we were interested in assigning blame, we could respond to such thoughtless statements with, "If only Adam would have taken his role to guard the Garden seriously!" Regardless of who was to blame, the fact remains that our Creator God in His infinite love and wisdom created the first man (in Hebrew the word is *ish*) and woman (*ishshah*) with free will to choose. God's desire is always for us to choose to love and obey Him, but for some reason Eve made a different choice. Let's look at the details of the instructions about the trees in the garden that God gave to Adam.

> Genesis 2:16–17: *The Lord God commanded the man, saying, "From any tree of the garden you may eat freely; but from the tree of the knowledge of good and evil you*

shall not eat, for in the day that you eat from it you will surely die."

Note here that God spoke directly to Adam, and it was Adam's job to communicate to the woman God's specific commands about the trees of the Garden of Eden (*Gan Eden*).

In the above verses, God gave Adam one prohibition for His Garden: to not eat of the tree of the knowledge of good and evil, because the penalty would be death. This death would not be physical death, but spiritual death resulting in separation from God's holy presence. And this command to *not eat* was the flashpoint of the free will the Lord gave humanity. Unfortunately, the woman misused her free will by choosing to please herself.

The Great Deception

Genesis 3:1: *Now the serpent was more crafty than any beast of the field which the LORD God had made. And he said to the woman, "Indeed, has God said, 'You shall not eat from any tree of the garden'?"*

The Scriptures describe this crafty animal as the shrewdest beast in the Garden. This serpent was the voice of Satan whose plan was to slander and defame God. Satan's goal was to create doubt about the goodness and trustworthiness of God in the woman's mind as he questioned her. His methods should not surprise us for we have Yeshua's description of the devil in John 8, where Yeshua calls him *"the father of lies."*

John 8:44: *You are of your father the devil, and you want to do the desires of your father. He was a murderer from the beginning, and does not stand in the truth because there is no truth in him. Whenever he speaks a lie, he speaks from his own nature, for he is a liar and the father of lies.*

The Woman Responds to the Serpent, but...

In the next verses in Genesis, we see the woman's response—and see that she added her own words to God's.

> Genesis 3:2–3: *The woman said to the serpent, "From the fruit of the trees of the garden we may eat; but from the fruit of the tree which is in the middle of the garden, God has said, 'You shall not eat from it **or touch it,** or you will die'"* (emphasis added).

In her response to the serpent, the woman was ninety-five percent correct when she quoted God's instructions. However, God did not say anything about *touching* the tree. Therefore, in her reply we have the first example of adding to the word of God incorrectly. When this is done it always opens the door for misinterpretation. I think it's significant to remember that Adam heard from God directly and it would have been his responsibility to communicate to the woman God's specific instructions.

> Genesis 3:4–5: *The serpent said to the woman, "You surely will not die! For God knows that in the day you eat from it your eyes will be opened, and you will be like God, knowing good and evil."*

After listening to the voice of lies, she began to mistrust God's voice of truth. Her ego got in the way and she decided, "*I* will determine what is right for *me*." Her doubting of God began in her thought life. The Apostle Paul gave us insight as to how the serpent deceived the woman in his letter to the congregation at Corinth. In communicating his zealous/jealous love for the Corinthian congregation, he cautioned them not to be led astray, like Eve, from the simplicity and purity of the Good News.

> 2 Corinthians 11:2–3 (definition added): *For I am jealous (zealous) for you with a godly jealousy; for I betrothed you to one husband, so that to Messiah I might present you*

as a pure virgin. But I am afraid that, as the serpent deceived Eve by his craftiness, your minds will be led astray from the simplicity and purity of devotion to Messiah.

What Happened to Her Thoughts?

Genesis 3:6 provides a description of the progress of the woman's sin, which I have annotated: *When the woman saw that the tree was good for food* (this appealed to her flesh), *and that it was a delight to the eyes* (it looked really good), *and that the tree was desirable to make one wise* (pride took over), *she took from its fruit and ate; and she gave also to her husband with her, and he ate.*

Eve's desire to be like God and not miss out on anything led her to listen to the voice of the *father of lies* instead of God's voice of truth. Paul said with certainty that she was *deceived … by his craftiness* and her mind *led astray.*

The word "mind" can also be translated "purpose" or "thought." The seeds of doubt that Satan sowed refocused Eve's thoughts away from the pure relationship she had with her Creator. Her deception began as she listened to the voice of the serpent and began to consider: *"Maybe God has not given me everything that I need; maybe God is shortchanging me."*

Consequences for Slandering God & Following Satan

After the advent of sin, God pronounced a curse, which contained His judgment and discipline upon the serpent and the woman.

First, God spoke to the woman in Genesis 3:13:

Then the Lord God said to the woman, "What is this you have done?" And the woman said, "The serpent deceived me, and I ate."

The question she was asked was, "What have *you* done?" but the answer she gave claimed no responsibility for her own actions. Instead, she shifted the blame to the serpent—who was the pawn of Satan.

Next, in Genesis 3:14-15, God spoke directly to the serpent:

> *The Lord God said to the serpent, "Because you have done this, cursed are you more than all cattle, and more than every beast of the field; on your belly you will go, and dust you will eat all the days of your life; and I will put enmity between you and the woman, and between your seed and her seed; He shall bruise you on the head, and you shall bruise him on the heel."*

This curse was a degradation to the serpent, which would be carried out by this creature eating dust all his life. "Eating the dust" is a sign of defeat. In battle, the Scriptures equate the eating of the dust with the enemy falling to the ground in defeat and humiliation (see Psalm 72:9).

God's Discipline for the Woman

After delivering His message to the serpent, God gave His verdict to Eve.

> Genesis 3:16: *To the woman He said, "I will greatly multiply your pain in childbirth, in pain you will bring forth children; yet your desire will be for your husband, and he will rule over you."*

To sum up, the judgment pronounced by God is as follows:

- Greatly increased pain in childbirth
- In pain you will bring forth children (Are these first two the same thing? We will explore that shortly.)
- Your desire will be for your husband
- Your husband will rule over you

THE RESTORATION

There is much to regret here. But let's look at these pronouncements one at a time, and see what God was already doing.

Even when delivering His judgment, it's not all bad news. When we look back at Genesis 3:15, we'll see God gave us the first promise of redemption which would come through the woman. In that verse, God establishes hostility to be present between the serpent's offspring and the woman's offspring in order to protect His people from identifying with Satan's evil seed. God declared, *"And I will put enmity between you and the woman, and between your seed* (offspring of Satan) *and **her seed*** (refers to Messiah and is the first promise of the Redeemer)*; He* (the seed of the woman) *shall bruise you on the head* (the death blow of Satan), *and you shall bruise him on the heel* (refers to Messiah's death for our sins which is interpreted as the enemy wounding His heel)."

This declaration of enmity established the spiritual warfare between those who follow God's truth and those who follow Satan's lies. Today we are called and equipped to be ready to destroy *"speculations and every lofty thing raised up against the knowledge of God, and we [take] every thought captive to the obedience of Messiah"* (2 Corinthians 10:5).

In context this verse was part of Paul's exhortation to the congregation at Corinth to be aware of the spiritual battle for their minds.

> 2 Corinthians 10:3–5: *For though we walk in the flesh, we do not war according to the flesh, for the weapons of our warfare are not of the flesh, but divinely powerful for the destruction of fortresses. We are destroying speculations and every lofty thing raised up against the knowledge of God, and we are taking every thought captive to the obedience of Messiah.*

Her Seed Is Our Hope

After declaring that the serpent would be the most cursed of any animal and eat dust continually, God then gave us the hope of redemption in the woman's seed.

> *"Her Seed"* is our hope... The *"seed"* of the woman? Do women have seed? Though *seed* in English is limited to males, in Hebrew it is used to the offspring that the woman produces as well. But why does the Scripture bother to refer to *"HER seed"* at all? For the Lord God's redemption... for all humanity brings restored honor to for the woman. The essential honor for all women is restored in Messiah's birth... By personal faith in Messiah, her seed become God's children. (*Messianic Marriage Matters*, Sam Nadler, p. 155)

Those Childbirth Pains

To *greatly multiply* our pain in childbirth so that *in pain* we *bring forth children* is a much discussed and deeply personal price we women all pay for the Fall. But consider, labor pains typify the sufferings that all of us endure because of the cursed earth and the pain of living. Our own disobedience and sinful living cause us pain. The world in which we live is full of grief and agony. Nonetheless this same pain also leads us to seek Messiah's grace as we come before His throne of grace.

> Hebrews 4:16: *Therefore let us draw near with confidence to the throne of grace, so that we may receive mercy and find grace to help in time of need.*

The New Covenant Gives a Perspective on the Pains of Childbirth

Yeshua used the example of the pain of labor to encourage His disciples in view of His upcoming death and resurrection.

> John 16:21-22: *Whenever a woman is in labor she has pain, because her hour has come; but when she gives birth to the child, she no longer remembers the anguish because*

of the joy that a child has been born into the world. Therefore you too have grief now; but I will see you again, and your heart will rejoice, and no one will take your joy away from you.

Paul encouraged us that our sufferings are only temporary—one day our pain and sorrows will be gone.

Romans 8:18–28 (emphasis added): *For I consider that the sufferings of this present time are not worthy to be compared with the glory that is to be revealed to us. For the anxious longing of the creation waits eagerly for the revealing of the sons of God. For the creation was subjected to futility, not willingly, but because of Him who subjected it, in hope that the creation itself also will be set free from its slavery to corruption into the freedom of the glory of the children of God. For we know that the whole creation groans and suffers the* **pains of childbirth together until now.** *And not only this, but also we ourselves, having the first fruits of the Spirit, even we ourselves groan within ourselves, waiting eagerly for our adoption as sons, the redemption of our body. For in hope we have been saved, but hope that is seen is not hope; for who hopes for what he already sees? But if we hope for what we do not see, with perseverance we wait eagerly for it. In the same way the Spirit also helps our weakness; for we do not know how to pray as we should, but the Spirit Himself intercedes for us with groanings too deep for words; and He who searches the hearts knows what the mind of the Spirit is, because He intercedes for the saints according to the will of God. And we know that God causes all things to work together for good to those who love God, to those who are called according to His purpose.*

Every day we must affirm in thankfulness our standing as God's beloved daughters. He created each of us to be His unique building. We are fearfully and wonderfully fashioned by His loving hand.

> Psalm 139:13–14: *For You formed my inward parts; You wove me in my mother's womb. I will give thanks to You, for I am fearfully and wonderfully made; wonderful are Your works, and my soul knows it very well.*

When Eve decided to use her free will to disobey the one commandment that God had put in place, her innocence turned to shame and guilt. She was deceived by Satan, the father of lies and immediately understood that she sinned against her Creator God. And I want to remind us that Adam was right there with her (Genesis 3:6) and was not being an effective guardian (*shomer*) as God had assigned him to be in Genesis 2:15.

To Summarize "Pain in Childbirth"

God's discipline for the woman to have pain in childbirth is not only a reminder of the consequences of sin but also a beacon of hope that one day the Messiah will conquer Satan and redeem us from the enemy by way of "her seed." The pain of childbirth is a reminder that we are weak, in need of His grace. The cry and groaning of creation, and our cries as well lead us to seek Messiah's grace and redemption—Hebrews 4:16, John 16:21–22, Romans 8:18–28. The pains of childbirth prophetically point us to a time when the curse of sin will be lifted, and God will restore this world.

> "Childbirth is a reminder not just of the painful consequences of our sin, but more importantly of the Messiah who will destroy Satan. For every childbirth reflects the cry of creation awaiting in pain Messiah's removal of the curse and of His redemption of the world." (*Messianic Marriage Matters*, Sam Nadler, p. 159)

In Pain You Shall "Bring Forth Children"

There is another aspect of God's discipline for women that I was challenged to consider as I was writing this book. The description of having pain in childbirth resonated with me because I know there was great pain (even though I have largely forgotten it) when I gave birth to my two sons and had a miscarriage too. That said, the phrase *"in pain you will bring forth children"* is referring to the raising of our children. After studying this section and related Scriptures I now understand that "the bringing forth of children" is speaking of raising our children through the pains and sorrows of motherhood. For believers we are called to be women who live for God's glory and represent His love to our children while enduring the pain of life. Both aspects of this discipline for us, giving birth and raising kids, point us to our need for Messiah's grace to be poured into our lives.

Let's take a moment to consider another New Covenant verse on this topic that is difficult to grasp. Considering what God was saying to Eve in Genesis 3:15–16, it is important for us to understand.

When Paul wrote to Timothy, who was ministering in Ephesus, he taught about the role of women in the congregation:

> 1 Timothy 2:14–15 (ESV, definitions added): *And Adam was not deceived, but the woman was deceived and became a transgressor. Yet she will be saved* (fulfilled) *through childbearing—if they continue in faith and love and holiness, with self-control* (saved/sound mind).

In this verse, Paul didn't dismiss the pain and suffering of raising children, but rather gave a heavenly perspective. Let's look at this more closely.

What Does it Mean to Have Self-Control, to be Sensible, of a Sound Mind, to be Discreet?

In addition to instructing Timothy about the role of women in the congregation, Paul also wrote to Titus. Many consider Titus 2:3–5 to be the definitive teaching for women's discipleship. My first book, published in 2012, was an exploration of this portion of Scripture, but I had been a believer and a ladies' Bible teacher for many years before I finally took the time to study and teach this important portion. In it, Paul's instruction to Titus regarding the discipleship of women in the new congregations in Crete is similar to his instruction to Timothy.

> *Older women likewise are to be reverent in behavior, not slanderers or slaves to much wine. They are to teach what is good and so train the young women to love their husbands and children, to be self-controlled, pure, working at home, kind, and submissive to their own husbands, that the word of God may not be reviled* (Titus 2:3–5 ESV).

When Paul referred to the *"older women [who]… are to teach … young women,"* this is referring to maturing women of God—and is not necessarily based on how many grey hairs one has. The women who are to be taught are called younger, referring to age and/or spiritual maturity. In the letter to Titus, Paul listed seven qualities to encourage in the young women, and the third quality is translated in various versions as to be *self-controlled,* or have a *sound mind,* be *sensible,* or *discreet.* In Greek, this third quality is a compound word combining *soza* (saved) and *frone* (mind). In other words, we women need to be put in our "saved minds." This same compound Greek word, *saved-mind,* is used in verb form in Titus 2:4; where it is translated "to encourage," or "to train," "teach" or "urge." The word signifies being saved and trained, or having our minds transformed. I find it difficult to relate to words like *sensible, discreet,* and *self-controlled,* because I know that in my flesh, I cannot be sensible, discreet, or especially self-controlled. But the point of the discipleship teaching that Paul is advocating is that we can—we must—have saved minds which we receive from God as His new creation in Messiah.

The reason I wanted to include this brief overview of Titus 2:3–5 is because of the words Paul used in 1 Timothy 2:14–15. In verse fifteen, Paul taught Timothy that women can be *saved* through childbearing. This word "saved" is *soza* which can also include the idea of being *fulfilled.* These instructions Paul wrote are for women who are already saved, in the sense that they are believers in Messiah, so the translation of being *fulfilled* or satisfied fits the context. Paul also included a conditional phrase that ensures *how* women can find this fulfillment in childbearing and childrearing. He said it is possible *if* women continue *"in faith and love and holiness, with self-control* (a saved, sound mind)". A saved mind is needed for all of us to live for the Lord and fulfill His will for our lives. This same compound word is found in 2 Timothy 1:7: *For God hath not given us the spirit of fear; but of power, and of love, and of a sound mind (sofronishmo*—a saved mind, KJV).

The Culture in Ephesus When Paul Wrote His Letters to Timothy

Timothy was teaching women from Ephesus who were new believers. These women had been raised with the false religion of the goddess Artemis which influenced every cultural and spiritual aspect of this important city. The Temple of Artemis (aka Diana) was in Ephesus and was renowned to be one of the Seven Wonders of the World. Artemis is the ancient Greek goddess of the hunt and the moon—she became combined with the Asian mother goddess Ishtar, the "mother of all life," who personified the reproductive powers of men and living things. As a major lunar Goddess, Artemis is very popular among modern witches today.

False worship emanated from this female goddess and it is still evident in the lies that undergird much of feminist culture today. According to mythology, Artemis was against motherhood. She remained a virgin and punished women who abandoned their virginity. Ironically, Artemis was the goddess of childbirth. But legend teaches that she frequently killed mothers especially during labor when she would send her arrows to kill them in their pains. She castrated the men who served in her temple. Young girls who were living in the temple and reached puberty were cast out if they decided to marry. Today we have the fruition of these underpinnings of 'man hatred and emasculation,' 'wholesale abortion,' and 'the despising of childrearing and motherhood.'

Your Desire Will Be for Your Husband

The next part of the Genesis 3:16 explains that not only will we have pain in childbirth and in raising children, but it's not going to be easy to submit to our husbands, either: *yet your desire will be for your husband, and he will rule over you.*

> The Hebrew word for desire (*tesukah*) means a longing, a desire like that of a beast to devour. As soon as the intimacy with God was broken by sin, Eve lost contentment in her role as the one who would be a strength corresponding (suitable helper) to her husband. Now her deep desire was not one of complementing and voluntarily submitting but rather a role of dominance over her husband. (*Honoring God* exposition book of Titus 2:3–5, Miriam Nadler, p. 178)

Your desire (*tesukah*) means a "longing to control." It is the same word used in the story of the life of Cain when he became angry at God for the rejection of his offering. Genesis 4:6–7:

> *Then the LORD said to Cain, "Why are you angry? And why has your countenance fallen? If you do well, will not your countenance be lifted up? And if you do not do well, sin is*

crouching at the door; and its desire (tesukah) *is for you, but you must master it."*

Submission (1 Peter 1:3): Our Example Is Yeshua

In Titus 2:5, women are exhorted *"to be sensible* (sophron, saved, sound mind), *pure, workers at home, kind, being subject* (hupotasso) *to their own husbands, so that the word of God will not be dishonored."*

The final phrase of Titus 2:5 instructs women to *"[be] subject to their own husbands."* Here we have the dreaded instruction to be submitted to our own husband. We must remember that *submission* is not *subjugation*. In 1 Peter 2:15–21 we have Yeshua as our ultimate example of One who submitted Himself and we are encouraged to *"follow in His steps."*

In fact, the Greek word for submission is *hupotasso* and means to "place under" or "rank under." In Titus 2:5 *"[be] subject to their own husbands"* is a verb participle that carries the idea of continually placing yourself in a subordinate position. I confess that the only way I can voluntarily place myself under my own husband's authority is if I have a "saved mind" and I am yielding myself to Yeshua's authority first and foremost.

And He Will Rule Over You

The final phrase in Genesis 3:16 states that Adam would rule over Eve. I'm encouraged by the teaching from Sam's book that explains what this means.

> "And he (Adam) will rule *(mashal)* over you." *Mashal* in Hebrew means to govern, to manage but not in an overbearing way—in Scripture and in Messiah there is total equality of male and female, with only functional subordination for the wife as to her divine calling as his helpmeet. The male's leadership calling is as a servant to all in his family. For him to either oppress his wife or abdicate

his leadership is to rebel against God's calling. Likewise, for her to resist the man's leadership or to usurp his leadership is to rebel against God's calling for her. (*Messianic Marriage Matters*, Sam Nadler p. 161-162)

An Aside: God's Discipline for the Man

Genesis 3:17–19: *Then to Adam He said, "Because you have listened to the voice of your wife, and have eaten from the tree about which I commanded you, saying, 'You shall not eat from it'; cursed is the ground because of you; in toil you will eat of it all the days of your life. Both thorns and thistles it shall grow for you; and you will eat the plants of the field; by the sweat of your face you will eat bread, till you return to the ground, because from it you were taken; for you are dust, and to dust you shall return."*

Though in this study we're going to focus on God's intervention in the lives of women, please note that the man did not escape God's discipline. In verse seventeen, God told Adam, *"You have listened to the voice of your wife instead of Me."* This implies that because Adam did not fulfill his leadership role to be the *shomer*—to guard her—in the garden, he would struggle to produce food until he died. In other words, instead of a perfect Garden to cultivate *(avad)*, now the work *(avad)* to produce food would be difficult and labor-intensive.

The end of verse nineteen mentions that there will be lots of dust or dirt in his physical labor. Our Creator knows each of us and in His great love pours out His lovingkindness and compassion on His dusty creation!

Psalm 103:11–14: *For as high as the heavens are above the earth, so great is His lovingkindness toward those who fear Him. As far as the east is from the west, so far has He removed our transgressions from us. Just as a father has compassion on his children, so the LORD has compassion*

on those who fear Him. For He Himself knows our frame;
He is mindful that we are but dust.

Adam Honors the Woman With Her Name

The woman *(ishsha)* received a name of honor and affirmation.

Genesis 3:20: *Now the man called his wife's name Eve, because she was the mother of all the living.*

Chayah Means "Life"

At this point Adam saw the discipline of God for the woman to be an affirmation and renewal of her call to motherhood—the mother of *all the living*—and in giving her this name he was also acknowledging and supporting that "her seed" will crush the head of Satan.

God knows what we need to be fulfilled in our lives and raising children is part of this fulfillment. But remember it is not only physical children but also those spiritual children we are privileged to minister to and disciple which can bring fulfilled joy.

God Provides Garments for Adam and Eve

Genesis 3:21: *The LORD God made garments of skin for Adam and his wife, and clothed them.*

In the next verses in Genesis, God provided the innocent animal for the repentant sinner. The animal skins represent the first deaths—not for food but for covering. This first sacrifice points to the Messiah's ultimate sacrifice in God's redemptive plan.

By way of application, take time to be thankful that God has given us new garments. In both the Hebrew Scriptures and the New Covenant, we have the assurance of His garments of salvation to cover our guilt and shame.

Isaiah 61:10: *I will rejoice greatly in the LORD, my soul will exult in my God; for He has clothed me with garments of salvation, He has wrapped me with a robe of righteousness, as a bridegroom decks himself with a garland, and as a bride adorns herself with her jewels.*

2 Corinthians 5:21: *He made Him who knew no sin to be sin on our behalf, so that we might become the righteousness of God in Him.*

Why Did God Kick Adam and Eve Out of Gan Eden?

Genesis 3:22–24: *Then the LORD God said, "Behold, the man has become like one of Us, knowing good and evil; and now, he might stretch out his hand, and take also from the tree of life, and eat, and live forever"—therefore the LORD God sent him out from the garden of Eden, to cultivate the ground from which he was taken. So He drove the man out; and at the east of the garden of Eden He stationed the cherubim and the flaming sword which turned every direction to guard the way to the tree of life* (etz chaim).

Both Adam and Eve were placed by God in a perfect garden with unbroken access and communion with their Creator! They had everything except the knowledge of evil. So, the knowledge of evil was how Satan deceived them into disobeying. The Tree of Life was not a temptation because they were created to have eternal life. But after their fall, God chose to protect them from eternally living in sin with no chance of redemption. It was in His mercy that He "kicked them out of the Garden." (The Cherubim guarded the Holy of Holies; see Exod 25:18–22, Ps 99:1.)

We Will Return to God's Garden

Revelation 22:1–5: *Then he showed me a river of the water of life, clear as crystal, coming from the throne of God and of the Lamb, in the middle of its street. On either side of the river was the tree of life, bearing twelve kinds of fruit, yielding its fruit every month; and the leaves of the tree were for the healing of the nations. There will no longer be any curse; and the throne of God and of the Lamb will be in it, and His bond-servants will serve Him; they will see His face, and His name will be on their foreheads. And there will no longer be any night; and they will not have need of the light of a lamp nor the light of the sun, because the Lord God will illumine them; and they will reign forever and ever.*

PERSONAL APPLICATION: ARE YOU A WORSHIPPER?

These same duties of serving/worshipping *(avad / avodah)* and guarding *(shomer)* that were given to Adam were also given to Aaron and his sons, who made up the Aaronic Priesthood. They ministered in the Tabernacle, the place where God chose to manifest His holy presence to the children of Israel. And in their worship and service, the priests had to be careful to honor the Lord and to guard His holiness as they interceded for the nation of Israel. Priests were chosen to do God's holy service.

Are you a worshipper and servant of the Lord? Do you guard His Holiness? Let's pause in our consideration of Adam's role in the Garden of God and apply these *"in the beginning"* principles to our walk as believers in Yeshua. Adam was to worship/serve in the Garden and to guard the Garden. We were created to worship Him. Ephesians 1:4 says, *"Just as He chose us in Him before the foundation of the world, that we would be holy and blameless before Him."* The only way we can be holy before Him is to worship and serve our King, because we are His royal priesthood.

> 1 Peter 2:9: *But you are a chosen race, a royal priesthood, a holy nation, a people for God's own possession, so that you may proclaim the excellencies of Him who has called you out of darkness into His marvelous light.*

We have practical application for how to guard the holiness of our King from Proverbs 4:23:

> *Watch* (netzer) *over your heart with all diligence* (shomer), *for from it flow the springs of life.*

Our thoughts begin in the heart! We are exhorted to be a guard *(netzer)* with diligence *(shomer,* watch, care). In Proverbs 4:23, there are two words for guarding your heart. We must be on the alert to any defilement of our hearts because this is the beginning of our thought life.

51

More Review and Application

1. How does the fact that God gives us His redemptive hope through the women's seed give all women His value? Remember, our worth is vindicated as it is through the seed of the woman that the evil one will be destroyed.

2. How many of us have said that having children and raising children is the most difficult yet the most fulfilling aspect of our lives? What does God's discipline for the woman—God said, "I will greatly multiply your pain in childbirth, in pain you will bring forth children (Gen 3:16)—point us to? Hint: Both aspects point us to our need for Messiah's grace to be poured into our lives.

   2 Corinthians 12:9: *My grace is sufficient for you, for power is perfected in weakness.*

3. Review these verses and pray about how you can apply them to your life:

   1 Timothy 2:14–15 (ESV, definitions added): *and Adam was not deceived, but the woman was deceived* (rebellion, "I'll do it my way") *and became a transgressor. Yet she will be saved* (fulfilled) *through childbearing* (raising children)—*if they continue in faith and love and holiness, with self-control* (saved mind).

   Titus 2:3 (definitions added): *Older women likewise are to be reverent in their behavior, not malicious gossips nor enslaved to much wine, teaching what is good, so that they may encourage* (sophronizo) *the young women to love their husbands, to love their children, to be sensible* (sophron—saved mind), *pure, workers at home, kind, being subject* (hupotasso) *to their own husbands, so that the word of God will not be dishonored* (blasphemeo—despise God's Word).

4. How should being in God's royal priesthood affect our walk as believers in Messiah Yeshua?

In Genesis 2:15 Adam's role to cultivate *(avad)* and keep *(shomer) Gan Eden* was pointing to the duties of the Aaronic priesthood in the Tabernacle:

> Numbers 18:7 (definitions added): *"But you and your sons with you shall attend* (shomer) *to your priesthood for everything concerning the altar and inside the veil, and you are to perform* (avad) *service. I am giving you the priesthood as a bestowed service, but the outsider who comes near shall be put to death."*

Today we are His *"royal priesthood, a holy nation, a people for his own possession, that [we] may proclaim the excellencies of him who called [us] out of darkness into his marvelous light"* (1 Peter 2:9, ESV).

Why do we need to guard our hearts? Proverbs 4:23 (definitions added)—*Watch* (netzer) *over your heart* (lev) *with all diligence* (mishmar, from shomar), *for from it flow the springs of life.*

Lev is "heart" in Hebrew, and it wasn't just a body part to the Israelites. In Biblical times the Israelites thought of the heart as not only the organ that gives physical life but more importantly as the place where you think and make sense of the world—where you feel emotions and make choices. So according to Proverbs 4:23, everything begins in your heart.

Satan's strategy has not changed as the battle for our hearts and minds continues. We must remember that God is the only One who can truly protect us, as is stated in Psalm 121:4–5 (definitions added): *Behold, He who keeps* (shomer) *Israel will neither slumber nor sleep. The LORD is your keeper* (shomer); *the LORD is your shade on your right hand.*

Just as God promises to be the guardian of Israel, He is the One who protects and guards those who love Him.

Psalm 145:20 (definition added): *The LORD keeps* (shomer) *all who love Him, but all the wicked He will destroy.*

Hear, O Lord,
and be gracious to me;
O Lord, be my helper. You have
turned for me my mourning into
dancing; You have loosed my
sackcloth and girded me with
gladness, that my soul may sing
praise to You and not be silent. O
Lord my God, I will give thanks
to You forever.

Psalm 30:10–12

Two

The Matriarch of Israel: *Sarah*

In this chapter we will continue to learn of God's unfolding plan of redemption where we meet Abraham and Sarah: the patriarch and matriarch of the nation of Israel.

THE PROMISE

God's Call to Abram: The Abrahamic Covenant

In Genesis 12, God called Abram to leave his country and follow Him to a land that God would reveal to him. God promised Abram that He would make Him a great nation, bless him, and give him a great name. Those who blessed Abram and his people would be blessed, but the individual who cursed him would be cursed. The final part of the verse speaks about all the families of the earth being blessed in Abram's family.

> Genesis 12:1–3: *Now the LORD said to Abram, "Go forth from your country, and from your relatives and from your*

father's house, to the land which I will show you; and I will
make you a great nation, and I will bless you, and make
your name great; and so you shall be a blessing; and I will
bless those who bless you, and the one who curses you I
will curse. And in you all the families of the earth will be
blessed."

How would all the families of the earth be blessed? The final promise *"in you all the families of the earth will be blessed"* would be accomplished through the family that God chose.

This is quite a promise to receive! Imagine its impact on Abram's wife, for at this point in the story we know only two things about her: she was called Sarai and she was barren (Genesis 11:29–30). In ancient times it was always seen as a blessing to have children; therefore being barren was a removal of blessing.

THE PROBLEM

So Abram and Sarai received the promise of having a child, a son, not once, but several times. Why did it have to take so long to be fulfilled? How long did it take, exactly? We'll look at this in a minute.

Another problematic factor in this history shows up in Sarai's relationship with Abram. In the course of their travels, Abram lied to the Pharoah and King Abimelech. Because Sarai was so beautiful, Abram was concerned about his own safety, so he told both the pharaoh and the king that Sarai was his sister. On the second occasion when he lied and said, "She is my sister," Abram tried to explain to King Abimelech his exact relationship with Sarai. Abram said to King Abimelech in Genesis 20:12:

Besides, she actually is my sister, the daughter of my
father (Terah), but not the daughter of my mother, and
she became my wife.

The first time Abram lied about Sarai was to the Egyptian Pharoah.

> Genesis 12:10-13: *Now there was a famine in the land; so Abram went down to Egypt to sojourn there, for the famine was severe in the land. It came about when he came near to Egypt, that he said to Sarai his wife, "See now, I know that you are a beautiful woman; and when the Egyptians see you, they will say, 'This is his wife'; and they will kill me, but they will let you live. Please say that you are my sister so that it may go well with me because of you, and that I may live on account of you."*

How do you think Sarai felt when Abram lied about her—twice—and both times she was put in danger because of his lies?! The first scenario with Pharaoh played out as follows in Genesis 12:14–16:

> *It came about when Abram came into Egypt, the Egyptians saw that the woman was very beautiful. Pharaoh's officials saw her and praised her to Pharaoh; and the woman was taken into Pharaoh's house. Therefore he treated Abram well for her sake; and gave him sheep and oxen and donkeys and male and female servants and female donkeys and camels.*

Both Pharaoh (Genesis 12:10–20) and King Abimelech (Genesis 20:1–18) were prevented by God from touching Sarai (when she was sixty-five and eighty-nine years old respectively!), but one of the female servants that Abram received as a gift from the Pharoah was named Hagar. She was added to their household and became one of Sarai's maids, and this isn't the last we'll hear of her.

Sarah Takes Matters into Her Own Hands!

The Timeline for the Promised Baby

- While he was in Ur, God promised Abram: "*Go forth from your country, and …I will make you a great nation…" Abram was seventy-five years old when he departed from Haran* (Genesis 12:2-4).

- Once they arrived in Canaan, the Lord promised: *To your descendants I will give this land* (Genesis 12:7).

- After they had settled in Canaan and Lot separated from them, the Lord said: *All the land which you see, I will give it to you and to your descendants forever. I will make your descendants as the dust of the earth, so that if anyone can number the dust of the earth, then your descendants can also be numbered* (Genesis 13:15–16).

- In Genesis 15:4–5, again the Lord promised, *"One who will come forth from your own body, he shall be your heir." And He took him outside and said, "Now look toward the heavens, and count the stars, if you are able to count them." And He said to him, "So shall your descendants be."*

- And at the end of Genesis 15, the Lord made more promises and again said, *"To your descendants I have given this land, from the river of Egypt as far as the great river, the river Euphrates"* (Genesis 15:18).

From the time of the first promise to Abram to this point in the story, despite the numerous repetitions of the promise, ten years had passed. Sarai was done waiting on the LORD. So we've arrived at Sarai's lowest point of faith. She decided to assist God in His plan for an heir.

Genesis 16:1–6 (definitions added): *Now Sarai, Abram's wife had borne him no children, and she had an Egyptian maid whose name was Hagar. So Sarai said to Abram, "Now behold, the Lord has prevented* (restrained) *me from bearing children. Please go into my maid; perhaps I shall obtain* (banah—build) *children through her." And Abram listened to the voice of Sarai. After Abram had lived ten years in the land of Canaan, Abram's wife Sarai took Hagar the Egyptian, her maid, and gave her to her husband Abram as his wife. He went in to Hagar, and she conceived; and when she saw that she had conceived, her mistress was despised* (treated with disrespect) *in her sight. And Sarai said to Abram, "May the wrong done me be upon you. I gave my maid into your arms, but when she saw that she had conceived, I was despised in her sight. May the Lord judge between you and me." But Abram said to Sarai, "Behold, your maid is in your power; do to her what is good in your sight." So Sarai treated her harshly, and she fled from her presence.*

This was the result of Sarai's grand plan. No child of her own; but forced to endure mockery in her own house. Broken relationships. In the conversation above, Sarai let Abram know that the disrespect and contempt Hagar showed to her should come back on Abram, and in the end the LORD would be the judge of what took place. Abram's response was to remind Sarai that her maid was under her power (*yad* in Hebrew means her "hand") and she could do what was *right in her sight*. Do you think that Sarai was remembering how Abram had lied to the Pharaoh about her being his sister, since from that interaction Pharoah came many gifts— including Hagar? Because of Hagar's attitude and actions against her, Sarai afflicted (*anah*) and humiliated Hagar so much so that Hagar ran away from her.

Can you identify with Sarah in her lowest point of faith when she says to Abram, *"Now behold, the LORD has prevented me from bearing children?"* How do we respond to God in our most disappointing and difficult situations? Blame Him? Lash out at others? Do we take matters into our own hands instead of trusting in God's promises, His timing, and His provision?

Well, the journey isn't over for Sarai. Genesis 12:4 tells us Abram was *seventy-five years old* when God made the promise of children, and the son promised them wouldn't show up until Abram was one hundred.

THE RESTORATION

What About Hagar?

What *about* Hagar? So far in this tale, she has had no say in her own fate. She was an Egyptian woman, a servant or concubine of the Pharaoh, given away to a Hebrew, going from a palace to a tent, then expected to bear the Hebrew's child. Who could blame her for making the best of her situation, or for feeling superior to her master's wife? For her mockery, though, the Scripture says Sarai oppressed her; so much so that she fled.

> Genesis 16:7–8: *Now the angel of the LORD found her by a spring of water in the wilderness, by the spring on the way to Shur. He said, "Hagar, Sarai's maid, where have you come from and where are you going?" And she said, "I am fleeing from the presence of my mistress Sarai."*

The Angel of the Lord was an appearance of Yeshua Himself. We will meet Him in Genesis 18 as well. But here, Yeshua was pouring out His comfort and mercy on Hagar and the son in her womb. He told her to return to Sarai and yield to her authority. He then gave her a promise about her unborn son.

> Genesis 16:9–12 (definition added): *Then the angel of the LORD said to her, "Return to your mistress, and submit yourself to her authority." Moreover, the angel of the LORD said to her, "I will greatly multiply your descendants so that they will be too many to count." The angel of the LORD said to her further, "Behold, you are with child, and you will bear a son; and you shall call his name Ishmael (God*

hears), *because the* LORD *has given heed to your affliction. He will be a wild donkey of a man, his hand will be against everyone, and everyone's hand will be against him; and he will live to the east of all his brothers."*

Hagar's Revelation of El Roi—The God Who Sees Me

Genesis 16:13–16 (definition added): *Then* [Hagar] *called the name of the* LORD *who spoke to her, "You are a God who sees"; for she said, "Have I even remained alive here after seeing Him?" Therefore the well was called Beer-lahai-roi* (well of the Living One who sees me); *behold, it is between Kadesh and Bered. So Hagar bore Abram a son; and Abram called the name of his son, whom Hagar bore, Ishmael. Abram was eighty-six years old when Hagar bore Ishmael to him.*

How could this revelation encourage Hagar and give her hope? The way Yeshua spoke to her indicated that there was a future for her and her son. He also assured her that God was aware of her situation and saw everything that was happening. Even the name of the water well—Beer-lahai-roi, "the well of the Living One who sees me"—testified to God's personal care and kindness to Hagar.

How does God's mercy poured out to Hagar speak to you? Yeshua—the Angel of the Lord appeared to her, and she called Him El Roi—the God who sees me.

Do you believe that Yeshua not only sees your specific needs but will also provide for you in His abundant grace?

Sarah—The Mother of Israel as Well as Many Nations!

Now back to Sarai. Where was her encouragement and hope?

First, in Genesis 17:5, God changed Abram's name (Abram means "exalted father") to Abraham, which means "father of a multitude." Then, in verse fifteen, God changed Sarai's name to Sarah.

> Genesis 17:15–16 (definitions added): *Then God said to Abraham, "As for Sarai your wife, you shall not call her name Sarai* (my princess), *but Sarah* (princess of many) *shall be her name. I will bless her, and indeed I will give you a son by her. Then I will bless her, and she shall be a mother of nations; kings of peoples will come from her."*

What a noble position God conferred on Sarah, that she would be a mother of nations and kings of people would come from her!

This message from God, however, caused Abraham to fall down and laugh in unbelief! Remember Abraham was ten years older than Sarah, and both were too old to have children, especially from Sarah's barren womb. Additionally, it had now been almost twenty-five years since the original promise of children for Abraham.

> Genesis 17:17: *Then Abraham fell on his face and laughed, and said in his heart, "Will a child be born to a man one hundred years old? And will Sarah, who is ninety years old, bear a child?"*

How disheartening, to hear your husband laugh at the notion of you bearing a child! Then, Abraham tried to reason with God that Hagar's son Ishmael could be the child of promise. But God responded immediately to that suggestion:

> *"No, but Sarah your wife will bear you a son, and you shall call his name Isaac; and I will establish My covenant with him for an everlasting covenant for his descendants after him.... My covenant I will establish with Isaac, whom Sarah will bear to you at this season next year." When He finished talking with him, God went up from Abraham* (Genesis 17:19, 21–22).

The son of promise would come from Sarah and Abraham's union! God affirmed that the *seed* that would bring redemption, first promised in Genesis 3:15, would grow from Sarah's womb, and this time He gave them a definitive due date for the baby.

Two Angels and Yeshua Visit and Renew the Promise

> Genesis 18:1-8: *Now the LORD appeared to him by the oaks of Mamre, while he was sitting at the tent door in the heat of the day. When he lifted up his eyes and looked, behold, three men were standing opposite him; and when he saw them, he ran from the tent door to meet them and bowed himself to the earth, and said, "My Lord, if now I have found favor in Your sight, please do not pass Your servant by. Please let a little water be brought and wash your feet, and rest yourselves under the tree; and I will bring a piece of bread, that you may refresh yourselves; after that you may go on, since you have visited your servant." And they said, "So do, as you have said." So Abraham hurried into the tent to Sarah, and said, "Quickly, prepare three measures of fine flour, knead it and make bread cakes." Abraham also ran to the herd, and took a tender and choice calf and gave it to the servant, and he hurried to prepare it. He took curds and milk and the calf which he had prepared, and placed it before them; and he was standing by them under the tree as they ate.*

Yeshua, the Angel of the LORD, and two angels came to visit Abraham and Sarah. According to Mideast hospitality, Abraham immediately gave them refreshments. He instructed Sarah, who was still in her tent, to prepare food and got a calf from his flock for his servants to prepare.

After lunch, God repeated His promise to do something that was impossible to expect to happen by human standards, and also confirmed the due date for the baby.

Genesis 18:9–12: *Then they said to him, "Where is Sarah your wife?" And he said, "There, in the tent." He said, "I will surely return to you at this time next year; and behold, Sarah your wife will have a son." And Sarah was listening at the tent door, which was behind him. Now Abraham and Sarah were old, advanced in age; Sarah was past childbearing. Sarah laughed to herself, saying, "After I have become old, shall I have pleasure, my lord being old also?"*

But the problems remained: the prospective parents were old; they were *advanced in age* and Sarah was *past childbearing.* God picked two people who couldn't have children to begin the Nation of Israel. They were a most unlikely couple to birth a nation. So why did He choose Abraham and Sarah?

God Gives Us His Reason When He was Speaking to Moses

Deuteronomy 7:6–8: *"For you are a holy people to the Lord your God; the Lord your God has chosen you to be a people for His own possession out of all the peoples who are on the face of the earth. The Lord did not set His love on you nor choose you because you were more in number than any of the peoples, for you were the fewest of all peoples, but because the Lord loved you and kept the oath which He swore to your forefathers, the Lord brought you out by a mighty hand and redeemed you from the house of slavery, from the hand of Pharaoh king of Egypt."*

God chose Israel to be His own special people in order to keep them by His promises, His redemption, and His provision. **He chose them because He loved them.**

Personal Application: Why Did God Choose You?

God chose Abraham and Sarah because He loved them. And that's exactly why God chose you to be His daughter! Lest I start to believe that I was so 'wise' to choose to follow God, I need to think about the truth of Scripture—that *He* chose *me* because He loves me. There was nothing I did to merit His love because it was all by His Grace—Yeshua's unmerited favor. I need to remember this at least a dozen times a day! Do you?

In speaking to His disciples, Yeshua told them,

> *You did not choose Me but I chose you, and appointed you that you would go and bear fruit, and that your fruit would remain, so that whatever you ask of the Father in My name He may give to you. This I command you, that you love one another* (John 15:16–17).

Do you believe that you are chosen, His royalty, and His holy, special possession?

> 1 Peter 2:9: *But you are a chosen race, a royal priesthood, a holy nation, a people for God's own possession, so that you may proclaim the excellencies of Him who has called you out of darkness into His marvelous light.*

Abraham Laughs and Sarah Laughs too!

Genesis 17:17 says that *"Abraham fell on his face and laughed, and said in his heart, 'Will a child be born to a man one hundred years old? And will Sarah, who is ninety years old, bear a child?'"* This was a laugh of incredulity. Abraham was in disbelief. Abraham wasn't the only one laughing, however.

> Genesis 18:13–15*: And the LORD said to Abraham, "Why did Sarah laugh, saying, 'Shall I indeed bear a child, when I am so old?' Is anything too difficult for the LORD? At the appointed time I will return to you, at this time next year, and Sarah shall have a son." Sarah denied it however, saying, "I did not laugh"; for she was afraid. And He said, "No, but you did laugh."*

The Scriptures indicate that Sarah's laugh was a combination of disbelief and fear. Genesis 18:15 indicates that she was afraid, and her laughter could have been an anxious response to God Himself. How did God respond to Sarah's laughter and her fear? God spoke directly to Sarah in verse fifteen. Wow, God spoke to her fears. He asked her the question, *"Is anything too difficult for the LORD?"* This question focused her heart and mind on who God is and what He alone can do. God let her know that He was aware of her laughter and her fear but His timing (*moed¹*) for her to have the son of promise was according to His appointment schedule. By the next year she would have Isaac in her arms.

Most of us know the answer to the question and can affirm that nothing is too difficult for the LORD! However when I learned that the word "difficult" in Hebrew is *palay*, this question took on a different dimension. *Palay* means "surpassing, extraordinary, wonderful." Let's ask the question again!

Is anything to surpassingly, extraordinarily wonderful for the LORD to perform for you?

This same word *palay* is used in Psalm 139:14 for "wonderfully" made. And to Jeremiah the prophet the LORD gave the same message in Jeremiah 32:27.

> Psalm 139:14 (definitions added): *I will give thanks to You, for I am fearfully and wonderfully* (palay) *made; wonderful are Your works, and my soul knows it very well.*

> Jeremiah 32:17, 27 (definitions added): *'Ah Lord GOD! Behold, You have made the heavens and the earth by Your great power and by Your outstretched arm! Nothing is too difficult* (palay) *for You. ... "Behold, I am the LORD, the God of all flesh; is anything too difficult* (palay) *for Me?"*

---

¹ *Moed* is Hebrew for God's appointments and is used in Leviticus 23:2 (definitions added): *"Speak to the sons of Israel and say to them, 'The Lord's appointed times* (moed) *which you shall proclaim as holy convocations—My appointed times* (moed) *are these.'"*

Palay is found in one of the names of Messiah as prophesied in Isaiah 9:6, "*Wonderful* (palay) *Counselor.*" When Yeshua gives us His counsel, it is extraordinary and surpasses all other counsel.

> Isaiah 9:6: *For a child will be born to us, a son will be given to us; and the government will rest on His shoulders; and His name will be called Wonderful Counselor, Mighty God, Eternal Father, Prince of Peace.*

Take time to meditate on these Scriptures and the truth that "there is nothing too wonderful and extraordinary that God cannot do for you!" To state in a positive way: "Nothing is too wonderful, too extraordinary for God to accomplish for you." He loves you!

According to God's Perfect Timing Isaac Is Born

As the Lord had said, Sarah did become pregnant and she gave birth at ninety years of age.

> Genesis 21:1–5 (definitions added): *Then the Lord took note of Sarah as He had said, and the Lord did (asah) for Sarah as He had promised. So Sarah conceived and bore a son to Abraham in his old age, at the appointed time (moed) of which God had spoken to him. Abraham called the name of his son who was born to him, whom Sarah bore to him, Isaac (he laughs). Then Abraham circumcised his son Isaac when he was eight days old, as God had commanded him. Now Abraham was one hundred years old when his son Isaac was born to him.*

Sarah Is Laughing for Joy Not Out of Fear and Disbelief

This time Sarah laughed for joy! And she didn't want to keep this miracle to herself. She wanted everyone who heard of God's miraculous act to also rejoice with her.

Genesis 21:6–7 (definitions added): *Sarah said, "God has made (asah) laughter for me; everyone who hears (shema) will laugh (laugh out loud) with me." And she said, "Who would have said to Abraham that Sarah would nurse children? Yet I have borne him a son in his old age."*

Her son's name Isaac means "laughter," reflecting the joy of this child of promise.

Does Sarah's joy resonate with you? Sarah's praise can definitely reverberate in all of as we remember all the blessings of God and praise Him together as a community. Has the LORD done great things for you in your community? Are you rejoicing together with praise and joyful shouting?

Psalm 103:1–2: *A Psalm of David. Bless the LORD, O my soul, and all that is within me, bless His holy name. Bless the LORD, O my soul, and forget none of His benefits.*

Psalm 30:10–12: *"Hear, O LORD, and be gracious to me; O LORD, be My helper." You have turned for me my mourning into dancing; You have loosed my sackcloth and girded me with gladness, that my soul may sing praise to You and not be silent. O LORD my God, I will give thanks to You forever.*

Psalm 126: *When the LORD brought back the captive ones of Zion, we were like those who dream. Then our mouth was filled with laughter and our tongue with joyful shouting; then they said among the nations, "The LORD has done great things for them." The LORD has done great things for us; we are glad. Restore our captivity, O LORD, as the streams in the South. Those who sow in tears shall reap with joyful shouting. He who goes to and fro weeping, carrying his bag of seed, shall indeed come again with a shout of joy, bringing his sheaves with him.*

Exodus 15:11: *"Who is like You among the gods, O LORD? Who is like You, majestic in holiness, awesome in praises, working wonders?"*

More Laughter, Not of Joy but of Ridicule and Derision

Sarah gave praise to God about the birth of the promised child Isaac.

> Genesis 21:8–9: *The child grew and was weaned, and Abraham made a great feast on the day that Isaac was weaned. Now Sarah saw the son of Hagar the Egyptian, whom she had borne to Abraham, mocking.*

This word "mocking" is based on the word "laughter" *(tzahak)*. In this context it can carry the meaning of ridiculing, make sport of, and jesting.

Sarah Tells Abraham What to Do and God Counsels Him to Listen to Her

> Genesis 21:10–13: *Therefore she said to Abraham, "Drive out this maid and her son, for the son of this maid shall not be an heir with my son Isaac." The matter distressed Abraham greatly because of his son. But God said to Abraham, "Do not be distressed because of the lad and your maid; whatever Sarah tells you, listen to her, for through Isaac your descendants shall be named. And of the son of the maid I will make a nation also, because he is your descendant."*

This promise of a nation through his son Ishmael is a fulfillment of the Abrahamic Covenant in Genesis 12:3 where God said to Abraham that through him "*all the families of the earth will be blessed.*" With the assurance of God's blessing for Hagar and Ishmael, Abraham listened to Sarah and the next morning sent them away with just a container of water and some bread. They both wandered into the wilderness of Beersheva, where God Himself met them.

First Mention of Tears: Both Hagar and Ishmael

> Genesis 21:14–21 (emphasis added): *So Abraham rose early in the morning and took bread and a skin of water*

71

and gave them to Hagar, putting them on her shoulder, and gave her the boy, and sent her away. And she departed and wandered about in the wilderness of Beersheba. When the water in the skin was used up, she left the boy under one of the bushes. Then she went and sat down opposite him, about a bowshot away, for she said, "Do not let me see the boy die." **And she sat opposite him, and lifted up her voice and wept. God heard the lad crying; and** *the angel of God called to Hagar from heaven and said to her, "What is the matter with you, Hagar? Do not fear, for God has heard the voice of the lad where he is. Arise, lift up the lad, and hold him by the hand, for I will make a great nation of him." Then God opened her eyes and she saw a well of water; and she went and filled the skin with water and gave the lad a drink. God was with the lad, and he grew; and he lived in the wilderness and became an archer. He lived in the wilderness of Paran, and his mother took a wife for him from the land of Egypt.*

Appropriately, Ishmael means "God hears," (combining *shema* and *El*). God heard and answered their prayers and dried their tears.

How does this first mention of tears speak to you? It reminds me that wherever I am and no matter how far I might wander God's merciful grace will find me. He gives me His perspective of my life and my situation. He opens my eyes to see that He is the source of living water just as he opened the eyes of Hagar and assured her of His presence and His provision. In the beginning of His earthly ministry, Yeshua met the Samaritan woman at the well and told her about the water of life that He alone could provide for her.

John 4:13–14: *Yeshua answered and said to her, "Everyone who drinks of this water will thirst again; but whoever drinks of the water that I will give him shall never thirst; but the water that I will give him will become in him a well of water springing up to eternal life."*

Yeshua's words brought her to faith, and she spread the message throughout her town that she had found the Messiah.

> John 4:39–42: *From that city many of the Samaritans believed in Him because of the word of the woman who testified, "He told me all the things that I have done." So when the Samaritans came to Yeshua, they were asking Him to stay with them; and He stayed there two days. Many more believed because of His word; and they were saying to the woman, "It is no longer because of what you said that we believe, for we have heard for ourselves and know that this One is indeed the Savior of the world."*

The Binding of Isaac: Abraham's Final Test

Genesis 22 is the famous account of Abraham obeying the Lord and taking Isaac to Mount Moriah for sacrifice. In retrospect, I love how these promises culminate in the first mention of a lamb/ram provided in the place of an individual as the sacrifice.

> Genesis 22:7–8 (emphasis added): *Isaac spoke to Abraham his father and said, "My father!" And he said, "Here I am, my son." And he said, "Behold, the fire and the wood, but where is the lamb for the burnt offering?" Abraham said, "**God will provide for Himself the lamb for the burnt offering**, my son." So the two of them walked on together.*

Abraham Believed God Could Raise Isaac from the Dead!

> Hebrews 11:17–19: *By faith Abraham, when he was tested, offered up Isaac, and he who had received the promises was offering up his only begotten son; it was he to whom it was said, "In Isaac your descendants shall be called." He considered that God is able to raise people even*

from the dead, from which he also received him back as a type (figuratively speaking, example).

Genesis 22:13–14 (definitions added): *Then Abraham raised his eyes and looked, and behold, behind him a ram caught in the thicket by his horns; and Abraham went and took the ram and offered him up for a burnt offering in the place of his son. Abraham called the name of that place The LORD Will Provide* (raah, see), *as it is said to this day, "In the mount of the LORD it will be provided"* (Jehovah Yireh—the LORD sees and provides).

Do you believe that the LORD is your Jehovah Yireh? I hope you can respond with a resounding "YES"! Because God already sees the needs in your own life and desires to meet those needs. We are encouraged to "pray without ceasing" because God will answer your prayers.

1 Thessalonians 5:16–24: *Rejoice always; pray without ceasing; in everything give thanks; for this is God's will for you in Messiah Yeshua. Do not quench the Spirit; do not despise prophetic utterances. But examine everything carefully; hold fast to that which is good; abstain from every form of evil. Now may the God of peace Himself sanctify you entirely; and may your spirit and soul and body be preserved complete, without blame at the coming of our Lord Yeshua the Messiah. Faithful is He who calls you, and He also will bring it to pass.*

Our Study of Sarah Concludes

Genesis 23:1–2: *Now Sarah lived one hundred and twenty-seven years; these were the years of the life of Sarah. And Sarah died in Kiriath-arba (that is, Hebron) in the land of Canaan; and Abraham went in to mourn for Sarah and to weep for her.*

And for four hundred shekels of silver, Abraham purchased the place where he buried his beloved wife Sarah.

Genesis 23:19–20: *After this, Abraham buried Sarah his wife in the cave of the field at Machpelah facing Mamre (that is, Hebron) in the land of Canaan. So the field and the cave that is in it, were deeded over to Abraham for a burial site by the sons of Heth.*

APPLICATION: THOUGHTS AND REFLECTIONS

Sarah's esteem in Israel's history is seen in how Isaiah exhorted the people of Israel and proclaimed:

> Isaiah 51:1–2 (CJB): *"Listen to me, you pursuers of justice, you who seek ADONAI: consider the rock from which you were cut, the quarry from which you were dug—consider Avraham your father and Sarah, who gave birth to you; in that I called him when he was only one person, then blessed him and made him many.*

Consider your purpose as His daughter. Remember that everything God did for Sarah was because of His choosing of her and by His miracle-working power in her life. He chose you! He pours out His grace and power for you to live as His faithful daughter.

Think about the names of God that were revealed in these sections and what these same names can mean for you.

- **El Roi**: The God Who Sees Me—Genesis 16:13 from Hagar
- **Jehovah Yireh**: The God Who Sees and Provides—Genesis 22:14 from Abraham
- **El Shaddai**: God Almighty—Genesis 17:1 from God to Abraham

Paul's prayer for us in light of our awesome El Shaddai who is exceedingly and abundantly powerful!

> Ephesians 3:16–21: *that He would grant you, according to the riches of His glory, to be strengthened with power through His Spirit in the inner man, so that Messiah may dwell in your hearts through faith; and that you, being rooted and grounded in love, may be able to comprehend with all the saints what is the breadth and length and height and depth, and to know the love of Messiah which surpasses knowledge, that you may be filled up to all the*

fullness of God. Now to Him who is able to do exceedingly abundantly beyond all that we ask or think, according to the power that works within us, to Him be the glory in the congregation and in Messiah Yeshua to all generations forever and ever. Amen.

1. Sarah is one of four women named in Hebrews 11. How does Hebrews 11:11 speak to you? Like Sarah, let's grow in our faith in Yeshua, to trust Him in every area of our lives.

   Hebrews 11:11: *By faith even Sarah herself received ability to conceive, even beyond the proper time of life, since she considered Him faithful who had promised.*

   Genesis 18:14, when two angels and Yeshua visit Abraham and Sarah (Genesis 18:11–14): *"Is anything too difficult for the LORD? At the appointed time I will return to you, at this time next year, and Sarah will have a son."*

In the question *"Is anything too difficult for the LORD?,"* the word "difficult" is *palay* in Hebrew and also carries the meaning of "too surpassing," "too extraordinary," "too wonderful."

   Psalm 139:14: *I will give thanks to You, for I am fearfully and wonderfully made; wonderful are Your works, and my soul knows it very well* (see also Jeremiah 32:17, 27; Exodus 15:11; Luke 1:35–38; Isaiah 9:6).

The, Extraordinary, Wonderful, Supernatural Birth of Our Messiah, Yeshua

   Luke 1:35–38: *The angel answered and said to her, "The Holy Spirit will come upon you, and the power of the Most High will overshadow you; and for that reason the holy Child shall be called the Son of God. And behold, even your relative Elizabeth has also conceived a son in her old age; and she who was called barren is now in her sixth month.*

For nothing will be impossible with God." And Miriam said, "Behold, the bondslave of the Lord; may it be done to me according to your word." And the angel departed from her.

2. Do you believe that ALL things are possible with God?

God's miraculous and mighty resurrection power is demonstrated through Sarah's womb. We have the same assurance in Yeshua: that which was dead becomes alive, that which was barren becomes fertile and fruitful, and our mourning is turned into dancing.

> Psalm 30:10–12: *Hear, O LORD, and be gracious to me; O LORD, be my helper. You have turned for me my mourning into dancing; You have loosed my sackcloth and girded me with gladness, that my soul may sing praise to You and not be silent. O LORD my God, I will give thanks to You forever.*

3. How does Sarah teach us to respond to our husbands who are not following the Lord?

In Genesis 18:12, Sarah's comment to herself became an example for each of us when she called Abraham lord—*adon*—in her heart and soul. She respected her husband in her heart and her thoughts reflected this respect when she called him "lord" or "master."

> 1 Peter 3:1–6 (NIV): *Wives, in the same way submit yourselves to your own husbands so that, if any of them do not believe the word, they may be won over without words by the behavior of their wives, when they see the purity and reverence of your lives. Your beauty should not come from outward adornment, such as elaborate hairstyles and the wearing of gold jewelry or fine clothes. Rather, it should be that of your inner self, the unfading beauty of a gentle and quiet spirit, which is of great worth in God's sight. For this is the way the holy women of the past who put their hope in God used to adorn themselves. They*

submitted themselves to their own husbands, like Sarah, who obeyed Abraham and called him her lord. You are her daughters if you do what is right and do not give way to fear (see also Proverbs 31:30).

Sarah's incredulous laughter was turned to rejoicing because of how God answered prayer:

Genesis 21:6–7 (definitions added): *Sarah said, "God has made* (asah) *laughter for me; everyone who hears* (shema) *will laugh* (laugh out loud) *with me." And she said, "Who would have said to Abraham that Sarah would nurse children? Yet I have borne him a son in his old age."*

We also noted some important verses where Sarah is recognized and honored throughout Scripture. I invite you to apply these truths and promises found in these verses in your own life as you read and follow up with prayer.

Isaiah 51:1–2 (CJB): *Listen to me, you pursuers of justice, you who seek Adonai: consider the rock from which you were cut, the quarry from which you were dug—consider Avraham your father and Sarah, who gave birth to you; in that I called him when he was only one person, then blessed him and made him many.*

Prayers of Thanksgiving Upon God's Promises:

Here are some prayers to get you started giving God thanks! Add your own prayers specifically remembering God's faithfulness to you.

Dear Lord, I'm remembering and praising You for Your covenant promises to Sarah and Abraham. Thank You for always keeping Your promises to me as well.

Romans 9:9: *For this is the word of promise: "At this time I will come, and Sarah shall have a son."*

Dear Lord, thank You for Your timing in Your redemptive plan and thank You for Your timing in my life. I praise You,

Lord, that You are never early or late. I have confidence that Your plan for me is always in the fullness of Your time.

> 1 Peter 3:6:*Just as Sarah obeyed Abraham, calling him lord, and you have become her children if you do what is right without being frightened by any fear.*

Dear Lord, help us to follow Sarah's example of godly submission and respect for our husbands—to win him without a word as we humble ourselves under Your mighty hand of grace.

> Hebrews 11:11: *By faith even Sarah herself received ability to conceive, even beyond the proper time of life, since she considered Him faithful who had promised.*

Dear Lord, help me to grow in trusting Your miracle-working power for Your timing and provision in my life.

For you have not come to a mountain that can be touched and to a blazing fire, and to darkness and gloom and whirlwind... But you have come to Mount Zion and to the city of the living God, the heavenly Jerusalem, and...to the congregation of the firstborn who are enrolled in heaven, and to God, the Judge of all, and to the spirits of the righteous made perfect, and to Yeshua, the mediator of a new covenant...

Hebrews 12:18, 22-24

Three

A Question of Twins & Trust: Rebekah

This chapter introduces to us the next woman in the line of redemption for all mankind. We will meet a very beautiful young virgin named Rebekah. We are given a snapshot of the first arranged marriage in the Scriptures. In this ancient culture, arranged marriages were commonplace and we will have a bird's eye view of how Rebekah was chosen.

Abraham had passed the test with flying colors as he was willing to offer up Isaac, the son of promise. In Genesis 22:16–18, the Lord let Abraham know that he had demonstrated that his love for God was primary:

> *By Myself I have sworn, declares the LORD, because you have done this thing and have not withheld your son, your only son, indeed I will greatly bless you, and I will greatly multiply your seed as the stars of the heavens and as the sand which is on the seashore; and your seed shall possess the gate of their enemies. In your seed all the nations of*

the earth shall be blessed, because you have obeyed My voice.

Since Abraham was very old and his son Isaac was pushing forty, Abraham felt the urgency to find a wife for his son of promise. He commissioned his most trusted servant, Eliezer, to carry out this most important task and be the matchmaker.

> Genesis 24:1–6 (definitions added): *Now Abraham was old* (one hundred forty), *advanced in age; and the LORD had blessed Abraham in every way. Abraham said to his servant* (Eliezer—see Gen 15:2), *the oldest of his household, who had charge of all that he owned, "Please place your hand under my thigh, and I will make you swear* (sheva—swear an oath) *by the LORD, the God of heaven and the God of earth, that you shall not take a wife for my son from the daughters of the Canaanites, among whom I live, but you will go to my country and to my relatives, and take a wife for my son Isaac." The servant said to him, "Suppose the woman is not willing to follow me to this land; should I take your son back to the land from where you came?" Then Abraham said to him, "Beware* (shamar—be on guard) *that you do not take my son back there!"*

This was an overwhelming duty for Eliezer whose name means, "my God is help." *Eli* means "my God" and *ezer* means "help." Giving him the assurance he needed, Abraham instructed him where he was to go. He also promised Eliezer that God's angel would go before him to guide him in the matchmaking role.

By the way, does the Hebrew word *ezer* sound familiar? We learned in Genesis 2:18 that God created women to be the "*ezer kenegdo*" for the man. God created the woman to be a strength and power *(ezer)* corresponding to or equal to the man. And we will continue to learn that to fulfill our calling as women of faith and courage, we must absolutely have the truth that "our God is our strength, power, help—Eliezer."

THE PROMISE

First, a Promise for Eliezer

Abraham continued to give Eliezer encouragement to let him know that he was equipped for this task to be the matchmaker. He shared his testimony of God's leadership in his life.

> Genesis 24:7–9 (definition added): *"The LORD, the God of heaven* (Elohai HaShamayim), *who took me from my father's house and from the land of my birth, and who spoke to me and who swore to me, saying, 'To your descendants I will give this land,' He will send His angel before you, and you will take a wife for my son from there. But if the woman is not willing to follow you, then you will be free from this my oath; only do not take my son back there." So the servant placed his hand under the thigh of Abraham his master, and swore to him concerning this matter.*

What do you do when God gives you a seemingly impossible task to accomplish? We can learn much from the actions of Eliezer as he immediately prayed to Abraham's God when he arrived at Abraham's former home.

Eliezer's prayer to God is in Genesis 24:12–15: He said,

> *"O LORD, the God of my master Abraham, please grant me success today, and show lovingkindness to my master Abraham. Behold, I am standing by the spring, and the daughters of the men of the city are coming out to draw water; now may it be that the girl to whom I say, 'Please let down your jur so that I may drink,' and who answers, 'Drink, and I will water your camels also'—may she be the one whom You have appointed for Your servant Isaac; and*

by this I will know that You have shown lovingkindness to my master." Before he had finished speaking, behold, Rebekah who was born to Bethuel the son of Milcah, the wife of Abraham's brother Nahor, came out with her jar on her shoulder.

Can you hear the humble spirit of Eliezer and his respect for Abraham as he prayed? His prayer was specific in asking God to show him the woman that God Himself had selected. Amazingly, before Eliezer's prayer was completed, God sent him Rebekah.

Genesis 24:16–19: *The girl was very beautiful, a virgin, and no man had had relations with her; and she went down to the spring and filled her jar and came up. Then the servant ran to meet her, and said, "Please let me drink a little water from your jar." And she said, "Drink, my lord"; and she quickly lowered her jar to her hand, and gave him a drink. Now when she had finished giving him a drink, she said, "I will draw also for your camels until they have finished drinking."*

YOU ALSO HAVE BEEN SENT

Consider with me that we also have a command from our Master Yeshua and it's found in Matthew 28:18–20. This passage is known as the Great Commission, which Yeshua gave to His disciples, including us. It included His parting instructions, just before He ascended to Heaven.

Matthew 28:18–20: *And Yeshua came up and spoke to them, saying, "All authority has been given to Me in heaven and on earth. Go therefore and make disciples of all the nations, baptizing them in the name of the Father and the Son and the Holy Spirit, teaching them to observe all that I commanded you; and lo, I am with you always, even to the end of the age."*

Compare Eliezer obeying the commission that Abraham gave him and the Great Commission that Yeshua gave us! Eliezer was commissioned to find a bride for Isaac. Jacob would be in the Messianic line of Yeshua. Whereas in Yeshua's Great Commission, He is calling us to go and make disciples of all nations who will become His bride for eternity.

INTERCESSORY PRAYER

1. Eliezer's prayer was an intercessor's prayer. He was praying on behalf of his master Abraham that he would be successful in accomplishing the task before him.

When we pray for others, do we pray in the Name of our Master Yeshua the Messiah? In this daunting task, we must remember that we are reaching those whom God has chosen. Do you consider yourself His servant willing to serve Him—wherever you go? What does Romans 8:34 teach us about Yeshua's ministry to us?

2. Eliezer took initiative and went to a specific place per Abraham's instructions to find Isaac a bride.

Are we willing to take the initiative in sharing the Good News and loving those around us? As the Holy Spirit leads us, will we go out of our way at times to share and disciple others?

3. Praying for success that will reflect upon God's lovingkindness *(chesed)* is always the right way to pray!

Genesis 24:12: *He said, "O Lord, the God of my master Abraham, please grant me success today, and show lovingkindness to my master Abraham."*

Do we pray that God would bring about success in what or who we are praying for and that this success would reflect on the character of our God and His lovingkindness? Do we pray to show the truth that God is a God of love and His mercies are new every morning?

4. In Genesis 24:13–25, Eliezer asked the LORD for specific signs and confirmation that the woman would be the chosen bride for Isaac. God wants us to come to Him with specific needs. If we don't know exactly how to pray for a person or situation, we have the promise of the Holy Spirit praying for us (Romans 8:26–28).

5. When God answered his prayer, Eliezer worshiped the LORD and praised Him (Genesis 24:26–27).

Do we remember to thank the LORD and to praise Him with others?

6. Abraham encouraged Eliezer that an angel would guide him and be with him.

We not only have God's angels around us, but we also have the very presence of Yeshua with us because He promised us in Matthew 28:20: *"I am with you always, even to the end of the age."*

ENTERTAINING ANGELS

Can you think of a time when angels protected you or enabled you to minister in a situation? In my life I believe that angels have protected me as I narrowly evaded a car accident. Also, as a single woman living and traveling abroad, I felt protected from danger by angels.

Let me share with you one story of an angelic visitor, This happened several years ago. I was enthusiastically involved in exercise classes at a local gym. One instructor, Rose, was so vivacious that I always enjoyed her classes. After she came down with cancer, she continued to teach for a short time then eventually she had to stop but would visit the class in her wheelchair. A few of us were diligently praying for Rose's healing and salvation. However, after a hard-fought battle, it came to the point that she was hospitalized with little time remaining. I asked Sophie, who was close to Rose, if Rose had professed faith in Yeshua. When Sophie responded that she didn't think so, I strongly urged Sophie to go the hospital and share the Good News with her.

The next week I saw Sophie after class, and she said, "I need to talk with you."

She explained to me: "The day Rose died; I was in her hospital room along with some of her family. Rose was nonresponsive and all the family members had left the room for a brief break. Suddenly a tall, lovely woman came into the room and took Rose's hand. She told Rose that God loved her as she bent over and spoke to her. All this time I was in shock. Moments later, a family member returned and was upset that this unknown person was in the room. He told her to leave. And as she walked out, I ran after her to thank her but there was no sign of this heavenly messenger. It was as if she just disappeared." Wow! Sophie and I rejoiced together thanking God for answering our prayers.

(Names have been changed for privacy.)

Insight from Stacy:

In Genesis 24:32, Eliezer recounted to Laban and his family all the answered prayers God did in the moments that brought him to Rebekah's family. He was so excited as he said,

"I will not eat until I have told you what I have to say" (Gen 24:33, NIV).

He then shares everything that happened step by step. We can see that all he wanted to do was glorify God in this story. We see that Eliezer was feeling the blessing from God in a big way.

Like Eliezer, have you ever experienced God working through you and answering prayer in such a way that you wanted to stop everything you were doing and tell the world? If so, take time to write it out or share with others. Then pray for God to put people in your life with whom you can also share your story about how God has worked in your life!

A Promising Young Woman

Like Sarah, Rebekah was very beautiful! We learn she was a young woman and a virgin. She gave Eliezer the water willingly, without hesitation—this phrase, "without hesitation" in Hebrew is *maher*, which is used in modern Hebrew for "quickly" or "rapidly." She energetically served him, including watering the ten camels in their caravan, which was no small feat. Eliezer was duly impressed and asked her,

> *"Whose daughter are you? Please tell me, is there room for us to lodge in your father's house?" She said to him, "I am the daughter of Bethuel, the son of Milcah, whom she bore to Nahor"* (Genesis 24:23–24).

She was the daughter of Bethuel and the granddaughter of Milcah and Nahor—Abraham's brother. Rebekah's brother was Laban and in the next chapter we will meet Laban again along with his daughters Leah and Rachel (see Gen 24:24, 29).

Eliezer was awestruck by the Lord's immediate answer to his prayer, and in response he worshipped God with praise and thanksgiving. Eliezer was a wonderful example of a man who knew that his impossible "matchmaker" assignment could only happen through God's power and supernatural guidance.

> Genesis 24:26–28 (definitions added): *Then the man bowed low and worshiped* (shahach—prostrate in worship) *the LORD. He said, "Blessed be the LORD, the God of my master Abraham, who has not forsaken His lovingkindness* (chesed) *and His truth* (emet) *toward my master; as for me, the LORD has guided me in the way to the house of my master's brothers." Then the girl ran and told her mother's household about these things.*

When Eliezer arrived at Rebekah's home, he immediately explained to her family that he had come to find a bride for his master, Abraham, and he included the details of answered prayer in Genesis 24. Notice how he included the blessings of God to Abraham and the LORD'S guidance in bringing him to their home.

Genesis 24:34–48: *So he said, "I am Abraham's servant. The LORD has greatly blessed my master, so that he has become rich; and He has given him flocks and herds, and silver and gold, and servants and maids, and camels and donkeys. Now Sarah my master's wife bore a son to my master in her old age, and he has given him all that he has. My master made me swear, saying, 'You shall not take a wife for my son from the daughters of the Canaanites, in whose land I live; but you shall go to my father's house and to my relatives, and take a wife for my son.' I said to my master, 'Suppose the woman does not follow me.' He said to me, 'The LORD, before whom I have walked, will send His angel with you to make your journey successful, and you will take a wife for my son from my relatives and from my father's house; then you will be free from my oath, when you come to my relatives; and if they do not give her to you, you will be free from my oath.' So I came today to the spring, and said, 'O LORD, the God of my master Abraham, if now You will make my journey on which I go successful; behold, I am standing by the spring, and may it be that the maiden who comes out to draw, and to whom I say, "Please let me drink a little water from your jar"; and she will say to me, "You drink, and I will draw for your camels also"; let her be the woman whom the LORD has appointed for my master's son.' Before I had finished speaking in my heart, behold, Rebekah came out with her jar on her shoulder, and went down to the spring and drew, and I said to her, 'Please let me drink.' She quickly lowered her jar from her shoulder, and said, 'Drink, and I will water your camels also'; so I drank, and she watered the camels also. Then I asked her, and said, 'Whose daughter are you?' And she said, 'The daughter of Bethuel, Nahor's son, whom Milcah bore to him'; and I put the ring on her nose, and the bracelets on her wrists. And I bowed low and worshiped the LORD, and blessed the LORD, the God of my master Abraham, who had guided me in the right way to take the daughter of my master's kinsman for his son."*

We have the response of her brother and father. They wisely allowed Rebekah to speak for herself and make her own decision.

Genesis 24:50–53: *Then Laban and Bethuel replied, "The matter comes from the LORD; so we cannot speak to you bad or good. Here is Rebekah before you, take her and go, and let her be the wife of your master's son, as the LORD has spoken." When Abraham's servant heard their words, he bowed himself to the ground before the LORD. The servant brought out articles of silver and articles of gold, and garments, and gave them to Rebekah; he also gave precious things to her brother and to her mother.*

Rebekah willingly responded to be Isaac's bride and go immediately with Eliezer. Eliezer then gave many gifts to both Rebekah and her family. These gifts were considered as a dowry or "bride price"—wedding gift.

Rebekah's name in Hebrew is *Rivkah* and means "tied up (as one ties a horse)," "secured," "captivated," and within this name lies the notion that individuals are placed together by something higher or smarter than they.

Eliezer spent the night and the next morning both Rebekah's mother and brother asked if she could stay a little longer—ten days—and Eliezer told them that he had to return to Abraham ASAP. When they asked Rebekah if she would go, she replied at once, "Yes, I'll go."

In Genesis 24:60, the family blessed Rebekah with a betrothal blessing: They blessed Rebekah and said to her,

"May you, our sister, become thousands of ten thousands, and may your descendants possess the gate of those who hate them." In other words they blessed her with fruitfulness, positions of authority, and victory over any enemies that would come upon them. Considering this family did not know the God of Israel personally, their blessing was an encouraging betrothal blessing that would actually be fulfilled in God's covenant blessings to Abraham, Isaac, and Jacob.

Love at First Sight? Rebekah and Isaac Tie the Knot!

I'm not sure I believe in "love at first sight," but this account seems to indicate that upon seeing Isaac, Rebekah was smitten and fell in love. Actually, the Hebrew word *naphal* indicates that when she saw him, she fell off her camel. So, we could say she fell "head over heels" for him! When she first saw him in the field, she didn't know that it was Isaac. However, Rebekah was already committed in her heart to marry him, and Isaac was committed to marry the woman that Eliezer brought to him. We can conclude it was not so much love at first sight, but the commitment to love each other in marriage at first sight! And once Isaac heard of how God answered Eliezer's prayers, he and Rebekah tied the knot.

> Genesis 24:61–67 (definitions added): *Then Rebekah arose with her maids, and they mounted the camels and followed the man* (Eliezer). *So the servant took Rebekah and departed. Now Isaac had come from going to Beer-lahai-roi* (the well of the Living One who sees me); *for he was living in the Negev. Isaac went out to meditate in the field toward evening; and he lifted up his eyes and looked, and behold, camels were coming. And Rebekah lifted up her eyes, and when she saw Isaac she dismounted* (naphal—fall down) *from the camel. She said to the servant, "Who is that man walking in the field to meet us?" And the servant said, "He is my master." Then she took her veil and covered herself.* (It was the custom for the bride

to be veiled on her wedding night. This would be a serious problem later for Jacob with Rachel and Leah!) *The servant* (Eliezer) *told Isaac all the things that he had done. Then Isaac brought her into his mother Sarah's tent, and he took Rebekah, and she became his wife; and he loved* (ahavah—dearly loved) *her; thus Isaac was comforted after his mother's death.*

Sarah died at age one hundred twenty-seven years old and Isaac was born when she was ninety. Isaac was forty when he married Rebekah, so if my math is correct, Sarah would have been gone for three years. It seems that Isaac was still grieving over Sarah's death, but when he took Rebekah into his mother's tent to consummate his marriage, he was consoled, and his time of mourning came to an end.

But if we fast forward twenty years, we find that they had no children yet.

> Genesis 25:21: *Isaac prayed to the LORD on behalf of his wife, because she was barren; and the LORD answered him and Rebekah his wife conceived.*

In Genesis 25:20, we learn that Isaac was forty years old when he married Rebekah. At this point, when he prayed for her to conceive, it was twenty years later. He was sixty years old when the Lord answered his prayer. She became pregnant.

What's Happening in My Womb?

This was not an easy pregnancy. Because of her suffering, Rebekah went to the LORD directly.

> Genesis 25:22–24: *But the children struggled together within her; and she said, "If it is so, why then am I this way?" So, she went to inquire of the LORD. The LORD said to her, "Two nations are in your womb; and two peoples will be separated from your body; and one people shall be stronger than the other; and the older shall serve the*

younger." When her days to be delivered were fulfilled, behold, there were twins in her womb.

She had two baby boys struggling with each other in her womb. Wow! Can you imagine being told by the Lord that you have two peoples/nations fighting each other in your womb? I can't fathom the physical discomfort that she must have been going through.

Additionally, she and Isaac needed to understand that the blessings of the firstborn and the rights of inheritance would be reversed as the older would serve the younger. This would be completely opposite of the traditional birthright protocol that they would have expected and understood.

Another Son of Promise

The twin boys were finally born. Esau represented the nation of Edom and Jacob represented the nation of Israel. Esau was born covered with hair and had a ruddy or red appearance!

> Genesis 25:25 (definition added): *Now the first (Esau) came forth red, all over like a hairy garment; and they named him Esau.*

Esau means "hairy" and Edom comes from a root meaning "red." Jacob is from the root word "heel" which is *akiev*—and it comes from the fact that Jacob was holding on to Esau's heel as they were being born.

> Genesis 25:26: *Afterward his brother came forth with his hand holding on to Esau's heel, so his name was called Jacob; and Isaac was sixty years old when she gave birth to them.*

THE PROBLEM

The Dysfunction of Favoritism

We have the picture of Isaac's and Rebekah's favoritism described for us in Genesis 25:27–28:

> *When the boys grew up, Esau became a skillful hunter, a man of the field, but Jacob was a peaceful man, living in tents. Now Isaac loved Esau, because he had a taste for game; but Rebekah loved Jacob.*

Does God treat his spiritual children with favoritism? No! His favor is poured out into each of our lives without measure and without partiality. He loves you with an everlasting love! That said, God's plan of redemption is His plan and He was working through these families to accomplish the promise of "her seed" that He gave in Genesis. It was God's sovereign choice that the line of the Messiah would come through Jacob and not Esau.

As parents and grandparents, we need to ask ourselves what we can do to avoid favoritism in raising our children and grandchildren. In the lives of Jacob and Esau, this partiality became a point of hostility and dysfunction for the whole family. Let's learn from Isaac and Rebekah what not to do.

The account of Esau selling his birthright comes in the next verses. The bottom line is that Jacob stole what was already his as promised by the God of Israel!

> Genesis 25:29–34 (definitions added): *When Jacob had cooked stew, Esau came in from the field and he was famished; and Esau said to Jacob, "Please let me have a swallow of that red stuff there, for I am famished." Therefore, his name was called Edom. But Jacob said, "First sell me your birthright." Esau said, "Behold, I am about to die; so of what use then is the birthright to me?" And Jacob said, "First swear (sheva) to me"; so he swore*

96

to him, and sold his birthright to Jacob. Then Jacob gave Esau bread and lentil stew; and he ate and drank, and rose and went on his way. Thus Esau despised (bazah—treated with contempt) *his birthright.*

This is the first use of *"bazah"* in the Scriptures. Esau is an example for us of lost spiritual opportunity because of his disdain *(bazah)* for God's promises in His Word.

Moses warned Israel against treating the Word of the Lord with contempt.

Numbers 15:31 (definition added): *"Because he has despised* (bazah) *the word of the LORD and has broken His commandment, that person shall be completely cut off; his guilt will be on him.'"*

Proverbs 1:7 teaches us that reverence for the LORD is the beginning of wisdom but fools disdain God's wisdom and truth:

The fear of the LORD is the beginning of knowledge; fools despise (bazah) *wisdom and instruction* (definition added).

What Does it Mean to Despise One's Birthright?

The birthright meant that as the firstborn, the son assumed leadership in the family and received a double portion of all the blessings. However, in the case of Esau and Jacob, there was much more at stake! This was because of God's covenant promise to Abraham and his descendants, that through His seed—which is the Messianic line—all the nations of the world would be blessed.

Believers are warned not to imitate Esau who, on impulse, gave away his birthright for a bowl of stew (Hebrews 12:16–17; Genesis 25:19–34). Because of his foolishness, Esau lost his birthright and the blessings of his father (Genesis 27). The lesson for us is to respect, honor, and treat as holy God's blessings and His position for us in His family. We should never throw away what is important, godly, or honorable for the sake of temporary pleasure. In the thoughts and reflection section at the end of this chapter I've included some important Scriptures about our birthrights as believers so we can understand that we are in *"the assembly ... of the firstborn"* (Hebrews 12:23).

Like Father Like Son!

Next in Genesis, we have an interlude of lying on Isaac's part, and the unraveling of Rebekah's trust.

> Genesis 26:6–8: *So Isaac lived in Gerar. When the men of the place asked about his wife, he said, "She is my sister," for he was afraid to say, "my wife," thinking, "the men of the place might kill me on account of Rebekah, for she is beautiful." It came about, when he had been there a long time, that Abimelech king of the Philistines looked out through a window, and saw, and behold, Isaac was caressing his wife Rebekah.*

Does this sound familiar? Isaac and Rebekah were living in the same area that Abraham and Sarah had lived in. The name Abimelech was a generic name for a ruler like Pharoah. Consequently over the years, there were a number of kings who ruled the Philistines named Abimelech. When Isaac told the people of Gerar that Rebekah was his sister, this was an outright lie. And his lie was exposed when the king noticed that Isaac was caressing or playing around with his wife in public.

The king admonished Isaac that he or one of his men could have violated Rebekah and incurred the wrath of God. Do you remember what happened to Abimelech and his household when Abraham was sojourning in Gerar (see Genesis 20:17)? In Genesis 26:11 this king gives instructions for everyone under his rule: *So Abimelech charged all the people, saying,*

"He who touches this man or his wife shall surely be put to death."

Why Was Isaac so Fearful and Insecure? He Forgot the Promises of His God

The reason I think it's important to add this detail is to show that at this point, even with all his wealth, prestige, a beautiful wife, two sons, and the covenant promises of God, Isaac was not trusting fully in God to protect him. He felt he had to protect himself.

Perhaps Isaac neglected to praise his God for His sure promises and provisions. Had what happened on Mount Moriah become a distant memory? We are instructed in Psalm 103:1–2,

> *Bless the LORD, O my soul, and all that is within me, bless His holy name. Bless the LORD, O my soul, and forget none of His benefits.*

We are to praise God with our entire being and in addition to our praise, we are to remember and not forget all of God's amazing blessings.

Nevertheless, it seems that Isaac had forgotten that he was being tested along with his father when he was there on Mount Moriah and was bound on the altar of sacrifice. The Scriptures tell us that Abraham, with his knife raised, was ready to plunge into his son's heart. At that point, Isaac was ready to be sacrificed, however God intervened in His perfect timing with His message of redemption by providing a lamb in his place.

> Genesis 22:10–18: *Abraham stretched out his hand and took the knife to slay his son. But the angel of the LORD called to him from heaven and said, "Abraham, Abraham!" And he said, "Here I am." He said, "Do not stretch out your hand against the lad, and do nothing to him; for now I*

know that you fear God, since you have not withheld your son, your only son, from Me." Then Abraham raised his eyes and looked, and behold, behind him a ram caught in the thicket by his horns; and Abraham went and took the ram and offered him up for a burnt offering in the place of his son. Abraham called the name of that place The LORD Will Provide, as it is said to this day, "In the mount of the LORD it will be provided." Then the angel of the LORD called to Abraham a second time from heaven, and said, "By Myself I have sworn, declares the LORD, because you have done this thing and have not withheld your son, your only son, indeed I will greatly bless you, and I will greatly multiply your seed as the stars of the heavens and as the sand which is on the seashore; and your seed shall possess the gate of their enemies. In your seed all the nations of the earth shall be blessed, because you have obeyed My voice."

That day Isaac was delivered from physical death by the lamb that God provided. His future was also secured through the covenant promises. When Yeshua, who is the angel of the Lord, spoke to his father Abraham, it was for him as well because the promise of redemption in the Messiah was to come through Isaac and Rebekah.

Why did Isaac lie to Abimelech and doubt God's promises to protect and prosper his family? I can ask myself the same type of question: Why do I doubt His many promises? Because I forget to praise my beloved Yeshua and trust in the position that He has given me as His daughter to live for Him *"according to the kind intention of His will to the praise of the glory"* of Messiah. As His adopted daughters, we have God's birthright.

Ephesians 1:5–6: *He predestined us to adoption as [daughters] through Yeshua the Messiah to Himself, according to the kind intention of His will, to the praise of the glory of His grace, which He freely bestowed on us in the Beloved.*

We are His daughters! As part of our birthright, God shows us His purpose for our lives:

Ephesians 1:9–14: *He made known to us the mystery of His will, according to His kind intention which He purposed in Him with a view to an administration suitable to the fullness of the times, that is, the summing up of all things in Messiah, things in the heavens and things on the earth. In Him also we have obtained an inheritance, having been predestined according to His purpose who works all things after the counsel of His will, to the end that we who were the first to hope in Messiah would be to the praise of His glory. In Him, you also, after listening to the message of truth, the gospel of your salvation—having also believed, you were sealed in Him with the Holy Spirit of promise, who is given as a pledge of our inheritance, with a view to the redemption of God's own possession, to the praise of His glory.*

These narratives of the families' struggles are in the Scriptures for our benefit to help us in our struggles. Since God is building His congregation through strong families, we need to have strong, godly families today.

Another Woman Takes Matters into Her Own Hands

More family drama ensued. Rebekah mistrusted Isaac's ability to follow what God had promised. And she neglected the truth that she didn't have to trust in people! So, she took matters in her own hands. In Genesis 27, Rebekah manipulated her son Jacob to lie to his father Isaac in order to obtain the firstborn blessing—which God had already promised to them. Remember what God told Rebekah when He spoke to her, *"And the older shall serve the younger"* (Genesis 25:23).

Jacob's Concern and Rebekah's Answer.

> Genesis 27:11–12: *Jacob answered his mother Rebekah, "Behold, Esau my brother is a hairy man and I am a smooth man. Perhaps my father will feel me, then I will be as a deceiver in his sight; and I shall bring upon myself a curse and not a blessing."*

Jacob's concern was commendable because he respected his father Isaac. He didn't want to be seen as a liar and a fraud who would bring a curse on himself.

Rebekah's response to Jacob was immediate and fierce. She said that she would take the curse for his actions and used her manipulation skills to get him to carry out her plan: *But his mother said to him, "Your curse be on me, my son; only obey my voice, and go, get them for me"* (Genesis 27:13).

Her plan was simple and devious. First, she would prepare Isaac's favorite meal that Esau would often make for him when he returned from hunting. Then she devised a clever disguise for Jacob using Esau's clothes and the hairy skins of the baby goats.

> Genesis 27:14–17: *So [Jacob] went and got [the young goats], and brought them to his mother; and his mother made savory food such as his father loved. Then Rebekah took the best garments of Esau her elder son, which were with her in the house, and put them on Jacob her younger son. And she put the skins of the young goats on his hands and on the smooth part of his neck. She also gave the savory food and the bread, which she had made, to her son Jacob.*

Jacob lied outright to his father.

> Genesis 27:18–19: *Then he came to his father and said, "My father." And he said, "Here I am. Who are you, my son?" Jacob said to his father, "I am Esau your firstborn; I*

have done as you told me. Get up, please, sit and eat of my game, that you may bless me."

Jacob took the Lord God's name in vain.

Genesis 27:20: Isaac said to his son, "How is it that you have it so quickly, my son?" And he said, "Because the LORD your God caused it to happen to me."

Isaac was taken in by Jacob's cunning and scheming.

Then Isaac said to Jacob, "Please come close, that I may feel you, my son, whether you are really my son Esau or not." So Jacob came close to Isaac his father, and he felt him and said, "The voice is the voice of Jacob, but the hands are the hands of Esau" (Gen 27:21–22).

Why Did Rebekah Deceive Her Husband?

She was full of fear and mistrust. Didn't God Himself promise her that the older would serve the younger in Genesis 25:23? God spoke to her and made this promise to her, yet years later she disregarded the word of God and decided to handle this problem herself. There were fissures in her relationship with her husband. She did not trust her husband to obey God and bestow the blessing of the firstborn to Jacob. Isaac had lied about her to Abimelech, exposing her to potential danger. It was obvious to Rebekah that Esau was Isaac's favorite son. So, from her perspective, she had to "take matters into her own hands." She trusted in her own schemes and skills to get the job done. Does this remind you of Sarah and her inability to wait on God for her promise?

What can we learn from this family of Abraham's son of promise? At this point, it seems that the entire family including Isaac, Rebekah, Jacob, and Esau were acting in a dysfunctional manner. Isaac should have obeyed God's choice of blessing his sons so that the older would serve the younger. Rebekah should have trusted in God's timing and His power to work in Isaac's heart to bring about obedience to His commands. And their godly influence in their sons' lives could have prevented the terrible scene where Jacob, in his clever disguise, lied repeatedly to his father. This is what happens when God, His power, His timing, and His grace are disregarded. Earlier in this chapter, we discussed the incident during which Isaac lied to Abimelech about Rebekah, but here the family has descended to a new level of lying and deceit.

Satan's Goal Is to Destroy Families—and Try to Prevent the Return of the Messiah!

Have you ever schemed and lied to have your desired outcome in a situation? I have many times! I have a passive-aggressive personality and unless I'm under the control of the Holy Spirit's anointing, I will fall back to my old sinful ways and listen to my flesh. I will try to use my 'skill set' as a passive aggressive way to manipulate and get the results that I desire.

Where does such lying and scheming originate? Those who follow Satan are under the influence of the father of lies. This is what Yeshua said to the Pharisees in John 8:44,

> *You are of your father the devil, and you want to do the desires of your father. He was a murderer from the beginning, and does not stand in the truth because there is no truth in him. Whenever he speaks a lie, he speaks from his own nature, for he is a liar and the father of lies.*

During the early development of the nation of Israel, Satan's goal would have been to destroy the nation outright, so that the promise of redemption could not be fulfilled through the first coming of the Messiah. Therefore, in the lives of the patriarchs, their wives, and their children, we see that Satan was constantly stirring up strife, jealousy, and destruction. This spiritual warfare will not end until Messiah returns to set up His kingdom. Presently, Satan is a defeated enemy, however this does not stop his evil schemes and wickedness from warring against believers. Satan is now trying to prevent the Messiah from returning. We need to always be aware that we are in a spiritual battle and put on the whole armor of God. Though we are Yeshua's beloved daughters, Satan's attempts to derail our trust and confidence in the Lord will succeed if we take our focus off Yeshua.

> Ephesians 6:10–12: *Finally, be strong in the Lord and in the strength of His might. Put on the full armor of God, so that you will be able to stand firm against the schemes of the devil. For our struggle is not against flesh and blood, but against the rulers, against the powers, against the world forces of this darkness, against the spiritual forces of wickedness in the heavenly places.*

To deal with our trust issues, we must obey God's voice as He speaks to us. He is always speaking to us through His Word. Proverbs 3:5–8 is an important passage of Scripture to memorize!

> Proverbs 3:5–8 (definitions added): *Trust* (batach—rely upon, have confidence in) *in the LORD with all your heart and do not lean on your own understanding. In all your ways acknowledge Him, and He will make your paths straight. Do not be wise in your own eyes; fear the LORD and turn away from evil. It will be healing to your body and refreshment to your bones* (etsem—substance, self; see Gen 2:23).

The aftermath of Jacob deceiving his father Isaac unfolded: Esau vowed to kill Jacob after their father died. Rebekah heard of this and told Jacob to go to her family and stay with her brother Laban. She then communicated to her husband Isaac the following:

> Genesis 27:46 (definitions added): *Rebekah said to Isaac, "I am tired of living because of the daughters of Heth (disgusted by the pagan practices of the Hittite girls); if Jacob takes a wife from the daughters of Heth, like these,*

from the daughters of the land, what good will my life be to me?"

THE RESTORATION

What happens to the promises of God when the people involved aren't faithful, or act selfishly, or make poor decisions? Though Isaac and Rebekah were imperfect parents, God is a perfect Father. His Word is sure and He makes it come to pass. Through this season, His plan for the redemption of mankind was progressing through His chosen family.

As much as Rebekah had distrusted Isaac, her desire to have their son Jacob marry a woman from their own family seems to be an indication that Rebekah was turning back to the LORD. She was understanding how important it would be for Jacob to find a wife from their own family rather than the local pagan Canaanite women.

Do you remember when we first met Rebekah? When she heard how God answered the prayers of Eliezer pointing to her as the chosen wife for Abraham's son Isaac, she willingly said yes. She was ready to be the wife of Isaac. I believe that God brought back to her heart and mind this special time of answered prayer and the reality that she was chosen to be part of God's plan in the life of Abraham's family. We learned that Rebekah was the first woman in Scripture *"to [have inquired] of the LORD"* (Gen 25:22). She went straight to God with her question to find out what was happening in her womb and the LORD gave her a prophetic explanation including the promise that her older son would serve the younger. God was not silent, and He spoke directly to her to assure her of what was happening in her womb and the future for her twins. The New Covenant explains this choosing in detail as both Sarah and Rebekah are honored to be part of God's redemptive plan in establishing the people of Israel.

New Covenant Confirmation

In Romans 9, Paul wrote that God's plan for redeeming the world came through the promises made to Abraham and Sarah, who would give birth to Isaac, then to Isaac and Rebekah's younger son Jacob. God's ways are higher than our ways and we cannot fully understand the mercy and compassion that He pours out to us. This passage reiterates that His mercy and compassion to us is based on His love and His grace, not on any merit of our own.

> Romans 9:6–16: *But it is not as though the word of God has failed. For they are not all Israel who are descended from Israel; neither are they all children because they are Abraham's descendants, but: "through Isaac your descendants will be named." That is, it is not the children of the flesh who are children of God, but the children of the promise are regarded as descendants. For this is the word of promise: "At this time I will come, and Sarah shall have a son." And not only this, but there was Rebekah also, when she had conceived twins by one man, our father Isaac; for though the twins were not yet born and had not done anything good or bad, so that God's purpose according to His choice would stand, not because of works but because of Him who calls, it was said to her, "The older will serve the younger." Just as it is written, "Jacob I loved, but Esau I hated." What shall we say then? There is no injustice with God, is there? May it never be! For He says to Moses, "I will have mercy on whom I have mercy, and I will have compassion on whom I have compassion." So then it does not depend on the man who wills or the man who runs, but on God who has mercy.*

Positive Steps!

A Blessing for Jacob from Isaac, Given on Purpose This Time

In Genesis 28, Isaac sent Jacob to the home of Rebekah's brother. Before Jacob left, Isaac blessed him: that he should find a wife, that she would be fruitful, and he would have many descendants—*"that you may become a company of peoples."* God did bless Jacob and in our next chapter, we meet his wives and his twelve sons.

> Genesis 28:1–5: *So Isaac called Jacob and blessed him and charged him, and said to him, "You shall not take a wife from the daughters of Canaan. Arise, go to Paddan-aram, to the house of Bethuel your mother's father; and from there take to yourself a wife from the daughters of Laban your mother's brother. May God Almighty bless you and make you fruitful and multiply you, that you may become a company of peoples. May He also give you the blessing of Abraham, to you and to your descendants with you, that you may possess the land of your sojournings, which God gave to Abraham." Then Isaac sent Jacob away, and he went to Paddan-aram to Laban, son of Bethuel the Aramean, the brother of Rebekah, the mother of Jacob and Esau.*

God Confirms His Covenant with Jacob Too

On Jacob's journey to Haran, God appeared to him in a dream and reconfirmed the Abrahamic Covenant to him. The next morning Jacob worshipped and named the place *Beth El*—House of God (Abraham had named it in Gen 12:8).

> Genesis 28:12–17 (definition added): *He had a dream, and behold, a ladder* (stairway) *was set on the earth with its top reaching to heaven; and behold, the angels of God were ascending and descending on it. And behold, the LORD stood above it and said, "I am the LORD, the God of your father Abraham and the God of Isaac; the land on which you lie, I will give it to you and to your descendants. Your descendants will also be like the dust of the earth, and you will spread out to the west and to the east and to the north and to the south; and in you and in your descendants shall all the families of the earth be blessed.*

Behold, I am with you and will keep you wherever you go, and will bring you back to this land; for I will not leave you until I have done what I have promised you." Then Jacob awoke from his sleep and said, "Surely the LORD is in this place, and I did not know it." He was afraid and said, "How awesome is this place! This is none other than the house of God, and this is the gate of heaven."

Years later, there would be a reconciliation between her two sons and their families, but unfortunately, Rebekah would not be alive to rejoice in this blessing. The Scriptures do not mention her again until Genesis 49:31–32:

There they buried Abraham and his wife Sarah, there they buried Isaac and his wife Rebekah, and there I buried Leah—the field and the cave that is in it, purchased from the sons of Heth.

THOUGHT QUESTIONS AND REFLECTIONS

1. What can we learn from the life of Rebekah?

What could Rebekah have done differently? She didn't trust Isaac and this lack of trust in him reflected on her inability to trust in the LORD'S sure promises!

I think that she was a helicopter mom and spent all her time focusing on Jacob. I wonder if she spent time teaching Jacob the history of his grandparents, Abraham and Sarah—and confirming the promises of God to his father.

She did tell Isaac to send Jacob back to the land of Abraham's family and her family, to her brother Laban, so Jacob wouldn't be tempted to marry a woman from the pagan cultures around them in Canaan. There are two firsts in this chapter. We learned about the first arranged marriage.

What surprised or impressed you the most about this arranged marriage? Some ideas: Eliezer—his praise and prayer life; Rebekah's willingness to go with Eliezer.

2. Why did God choose the older to serve the younger?

God's choosing in His sovereign choice because He is in charge! In the case of Esau and Jacob, God had predetermined that the younger, physically weaker brother would be the leader. God does the choosing. He chose David, who was the insignificant youngest son of Jesse. God had Samuel anoint him to be the next king of Israel. He was teaching us that man looks on the outside, but God looks on the heart (see 1 Samuel 16:7).

When the Scripture declares: *"Jacob I loved, but Esau I hated,"* it is literally saying, "Jacob I have chosen, but Esau is not chosen." As we noted, Paul explains this choosing in Romans 9:6–16:

> *"I will have mercy on whom I have mercy, and I will have compassion on whom I have compassion." So then it does*

not depend on the man who wills or the man who runs, but on God who has mercy.

3. When Esau despised his birthright, we discovered that this was the first time for the usage of the Hebrew word, *bazah*, which means, "to treat with contempt." Do we understand what it means to be the firstborn of the assembly of God? Why did God choose you to be His daughter?

Read through Ephesians 1:3–14 and take note of your standing by grace in the LORD and the amazing blessings He gives you. As you write down your birthright and your inheritance as His daughter, include praise and thanksgiving. Also ask the LORD to show you if you have treated with contempt aspects of your birthright in Messiah Yeshua.

Ephesians 1:3–14: *Blessed be the God and Father of our Lord Yeshua the Messiah, who has blessed us with every spiritual blessing in the heavenly places in Messiah, just as He chose us in Him before the foundation of the world, that we would be holy and blameless before Him. In love He predestined us to adoption as [daughters] through Yeshua the Messiah to Himself, according to the kind intention of His will, to the praise of the glory of His grace, which He freely bestowed on us in the Beloved. In Him we have redemption through His blood, the forgiveness of our trespasses, according to the riches of His grace which He lavished on us. In all wisdom and insight He made known to us the mystery of His will, according to His kind intention which He purposed in Him with a view to an administration suitable to the fullness of the times, that is, the summing up of all things in Messiah, things in the heavens and things on the earth. In Him also we have obtained an inheritance, having been predestined according to His purpose who works all things after the counsel of His will, to the end that we who were the first to hope in Messiah would be to the praise of His glory. In*

Him, you also, after listening to the message of truth, the gospel of your salvation—having also believed, you were sealed in Him with the Holy Spirit of promise, who is given as a pledge of our inheritance, with a view to the redemption of God's own possession, to the praise of His glory.

Here is another Scripture passage that instructs us as part of the congregation of the firstborn:

Hebrews 12:14–24 (emphasis added): *Make every effort to live in peace with everyone and to be holy; without holiness no one will see the Lord. See to it that no one falls short of the grace of God and that no bitter root grows up to cause trouble and defile many. See that no one is sexually immoral, or is godless like Esau, who for a single meal sold his inheritance rights as the oldest son. Afterward, as you know, when he wanted to inherit this blessing, he was rejected. Even though he sought the blessing with tears, he could not change what he had done. You have not come to a mountain that can be touched and that is burning with fire; to darkness, gloom and storm; to a trumpet blast or to such a voice speaking words that those who heard it begged that no further word be spoke to them, because they could not bear what was commanded: "If even an animal touches the mountain, it must be stoned to death." The sight was so terrifying that Moses said, "I am trembling with fear."* **But you have come to Mount Zion, to the city of the living God, the heavenly Jerusalem. You have come to thousands upon thousands of angels in joyful assembly, to the congregation of the firstborn, whose names are written in heaven. You have come to God, the Judge of all, to the spirits of the righteous made perfect, to Yeshua the mediator or a new covenant, and to the sprinkled blood that speaks a better word than the blood of Abel.**

Not that I speak from want, for I have learned to be content in whatever circumstances I am. I know how to get along with humble means, and I also know how to live in prosperity; in any and every circumstance I have learned the secret of being filled and going hungry, both of having abundance and suffering need. I can do all things through Him who strengthens me.

Philippians 4:11–13

Four

Two Sisters & Twelve Sons: *Rachel & Leah*

In this chapter we'll discuss the life and times of the family that Jacob built. This was a big step in God's restoration plan for mankind, and this is a big chapter. We'll take a few breaks along the way for reflection and application.

There was much dysfunction in the family of Isaac and Rebekah. When we left the brothers Esau and Jacob, one was threatening to kill and the other had departed hurriedly for his brother's house, for shelter and so Jacob could find a wife from among their people.

THE PROMISE (PART ONE)

The Covenant

On his way, God gave Jacob a wonderful dream which pictured angels going up and down a ladder to heaven.

> Genesis 28:12–15: *He had a dream, and behold, a ladder was set on the earth with its top reaching to heaven; and*

behold, the angels of God were ascending and descending on it. And behold, the LORD stood above it and said, "I am the LORD, the God of your father Abraham and the God of Isaac; the land on which you lie, I will give it to you and to your descendants. Your descendants will also be like the dust of the earth, and you will spread out to the west and to the east and to the north and to the south; and in you and in your descendants shall all the families of the earth be blessed. Behold, I am with you and will keep you wherever you go, and will bring you back to this land; for I will not leave you until I have done what I have promised you."

In this dream there was a reconfirmation of the Abrahamic Covenant. The promise was the same, and so were the problems: Jacob had no descendants. At this point he was still on his way to seek a wife.

Two Wives in One Week!

God led Jacob to the house of Laban where he met the love of his life, Rachel. She was a perfect match, a lovely young woman from his own family, *the daughter of Laban his mother's brother* (Genesis 29:10). Laban agreed that Jacob could marry his daughter in exchange for seven years of service. Seven years' worth of Jacob's labor was the bride price for Rachel. It should have all worked out.

Genesis 29:21–25: *Then Jacob said to Laban, "Give me my wife, for my time is completed, that I may go in to her." Laban gathered all the men of the place and made a feast. Now in the evening he took his daughter Leah, and brought her to him; and Jacob went into her. Laban also gave his maid Zilpah to his daughter Leah as a maid. So it came about in the morning that, behold, it was Leah! And he said to Laban, "What is this you have done to me? Was it not for Rachel that I served with you? Why then have you deceived me?"*

116

Jacob, who had deceived his father Isaac, found himself on the receiving end of deception from his new father-in-law. Laban had a perfectly logical explanation—their family protocol for marriage was always to have the older daughter married first. He then offered Jacob a deal so he could still marry Rachel. All Jacob had to do was agree to serve Laban for an additional seven years.

> Genesis 29:26–30 (definition added): *But Laban said, "It is not the practice in our place to marry off the younger before the firstborn. Complete the week* (shavuah) *of this one, and we will give you the other also for the service which you shall serve with me for another seven years." Jacob did so and completed her week, and he gave him his daughter Rachel as his wife. Laban also gave his maid Bilhah to his daughter Rachel as her maid. So Jacob went in to Rachel also, and indeed he loved Rachel more than Leah, and he served with Laban for another seven years.*

Who Were these Girls: Leah and Rachel?

In Genesis 29:17, the Scriptures portray the contrast between Leah and Rachel:

> *And Leah's eyes were* weak (tender, indicating poor eyesight)*, but Rachel was beautiful* (yaffa) *of form and face* (definitions added).

Apparently Leah had some sort of eye condition that made her unattractive. By contrast Rachel was *beautiful of form and face.* In other words, she had a great figure and a gorgeous face.

THE PROBLEM (PART ONE)

So What Is the Problem?

So far things aren't too bad, are they? Jacob found his mother's family and he got for himself two wives. He had the covenant promise of blessing from God for his offspring. The problem was, there were still no offspring. There is another revealing description in Genesis 29:31:

> *Adonai saw that Leah was unloved, so He made her fertile,*
> *but Rachel remained childless* (CJB).

The implication is that both ladies Jacob married could not have children. But then we have insight into our compassionate God. He saw that Leah was unloved and He opened her womb—gave her the blessing of children first. On the other hand, Rachel had all the love from her husband, but she remained barren for a long time, unable to have children.

THE RESTORATION (PART ONE)

The question of ensuring offspring for Jacob seemed to have an answer. God opened Leah's womb! God's blessings were just beginning to pour out to Leah, though. She had her first son.

> Genesis 29:32: *Leah conceived and bore a son and named him Reuben, for she said, "Because the Lord has seen my affliction; surely now my husband will love me."*

The next verse tells us that Leah had son number two:

> Genesis 29:33: *Then she conceived again and bore a son and said, "Because the LORD has heard that I am unloved, He has therefore given me this son also." So she named him Simeon.*

Leah's third son was named Levi.

> Genesis 29:34 (definition added): *She conceived again and bore a son and said, "Now this time my husband will become attached (joined) to me, because I have borne him three sons." Therefore he was named Levi.*

When Leah gave birth to her fourth son, her attitude changed.

Genesis 29:35: *And she conceived again and bore a son and said, "This time I will praise the LORD." Therefore she named him Judah. Then she stopped bearing.*

What About Rachel?

While Leah was giving birth to four sons, what was beautiful and greatly loved Rachel doing? She was consumed with jealousy over the Lord's blessings on her sister.

Genesis 30:1-2: *Now when Rachel saw that she bore Jacob no children, she became jealous of her sister; and she said to Jacob, "Give me children, or else I die." Then Jacob's anger burned against Rachel, and he said, "Am I in the place of God, who has withheld from you the fruit of the womb?"*

Jacob became angry with her outrageous demand. His response seemed harsh, didn't it? He didn't realize that Rachel was feeling desperate and consumed by jealousy because she didn't have any children and Leah already had four sons.

So, Rachel decided to give Jacob her maid Bilhah to have a baby. This was common practice as we noted with Sarah giving Abraham her maid Hagar to birth a child. A son was born to them, which would have been considered Rachel's son. She named him Dan, meaning, "judge."

Genesis 30:3-6 (definitions added): *She said, "Here is my maid Bilhah, go in to her that she may bear on my knees, that through her I too may have children." So she gave him her maid Bilhah as a wife, and Jacob went into her. Bilhah conceived and bore Jacob a son. Then Rachel said, "God has vindicated* (judged) *me, and has indeed heard* (shema) *my voice and has given me a son." Therefore she named him Dan.*

The word judge *(danan* in Hebrew) can also mean "vindicate." Rachel gave God the credit for vindicating her by allowing Bilhah to have her son and hearing her prayer, literally her voice *(kol* in Hebrew). Her attitude changed. She proclaimed that God had given her this son.

Bolstered by the success of Dan's birth, Rachel gave her maid to Jacob again.

> Genesis 30:7–8: *Rachel's maid Bilhah conceived again and bore Jacob a second son. So Rachel said, "With mighty wrestlings I have wrestled with my sister, and I have indeed prevailed." And she named him Naphtali.*

And Back to Leah

In the face of this blatant competition, with her sister demeaning her, *(I have wrestled with my sister, and I have indeed prevailed)* Leah decided to have her own maid sleep with Jacob. By this means, she had two more sons. Number seven was named Gad.

> Genesis 30:9–10: *When Leah saw that she had stopped bearing, she took her maid Zilpah and gave her to Jacob as a wife. Leah's maid Zilpah bore Jacob a son. Then Leah said, "How fortunate!" So she named him Gad.*

And number eight was called Asher.

> Genesis 30:12–13: *Leah's maid Zilpah bore Jacob a second son. Then Leah said, "Happy am I! For women will call me happy." So she named him Asher.*

Mandrakes: Love Apples!

Before we meet the ninth son, we will learn about love apples.

Genesis 30:14–21 is an interesting portion of Scripture that highlights the bargaining over the mandrakes that Rueben had found for his mother Leah. Rachel went to Leah and asked her to share the mandrakes with her. Mandrakes in Hebrew is *dudaim,* literally, "love apples." The fruits are actually berries; the plants have white and reddish blossoms and a yellow fruit similar to small apples. The Hebrew root for *dudaim* is *dodi*, meaning "my lover" and is used in Song of Solomon 7:13:

> *The mandrakes have given forth fragrance; and over our doors are all choice fruits, both new and old, which I have saved up for you, my beloved* (dodi).

Two More Boys for Leah

Rachel wanted some of this fruit for herself because it was considered to be an aphrodisiac. Leah's response to Rachel's request revealed the depth of the bitterness in her heart.

> *But [Leah] said to her, "Is it a small matter for you to take my husband? And would you take my son's mandrakes also?" So Rachel said, "Therefore he may lie with you tonight in return for your son's mandrakes"* (Gen 30:15).

First my husband, now even the mandrakes?! Nevertheless, Rachel made an offer to Leah that she couldn't refuse. She told Leah that Jacob would sleep with her that very night.

After the mandrake bargain, Leah became pregnant and Issachar, who was Jacob's ninth son (and Leah's fifth), was born.

> Genesis 30:17–18: *God gave heed to Leah, and she conceived and bore Jacob a fifth son. Then Leah said, "God has given me my wages because I gave my maid to my husband." So she named him Issachar.*

Son ten, Leah's sixth child, was named Zebulun.

> Genesis 30:19–20: *Leah conceived again and bore a sixth son to Jacob. Then Leah said, "God has endowed me with a good gift; now my husband will dwell with me, because I have borne him six sons." So she named him Zebulun.*

A Daughter for Leah

> Genesis 30:21: *Afterward she bore a daughter and named her Dinah.*

After the birth of her sixth son, Leah gave birth to Dinah. Her name was the feminine form of the name Dan and also means "judge." Jacob had other daughters (see Genesis 37:35; 46:7, 15), but Dinah is the only one named in the Scriptures. We know Dinah's name because of the role she played in the drama of Genesis 34, due to the rape she endured at the hands of Shechem the son of Hamor the Hivite.

The Saga of the Two Sisters

> Psalm 34:18: *The LORD is near to the brokenhearted and saves those who are crushed in spirit.*

Even with all the sons Leah gave to Jacob, her heart was still broken. She was crushed in her spirit because she was "not chosen" and she was "unloved." However, like David before he became king, she began to understand the truth of God's compassionate heart. God was always near to her and desiring to bless Leah as well as Rachel. Again, these are the mothers of Israel. The twelve tribes come from their wombs and the surrogate wombs of their handmaids.

These sisters spent much of their time and energy competing for the love of Jacob. Why? Why do we seek to have someone love us like Leah was desperately desiring Jacob's love? I believe we are hoping that along with the love will come acceptance, connection, affection, appreciation to validate who we are. We are longing like Leah and Rachel to have our innermost desires supported and affirmed by someone's love and meet those unspoken needs. The truth is that only my beloved Yeshua can meet those innermost needs to save me from my sinful flesh.

If Leah and Rachel only understood that the God who loved them chose them to be "mothers in Israel" because He already loved them completely. They didn't have to compete to receive God's love. His love is poured out to His daughters without measure. He loves each of us with an everlasting love. Both Leah and Rachel needed to look to God first for their needs; then Jacob's love, his attention, their children, their validation would be added to their lives. They needed to learn the same truth that Yeshua taught us:

> Matthew 6:33-34: *But seek first His kingdom and His righteousness, and all these things will be added to you. So do not worry about tomorrow; for tomorrow will care for itself. Each day has enough trouble of its own.*

How does misplaced competition and jealousy affect a believer in Messiah? Do you ever envy other believers in your fellowship who seem to have it all, desiring what they have?

What will it take for us to realize that we have everything we need from our King Himself? We have all His grace and love poured out to us as we serve Him. It took Leah giving birth to four sons to finally praise the Lord and realize that *"children are a gift of the LORD"* (Psalm 127:3).

Leah's heart was never truly healed. Rachel was always Jacob's true love and Leah remained unloved by him. However, God's love for her did not waver or diminish. It's sad to think that instead of seeking God, she sought for love and validation from the wrong source.

Pause and take a few minutes to ask God to show you if you are allowing jealousy, envy, or a competitive attitude to creep into your heart and mind. Are you convinced of God's purpose and provision for you as His daughter?

Paul Had To Learn To Be Content:

> Philippians 4:11–13: *Not that I speak from want, for I have learned to be content in whatever circumstances I*

am. I know how to get along with humble means, and I also know how to live in prosperity; in any and every circumstance I have learned the secret of being filled and going hungry, both of having abundance and suffering need. I can do all things through Him who strengthens me.

Finally, Children for Rachel

Years and years after her marriage, after watching her sister give birth seven times, God remembered Rachel and gives her a son from her own womb.

Genesis 30:22–24: *Then God remembered Rachel, and God gave heed to her and opened her womb. So she conceived and bore a son and said, "God has taken away my reproach." She named him Joseph, saying, "May the LORD give me another son."*

This hope was answered in the birth of Benjamin much later, the twelfth son. We'll discuss this later in this chapter.

How Did God Build His Nation?

Leah attempted to cause Jacob to love her by giving him sons, healthy boys that God in His compassion granted her. Then both the handmaids of Rachel and Leah got involved with birthing sons. Finally, Rachel was granted a pair of sons, and this awesome group of twelve sons was completed.

It's important for us to understand that God was using Abraham, Isaac, and now Jacob to build the nation of Israel. On the surface it seems He picked poorly. If God's plan was to build a nation, why did He choose people who, generation after generation, couldn't have children? Why did God choose this *least likely to succeed nation of any of the nations*? This passage from Deuteronomy 7 gives us God's explanation as He spoke to His people Israel.

Deuteronomy 7:6–9 (emphasis added): *"For you are a holy people to the LORD your God; the LORD your God has chosen you to be a people for His own possession out of all the peoples who are on the face of the earth. The LORD did not set His love on you nor choose you because you were more in number than any of the peoples, for you were the fewest of all peoples,* **but because the LORD loved you and kept the oath which He swore to your forefathers**, *the LORD brought you out by a mighty hand and redeemed you from the house of slavery, from the hand of Pharaoh king of Egypt. Know therefore that the LORD your God, He is God, the faithful God, who keeps His covenant and His lovingkindness to a thousandth generation with those who love Him and keep His commandments."*

The Scriptures are clear that it was because God loves Israel. He established His nation through the forefathers—through Abraham and Sarah then Isaac and Rebekah and here through Jacob with Leah and Rachel. God nurtured and cared for them. It's amazing to me that these twelve tribes of Israel (from the twelve sons) will be forever memorialized in the gates of the New Jerusalem.

About the New Jerusalem: Revelation 21:12–13: *It had a great and high wall, with twelve gates, and at the gates twelve angels; and names were written on them, which are the names of the twelve tribes of the sons of Israel. There were three gates on the east and three gates on the north and three gates on the south and three gates on the west.*

APPLICATION: THE BIRTH AND NAMING OF THE TWELVE SONS:

1. **Reuben** is taken from two Hebrew words: *roeh*—to see, and *ben*, which means son—put together the name means "see the son." Leah confessed that the Lord saw her affliction, her neediness, and gave her Reuben. Nevertheless, her true hope was that after she presented him with a son, Jacob would love her more than her sister.

How can we apply this to our lives? In Genesis 22:14, God appears to Abraham and His name is *Jehovah Yireh*—The God who sees and provides what we need. Do you believe that God not only sees the overview of your life, including the miserable situations, but also cares for you and will provide for you?

Yeshua, the Angel of the Lord, spoke to Hagar when she was running away from Sarah. He revealed His care for her and her response is found in Genesis 16:13:

> Then [Hagar] called the name of the Lord who spoke to her, "You are a God who sees"; for she said, "Have I even remained alive here after seeing Him?"

This encounter with the Living God convinced her that He is a personal God— she called Him *El Roi*, the God who sees *me*. This is what the LORD desires you to do as well. Each day may you be encouraged and fearless because He sees your life and will provide for you in every situation.

2. **Simeon** is from the Hebrew root *Shema* meaning, "to hear." Leah once again gave God the credit for His compassion on her as He heard that she was "hated" or "the one not chosen."

Do you sometimes feel unloved and unchosen? God's Word tells you that you are chosen and you are greatly loved. Focusing upon His sure promises and not our fickle feelings is our sure foundation of security in His love.

About Choosing, Yeshua Said to His Disciples:

> John 15:16: *"You did not choose Me but I chose you, and appointed you that you would go and bear fruit, and that your fruit should remain, so that whatever you ask of the Father in My name He may give to you."*

About His Love for You:

> 1 John 3:1–2: *See how great a love the Father has bestowed on us, that we would be called children of God; and such we are. For this reason the world does not know us, because it did not know Him. Beloved, now we are children of God, and it has not appeared as yet what we will be. We know that when He appears, we will be like Him, because we will see Him just as He is.*

Can You Praise the Lord Along with King David for Adonai Who Always Hears You?

> Psalm 116:1–2 (emphasis added): *I love the LORD, because He **hears** (shema) my voice and my supplications. Because He has inclined His ear to me, therefore I shall call upon Him as long as I live.*

3. **Levi** is from the Hebrew, *lavah*, which means, "to join" or "attach." Leah named her third son Levi hoping that this son would be the one who caused Jacob to love her and be joined to her over Rachel.

The use of this word "joined" is used in some beautiful passages that reveal God's heart for all people.

> Isaiah 56:6–7 (definition, emphasis added): *"Also the foreigners who **join** (lavah) themselves to the LORD, to minister to Him, and to love the name of the LORD, to be His servants, every one who keeps from profaning the Sabbath and holds fast My covenant; even those I will bring to My holy mountain and make them joyful in My house of prayer. Their burnt offerings and their sacrifices*

*will be acceptable on My altar; for My house will be called
a house of prayer for all the peoples."*

Yeshua is our Beloved Groom, and we are His bride—
joined together with Him.

4. Judah—*Yehudah*—means "praise" or more literally, "He
   will be praised." Leah said, "This time I will praise the
   LORD." What is the difference in her attitude and
   acceptance before God? She declares that for this son she
   will praise the Lord. How could God heal the heart of Leah?
   Even through an unplanned and unwanted marriage.
   From her womb, from the child she called Levi, would
   develop the Levitical priesthood, the priestly line of Aaron
   and his sons. These sons would be tasked with the sacred
   duties of caring for the Tabernacle and then the Temple,
   leading the children of Israel in worship with the
   accompanying sacrifices needed to atone for the sins of the
   people. But even more astonishing was the birth of this
   fourth son Judah. Through God's infinite grace for her, she
   had come to the place of praise to God and so she named
   him Judah—He will be praised.

There is a blessing that Jacob gave Judah which speaks to
the fact that the royal line of Messiah will come from Judah's
descendants.

> Genesis 49:10: *"The scepter shall not depart from Judah,
> nor the ruler's staff from between his feet, until Shiloh
> comes, and to him shall be the obedience of the peoples."*

The phrase, *"until Shiloh comes"* is a reference to the
coming Messiah of Israel, God's ultimate redemption plan.
This verse prophesied that out of Judah's lineage would come
the royal line of Messiah, from his lineage would come the
Redeemer promised in "her seed."

How Can Praising the Lord Make a Difference in Your Life?

Consider Psalm 30:1–5 and the results of his praising the LORD. Consider that David was praising God for God's victory, God's healing, His deliverance, His forgiveness, restoration, and joy.

> Psalm 30:1–5: *A Psalm; a Song at the Dedication of the House. A Psalm of David. I will extol You, O LORD, for You have lifted me up, and have not let my enemies rejoice over me. O LORD my God, I cried to You for help, and You healed me. O LORD, You have brought up my soul from Sheol; You have kept me alive, that I would not go down to the pit. Sing praise to the LORD, you His godly ones, and give thanks to His holy name. For His anger is but for a moment, His favor is for a lifetime; weeping may last for the night, but a shout of joy comes in the morning.*

5. **Dan**, means, as we said, "judge." The word judge (*danan* in Hebrew) can also mean "vindicate." Though this baby was born from Bilhah, Rachel named him, saying, *"God has vindicated (judged) me, and has indeed heard (shema) my voice and has given me a son."*

How can this idea of vindication apply to us? When we think about the fact that Yeshua has taken our judgment and we stand in His righteousness, it can be life changing.

> Psalm 26:1–2: *A Psalm of David. Vindicate me, O LORD, for I have walked in my integrity, and I have trusted in the LORD without wavering. Examine me, O LORD, and try me; test my mind and my heart.*

We our clothed in the righteousness of Messiah because of His sin offering and we are no longer under the judgement or condemnation of God.

2 Corinthians 5:21 (definition added): *He made Him who knew no sin to be sin* (offering) *on our behalf, so that we might become the righteousness of God in Him.*

Romans 8:1–2: *Therefore there is now no condemnation for those who are in Messiah Yeshua. For the law of the Spirit of life in Messiah Yeshua has set you free from the law of sin and of death.*

6. **Naphtali** is based on a Hebrew phrase, "mighty wrestlings," literally, "the wrestlings of God I have wrestled." Again with this baby of Bilhah's, Rachel named him, and in this case indicated that she overcame or prevailed in the wrestling match. So, she named this son Naphtali which means, "my wrestling." The same word is used when Jacob wrestled with God on his way back to Canaan.

   Genesis 32:24: *Then Jacob was left alone, and a man wrestled with him until daybreak.*

   Can you think of a promise from the LORD to let you know that in all your struggles He is with you and will give you His victory?

   Psalm 60:12: *Through God we shall do valiantly, and it is He who will tread down our adversaries.*

7. Gad, from *bagad* in Hebrew means "fortunate" or "good fortune, fortune has come." Though this was a child of Zilpah's, Leah named him. The name showed that she felt blessed to have another son. This is an indication of her growing thankfulness to the Lord. That thankfulness extends to the next child Zilpah had for her that Leah named.

8. Asher means "happy." It literally means, "with my happiness" or "others will call me happy."

Perhaps the name Asher is familiar to some of you. It's a wonderful name to choose for your son because it reflects the desire for your son to grow in happiness blessed by God. In Psalm 1 we find God's protocol to be happy. Have you thought much about the fact that God desires for you to be happy and to understand happiness from His perspective? *Ashrei* in Hebrew and *makarios* in Greek literally mean "happy." In the Scriptures, such as in Psalm 1 and Matthew 5, those words are translated as "blessed," but the literal definition is "happy."

> Psalm 1:1–3 (definition, emphasis added*): How **blessed (ashrei—happy)** is the man who does not walk in the counsel of the wicked, nor stand in the path of sinners, nor sit in the seat of scoffers! But his delight is in the law of the LORD, and in His law he meditates day and night. He will be like a tree firmly planted by streams of water, which yields its fruit in its season, and its leaf does not wither; and in whatever he does, he prospers.*

How is happiness defined by Yeshua different from the world's idea of happiness? Read His Sermon on the Mount. Yeshua uses the Greek *Makarios*, but remember each "blessed" can be translated "happy."

> Matthew 5:1–11 (definition added): *When Yeshua saw the crowds, He went up on the mountain; and after He sat down, His disciples came to Him. He opened His mouth and began to teach them, saying, "Blessed are the poor in spirit, for theirs is the kingdom of heaven. Blessed are those who mourn, for they shall be comforted. Blessed are the gentle, for they shall inherit the earth. Blessed are those who hunger and thirst for righteousness, for they shall be satisfied. Blessed are the merciful, for they shall receive mercy. Blessed are the pure in heart, for they shall see God. Blessed are the peacemakers, for they shall be called sons of God. Blessed are those who have been*

persecuted for the sake of righteousness, for theirs is the kingdom of heaven. Blessed are you when people insult you and persecute you, and falsely say all kinds of evil against you because of Me."

9. *Issachar* means "to hire." Leah named the next baby she bore after saying, "God has given me my wages." Leah is alluding to the fact that she used the mandrakes—the aphrodisiac—to hire her husband to sleep with her resulting in the conception of Issachar.

She purchased the right to sleep with her husband by giving her sister/rival Rachel the mandrakes Reuben had found in the field. Naming her son after the price she had to pay to rent her own husband from his other wife showed her continual heartbreak over the lack of love from Jacob.

10. **Zebulun** is from the Hebrew word for "dwell," *zaval*. In naming this son Zebulun, Leah was naming him, "dwelling," with the hope that Jacob will now live with her. This Hebrew word can also mean to "exalt" and "to honor." Further insight into this word implies it is not only a dwelling, but a place where God is pleased to dwell. The verb *zaval* (זבל) occurs only once in Scripture, here in Genesis 30:20, in a word play on the name Zebulun. When Leah gave birth to her sixth son, she was literally saying, "Now my husband will feel honored to dwell with me, because I have borne him six sons."

As followers of Messiah Yeshua, we would flip this statement and praise the Lord that we can honor and exalt Him as we dwell in His presence.

In 1 Kings 8:13, Solomon gave his Temple initiation speech. He addressed God and spoke of the temple he made for the Lord. He proclaimed:

> *But I have built you a magnificent house* (zevul, from the root word "zaval") *a place for you to live forever* (CJV).

Solomon's desire for this magnificent Temple was that it be the place where God was honored and exalted. What is your desire for the temple God has given you? Paul asked the congregation at Corinth this question:

> 1 Corinthians 3:16: *Do you not know that you are a temple of God and that the Spirit of God dwells in you?*

And later he exhorted them in light of being the temple of the living God:

> 2 Corinthians 6:16–18: *Or what agreement has the temple of God with idols? For we are the temple of the living God; just as God said, "I will dwell in them and walk among them; and I will be their God, and they shall be My people. Therefore, come out from their midst and be separate," says the Lord. "And do not touch what is unclean; and I will welcome you. And I will be a father to you, and you shall be sons and daughters to Me," says the Lord Almighty.*

11. **Joseph** in Hebrew is *Yoseph* and means "addition" and "He will add." Rachel was thanking God for taking away her barrenness. When she named Joseph, she expressed the hope that God would add *(asaf)* another son to her. Her deep desire was that Joseph would not be the only biological son she would have. Later she would indeed have another son from her own womb.

12. **Benjamin** was the fulfillment of Rachel's hope, but his birth resulted in Rachel's death.

All eleven sons were given their names by either Leah or Rachel. Benjamin was the exception because Jacob renamed him; we'll get to that a bit later. Joseph and Benjamin were a wonderful blessing to their father.

THE PROMISE (PART TWO)

God Spoke to Jacob! It's Time to "Return to the Land of Your Fathers."

Jacob had been working for Laban for at least twenty years and Laban's sons were growing jealous. Genesis 31:1 describes how Laban's sons were accusing Jacob of taking from their father and getting his wealth through stealth. Then in verse two, we learn that Laban's countenance toward his son-in-law was not favorable, as it had been before. Verse three is very important for our study as we begin this section.

> Genesis 31:3: *Then the LORD said to Jacob, "Return to the land of your fathers and to your relatives, and I will be with you."*

Remember the covenant promise God made to Jacob back in Genesis 28:13-15?

> *I am the LORD, the God of your father Abraham and the God of Isaac; the land on which you lie, I will give it to you and to your descendants. Your descendants will also be like the dust of the earth, and you will spread out to the west and to the east and to the north and to the south; and in you and in your descendants shall all the families of the earth be blessed. Behold, I am with you and will keep you wherever you go, and will bring you back to this land; for I will not leave you until I have done what I have promised you.*

The first part of the promise, the fact that he had no descendants, God had taken care of through the birth of twelve sons for Jacob. The promise of Jacob having descendants *like the dust of the earth* was underway. Now it was time to address the second part of the promise, to bring Jacob back into "this land."

Jacob wasted no time and called both Rachel and Leah from their tents to meet him in the field with his flocks. There he had a private conversation with them and reviewed the deceit and treachery that he suffered from Laban's tactics by changing his wages ten times. To Jacob's credit, he gave God the praise for His protection and His blessings of prosperity.

Jacob explained to Rachel and Leah,

> *"I see your father's attitude, that it is not friendly toward me as formerly, but the God of my father has been with me. You know that I have served your father with all my strength"* (Gen 31:5–6).

The response of his wives revealed animosity and bitterness toward their own father. Note their reply after Jacob told them how God intervened by describing his dream to them.

Describing His Dream

> Genesis 31:11–13: *"Then the angel of God said to me in the dream, 'Jacob,' and I said, 'Here I am.' He said, 'Lift up now your eyes and see that all the male goats which are mating are striped, speckled, and mottled; for I have seen all that Laban has been doing to you. I am the God of Bethel, where you anointed a pillar, where you made a vow to Me; now arise, leave this land, and return to the land of your birth.'"*

Their Response

> Genesis 31:14–16: *Rachel and Leah answered and said to him, "Do we still have any portion or inheritance in our father's house? Are we not reckoned by him as foreigners? For he has sold us, and has also entirely consumed our purchase price. Surely all the wealth which God has taken away from our father belongs to us and our children; now then, do whatever God has said to you."*

Wait. Does it seem that the sisters were actually in agreement? What did their agreement reveal about their feelings for their father? For Jacob and his God?

1. Both sisters were united in their support of leaving their father's home.
2. They both realized that because Laban had sons, they would inherit nothing from him because as they stated—*we are reckoned as foreigners or aliens*
3. They declared that their own father profited from the bride price of Jacob's fourteen years of labor. Laban treated them like merchandise.
4. They acknowledged that God was the One who oversees the "wealth distribution" and they agreed to follow Jacob wherever God led him.

I find their responses to be encouraging because they both recognized that Jacob's prosperity was the result of God's divine justice and blessing.

What Can We Learn from the Sisters' Agreement?

I think we can agree that in our families and congregations there are areas of disagreement, jealousy, and disappointment over various decisions which arise. How can we give these feelings to the Lord and be in unity and agreement? When we *"[fix] our eyes on Yeshua, the author and perfecter of [our] faith"* (Heb 12:2), we will discover that focusing on Yeshua and His redemptive purposes will keep us looking to Him and not the disagreements causing pain. In Yeshua's forgiveness for us, we can continue to be forgiving and loving to those in our families and congregational families.

What Yeshua taught His disciples at their final Passover meal together is still true for us today:

John 13:35: *By this all men will know that you are My disciples, if you have love for one another.*

Can I withhold forgiveness from others when Yeshua has lavishly forgiven me?

> Ephesians 1:7–8: *In Him we have redemption through His blood, the forgiveness of our trespasses, according to the riches of His grace which He lavished on us.*

THE PROBLEM (PART TWO)

From Outside: Laban, and from Inside: Rachel

Jacob assembled his entire family along with his wives, his sons, camels, and cattle, and all the substance that he had gathered. He left while Laban was away shearing sheep. When Laban found out three days later, he took off in hot pursuit of Jacob.

> Genesis 31:17–18: *Then Jacob arose and put his children and his wives upon camels; and he drove away all his livestock and all his property which he had gathered, his acquired livestock which he had gathered in Paddan-aram, to go to the land of Canaan to his father Isaac.*

Rachel Stole Her Father's Idols

> Genesis 31:19: *When Laban had gone to shear his flock, then Rachel stole the household idols that were her father's.*

These household idols were valuable in that they gave the owner a claim to his property. Was Rachel taking this chance to gain Laban's property for her husband? Or was this her way of getting self-validation—gaining a sense of power when she had spent her whole life feeling powerless?

Laban chased after Jacob, but in his pursuit God spoke to him in a dream:

> Genesis 31:24–25: *God came to Laban the Aramean in a dream of the night and said to him, "Be careful that you do not speak to Jacob either good or bad." Laban caught*

up with Jacob. Now Jacob had pitched his tent in the hill country, and Laban with his kinsmen camped in the hill country of Gilead.

Laban used false family affection and guilt to accuse Jacob, saying,

"What have you done by deceiving me and carrying away my daughters like captives of the sword? Why did you flee secretly and deceive me, and did not tell me so that I might have sent you away with joy and with songs, with timbrel and with lyre; and did not allow me to kiss my sons and my daughters? Now you have done foolishly. It is in my power to do you harm, but the God of your father spoke to me last night, saying, 'Be careful not to speak either good or bad to Jacob'" (Genesis 31:26–29).

Why Did You Steal My Idols?

"Now you have indeed gone away because you longed greatly for your father's house; but why did you steal my gods" (Gen 31:30)?

Jacob's Interesting and Harsh Response

Then Jacob replied to Laban, "Because I was afraid, for I thought that you would take your daughters from me by force. The one with whom you find your gods shall not live; in the presence of our kinsmen point out what is yours among my belongings and take it for yourself." For Jacob did not know that Rachel had stolen them (Gen 31:31–32).

It seems to me that Jacob's reason for not telling Laban he was leaving was, at best, lame. Was he really afraid of Laban? The God of Israel had told him to leave with the assurance of His protection. However, considering Laban's behavior up to this point, it would be logical to assume that Laban would try to force Jacob to remain and to keep his daughters from leaving.

When Jacob made the declaration that he would take the life of the one who stole the idols, he had no idea that it was his beloved Rachel who had stolen them. Laban kept searching and finally got to Rachel's tent.

Rachel Continues to Deceive Her Dad:

Genesis 31:33–35: *So Laban went into Jacob's tent and into Leah's tent and into the tent of the two maids, but he did not find them. Then he went out of Leah's tent and entered Rachel's tent. Now Rachel had taken the household idols and put them in the camel's saddle, and she sat on them. And Laban felt through all the tent but did not find them. She said to her father, "Let not my lord be angry that I cannot rise before you, for the manner of women is upon me." So he searched but did not find the household idols.*

Deception seemed to run in the family. Rachel told Laban that she was having her monthly period and could not get off of her camel because she was not feeling well. This was a perfect excuse for her to stay put and keep the stolen idols concealed. This leads us back to the question, *why* did Rachel steal from her father? Jacob had grown wealthy over the years of serving her father and in turn her father had also become wealthy. The wealth and prestige of Laban's family would go to his sons. From Rachel's perspective, her father had treated her despicably. Laban would give the wealth he had gained from Jacob's hard work to his own sons. Nothing about the whole situation seemed fair. She spent her life feeling powerless and abused and perhaps she had a root of bitterness against her father—and possibly against the circumstances of her life. She was filled with resentment. Remember, if she had his idols, she had the right to the inheritance of her father. Forgiving her father for the way he had treated her was not an option that she considered.

Do you find this difficult to understand? I do! Rachel was the beautiful sister. She was the beloved of Jacob's heart. Why wouldn't those circumstances heal her and give her the value she longed for? However, the fact that she was gorgeous and loved did not make a difference in her attitudes toward her father or her sister Leah. What would have changed this situation into a different scenario? She needed to forgive her father and her sister. She needed to look to her Creator, the God of Israel, and trust in His plan for her.

APPLICATION: FORGIVENESS IS THE KEY!

Do you sometimes despise an unfair situation that was caused by a parent, a grown child, or a friend? Do you desire to get revenge to validate your feelings of powerlessness and humiliation? Do you allow unforgiveness to consume you and prevent you from trusting in the fullness of God's love and grace? If you can relate to any of these questions, this would be a good time to examine your heart and ask God to show you if there is someone, like a parent, a grown child, another relative or a friend, who has caused you great pain and anguish. By confessing this to the Lord and asking for His healing power to mend your broken, bitter heart, He will give you the opportunity to live in His lavish grace. God forgives you so you can, in turn, forgive the one who is causing you so much distress. First, confess to the Lord and accept His forgiveness, then rely on His courage to forgive the person who has abused you.

Forgiving someone does not mean that the person can 'get away with it' because God is the One who is the judge and He is in charge. He is sovereign and will bring His justice to the situation. Consequently, for those who choose to forgive in the strength of the Lord, they will discover a new freedom and a cleansing time of renewal. The bitter well will be emptied and filled with the living waters of Yeshua.

Like Isaiah the prophet you can joyously draw waters from the springs of salvation:

> Isaiah 12:2: *Behold, God is my salvation, I will trust and not be afraid; for the LORD GOD is my strength and song, and He has become my salvation.*

Rachel knew that Jacob's prosperity was a direct result of the Lord's blessings (see Genesis 30:43, 31:9–21). Rachel heard these truths directly from Jacob that would reinforce her understanding that her blessings and prosperity would come from the hand of God but unfortunately, she didn't trust fully in God. Do we realize each day that we need to declare the source of our blessings every day, as Paul said?

Ephesians 1:3: *Blessed be the God and Father of our Lord Yeshua the Messiah, who has blessed us with every spiritual blessing in the heavenly places in Messiah?*

THE RESTORATION (PART TWO)

Can There Be Peace for Jacob and Laban?

After Laban finished his search for his idols and found nothing, Jacob became angry:

Genesis 31:36: *Then Jacob became angry and contended with Laban; and Jacob said to Laban, "What is my transgression? What is my sin, that you have hotly pursued me?"*

Jacob then explained how he worked very hard in all kinds of inclement weather, and how he had never stolen so much as a lamb from Laban's flock in all the years he worked for him. He went on to say,

These twenty years I have been in your house; I served you fourteen years for your two daughters and six years for your flock, and you changed my wages ten times. If the God of my father, the God of Abraham, and the fear of Isaac, had not been for me, surely now you would have sent me away empty-handed. God has seen my affliction and the toil of my hands, so He rendered judgment last night (Gen 31:41–42).

Jacob gave the glory to the God of his father (Isaac) and the God of Abraham (his grandfather) and again by the fear of Isaac (his father) to identify who he was serving. God led him to Laban's household, but God was watching him the entire time and prospered him in all his work. The fact that the God of Jacob's fathers appeared to Laban in a dream to admonish

Laban not to touch Jacob was proof that God is the supreme judge and aware of everything that concerns His people. As I read these verses, I'm struck by the fact that it's not about Jacob, but rather it's all about God—the God of his father and grandfather.

We need to remember that Laban's sister Rebekah became Isaac's wife and was brought into the covenant family. This was God's doing and had nothing to do with Laban. God's redemptive program which would continue through Abraham, Isaac, Jacob and his sons, specifically Judah, was always based on God's promises and His covenant love alone.

What Nerve Laban Has: Chutzpah on Steroids!

Laban's response to Jacob was self-centered and materialistic. He claimed that Leah, Rachel, and their sons belonged to him:

> Genesis 31:43: *Then Laban replied to Jacob, "The daughters are my daughters, and the children are my children, and the flocks are my flocks, and all that you see is mine. But what can I do this day to these my daughters or to their children whom they have borne?"*

Acknowledging that he had lost the battle to have his children and grandchildren remain with him, Laban then suggested they make a covenant to cease fighting:

> Genesis 31:44–46: *"So now come, let us make a covenant, you and I, and let it be a witness between you and me." Then Jacob took a stone and set it up as a pillar. Jacob said to his kinsmen, "Gather stones." So they took stones and made a heap, and they ate there by the heap.*

What Is this Covenant Really About?

Scripture gives us description of this covenant known by a few different names. Laban called it *Jegar-sahadutha*, but Jacob called it *Galeed*.

143

Genesis 31:47–49: *Laban said, "This heap is a witness between you and me this day." Therefore it was named Galeed, and Mizpah, for he said, "May the LORD watch between you and me when we are absent one from the other."*

In Hebrew, the name *Galeed* means, "the heap of witnesses," and the name *Mizpah* means "watchtower." This name was linked to the phrase, *"May the LORD watch between you and me when we are absent one from the other."* I always thought that this was a wonderful blessing and was surprised to learn that the original meaning in this context was not a benediction, but a warning. This was a warning between two men who could not trust each other. The pillar or heap of stones marked a border which neither one was to cross over.

Remember the idols that Rachel took? Laban was convinced that Jacob had these household idols and, in the future, would return using those idols to claim some of Laban's territory. Laban felt he needed protection from Jacob. Ironically, this covenant was an assurance to Leah and Rachel and their sons that Laban had no authority in their lives and could no longer try to steal what the God of Abraham, Isaac, and Jacob had given them.

APPLICATION OF THIS BLESSING

As believers in the God of Israel, we can turn this *Mizpah* covenant into a true blessing by considering the Hebrew word, "watch" or *shomer*. In the garden, Adam was given the role to guard or keep the garden. We learned that his guarding skills did not turn out to be adequate therefore he and Eve were kicked out of the garden while those awesome cherubim with the flaming swords guarded the entrance.

Let's consider for our own encouragement the Lord who is our ultimate *Shomer*—Guardian—from Psalm 121. In this psalm we have a description of the ultimate *shomer* of all time. Remember *shomer* is a Hebrew word that means, "to watch, guard, or keep." When David wrote Psalm 121, he utilized *shomer* six times. I highlighted the usage of *shomer* in this psalm. Take time to personalize this psalm for your own life and your family. Thank Him for being your guardian in every situation.

- Praise Him that He is your stability and guard who never sleeps: Ps 121:4–5.
- He is your protector day and night: Ps 121:5–6.
- He is your guardian from all evil, watching over your soul everywhere you go forever: Ps 121:7–8.

Psalm 121 (emphasis added): *A Song of Ascents. I will lift up my eyes to the mountains; from where shall my help come? My help comes from the L*ORD*, who made heaven and earth. He will not allow your foot to slip; He who* **keeps** *you will not slumber. Behold, He who* **keeps** *Israel will neither slumber nor sleep. The L*ORD *is your* **keeper***; the L*ORD *is your shade on your right hand. The sun will not smite you by day, nor the moon by night. The L*ORD *will* **protect** *you from all evil; He will* **keep** *your soul. The L*ORD *will* **guard** *your going out and your coming in from this time forth and forever.*

Can There Be Peace for Jacob and Esau?

Once the threat of Laban had passed, a new one—or perhaps an old one—awaited them: Esau. But Jacob didn't continue his journey alone. He had a company of angels.

> Genesis 32:1–2: *Now as Jacob went on his way, the angels of God met him. Jacob said when he saw them, "This is God's camp." So he named that place Mahanaim.*

With the many angels there, Jacob concluded this was God's camp. The plural for "camp" in Hebrew is *mahanaim*. He sent his messengers ahead to meet Esau with the promise of many gifts to be a sign of goodwill, so that he might find favor in his sight. We know his state of mind when these messengers returned and told him that Esau was coming to meet him with four hundred men.

His Plan from a Fearful Heart

> Genesis 32:7–8: *Then Jacob was greatly afraid and distressed; and he divided the people who were with him, and the flocks and the herds and the camels, into two companies; for he said, "If Esau comes to the one company and attacks it, then the company which is left will escape."*

In his fearful state, he prays to his faithful God:

> Genesis 32:9–12: *Jacob said, "O God of my father Abraham and God of my father Isaac, O LORD, who said to me, 'Return to your country and to your relatives, and I will prosper you,' I am unworthy of all the lovingkindness and of all the faithfulness which You have shown to Your servant; for with my staff only I crossed this Jordan, and now I have become two companies. "Deliver me, I pray, from the hand of my brother, from the hand of Esau; for I fear him, that he will come and attack me and the mothers with the children. "For You said, 'I will surely prosper you and make your descendants as the sand of the sea, which is too great to be numbered.'"*

Jacob first reminded God that it was God's idea for him to go back to his country. Then he humbled himself and acknowledged that God prospered him, transforming him from a one-person family to a family of so many that he had to split them into two companies. He begged for God's protection from Esau and ended the prayer reminding God of His Abrahamic Covenant promise.

Consider Jacob's prayer as an example for you when you are distressed and greatly afraid:

- *I'm following Your instructions* (Genesis 32:9). Apply God's Word and seek Him first.
- *I acknowledge that I am unworthy and owe my success to Your grace* (Genesis 32:10). Humbly acknowledge that all you have is by His grace.
- *Please save me from this imminent danger* (Genesis 32:11). Be honest with the LORD about your fears.
- *I remind You of Your covenant promise* (Genesis 32:12). Come to Him based on His New Covenant promises.

Still Fighting Fear and Despair

Considering his inevitable meeting with his brother Esau, Jacob divided his large family into two camps or companies. His thinking was that if one company was attacked, the other one would be saved. Jacob had apparently forgotten the promises for protection that the God of Abraham and Isaac had given him.

Face to Face with God and a New Name

Jacob sent his family groups across the river. Then he decided to return to the other side where he encountered God and wrestled with Him all night long.

> Genesis 32:22–32: *Now he arose that same night and took his two wives and his two maids and his eleven children, and crossed the ford of the Jabbok. He took them*

and sent them across the stream. And he sent across whatever he had. Then Jacob was left alone, and a man wrestled with him until daybreak. When he saw that he had not prevailed against him, he touched the socket of his thigh; so the socket of Jacob's thigh was dislocated while he wrestled with him. Then he said, "Let me go, for the dawn is breaking." But he said, "I will not let you go unless you bless me." So he said to him, "What is your name?" And he said, "Jacob." He said, "Your name shall no longer be Jacob, but Israel; for you have striven with God and with men and have prevailed." (Israel—he wrestles with God, Prince of God, striving with God.) *Then Jacob asked him and said, "Please tell me your name." But he said, "Why is it that you ask my name?" And he blessed him there. So Jacob named the place* **Peniel,** *for he said,* **"I have seen God face to face, yet my life has been preserved."** *Now the sun rose upon him just as he crossed over Penuel, and he was limping on his thigh. Therefore, to this day the sons of Israel do not eat the sinew of the hip which is on the socket of the thigh, because he touched the socket of Jacob's thigh in the sinew of the hip* (definition, emphasis added).

What Can We Learn from Jacob's All-Night Struggle with Yeshua?

When we meet Yeshua, He gives us a new name. Do you believe the Messiah Yeshua has given you a new name and that you are called a "daughter of the King"?

In his struggle with the Lord, Yeshua touched Jacob's hip, weakening him so he would have to limp for the rest of his life. What a blessing to be reminded of our weaknesses, so we realize that we need to depend totally upon the Lord. Can you praise Him for weak areas in your life? Remember when you are weak, the Lord is strong in you (2 Cor 12:9).

A Wonderful Reunion—Once Estranged and Now United

Remember, it had been twenty years since Jacob and Esau last met. Jacob left with a death threat from Esau hanging over his head.

> Genesis 33:1–5: *Then Jacob lifted his eyes and looked, and behold, Esau was coming, and four hundred men with him. So he divided the children among Leah and Rachel and the two maids. He put the maids and their children in front, and Leah and her children next, and Rachel and Joseph last. But he himself passed on ahead of them and bowed down to the ground seven times, until he came near to his brother. Then Esau ran to meet him and embraced him, and fell on his neck and kissed him, and they wept. He lifted his eyes and saw the women and the children, and said, "Who are these with you?" So he said, "The children whom God has graciously given your servant."*

Jacob arranged his family in a certain way to introduce them. Jacob divided the family into three sections: the first division was the handmaids and their children, the second group was Leah and her children, and the third group was Rachel and her son Joseph. Jacob went in front of all the groups and humbled himself before Esau. According to the protocol of the day, he bowed himself to the ground seven times as he approached his brother. What a beautiful picture of reconciliation as Esau ran to him, hugged him, with kisses and weeping. After this Esau asked Jacob who the women and children belonged to. Jacob not only gave glory to the graciousness of God, but he also described himself as Esau's servant.

Esau was introduced to everyone and then he accepted the gifts that Jacob lavishly gave him in order to *"find **favor** in the sight of my lord"* (Gen 33:8, emphasis added). Esau told Jacob, *"I have plenty, my brother."* Esau had also become wealthy over the twenty years, but Jacob had two reasons he wanted Esau to receive his gifts:

> Gen 33:10-11, emphasis added: *Jacob said, "No, please, if now I have found **favor** in your sight, then take my present from my hand, for I see your face as one sees the face of God, and you have received me **favorably**. Please take my gift which has been brought to you, because God has **dealt graciously** with me and because I have plenty." Thus he urged him and he took it.*

Returning the Blessing of the Birthright of His Wealth to Esau

Jacob was so glad to see the face of his brother that he compared it to seeing the face of God. The phrase, *"Please take my gift* (berachah) *which has been brought to you"* (Gen 33:10, definition added), uses a special word for gift *(berachah)* because it carries the meaning of "my blessing." In other words, this was a reference to the patriarchal blessing of their father Isaac that he now wanted to share with Esau. Jacob urged Esau to receive the gifts and he finally took them.

I want us to note that both Leah and Rachel were witnesses to all that was happening. Although the Scriptures do not tell us specifically how they were feeling, I think we can presume that it must have been very encouraging for both of them. Leah and Rachel along with their handmaids and their children could see the graciousness of God in the brothers' reunion. Forgiveness and graciousness can only happen as a result of God giving them His grace and His favor first. What must it have been like for these sisters to see the grace of God in action? What is it like for us when we acknowledge His grace in all things?

Preparation Instructions from God for Renewal at Bethel

> Genesis 35:1-4: *Then God said to Jacob, "Arise, go up to Bethel and live there, and make an altar there to God, who*

*appeared to you when you fled from your brother Esau."
So Jacob said to his household and to all who were with
him, "Put away the foreign gods which are among you,
and purify yourselves, and change your garments; and let
us arise and go up to Bethel; and I will make an altar there
to God, who answered me in the day of my distress, and
has been with me wherever I have gone." So they gave to
Jacob all the foreign gods which they had and the rings
which were in their ears, and Jacob hid them under the
oak which was near Shechem.*

Jacob obeyed the voice of his God and exhorted his
household and all who were with him to get rid of their foreign
gods and purify themselves (purify is *tahor*—be ceremonially
clean) and put on different clothes. He told them they were
going to Bethel where he would build an altar to God. Note the
way Jacob described his God to them: Jacob told them that
God always answered him when he was in trouble, and then
he confessed something quite astounding! He said that God
had been with him wherever he had gone, declaring to them
that his God was always with him.

Is There an Application for Us?

How can we apply this portion to our own lives? Do I have
any idols in my life that I put before the Lord? Initially I would
answer "no" until I'm reminded of Colossians 3:4–5 which says
that greed is idolatry.

Colossians 3:4–5 (emphasis added): *When Messiah, who
is our life, is revealed, then you also will be revealed with
Him in glory. Therefore consider the members of your
earthly body as dead to immorality, impurity, passion, evil
desire, **and greed, which amounts to idolatry.***

If greed is idolatry, then idol worship becomes a different
question for me. Am I allowing materialism that has me
longing for more to creep into my life? Is there an area of my
life that I am making into an idol by my desire for *more*—stuff

or a better position, etc.? If so, I need to confess these sins and be cleansed. This cleansing is tied together with Jacob's exhortation that they should purify themselves. This word "purify" means "to be ceremonial clean" in order to come into the presence of our Holy God in worship.

Learn from King David

After he confessed to God his sins of adultery and murder, King David prayed in Psalm 51:10: *Create in me a clean heart, O God, and renew a steadfast spirit within me.* David used the words *lev* (heart), *tahor* (ceremonially clean), *barah lee* (create in me), and *Elohim* (God). David was not talking about his human heart, but rather his inner being that needed to be made new. In Judaic thinking, the heart represents the spiritual center of a person. Only our creator God can create a clean heart and renew His Spirit within us. David had plenty to confess with all that he had done, but God forgave him, purified him, and renewed him in his role as king of Israel.

For us as well when we sin and we need to be cleansed, we can follow the instructions of 1 John 1:9:

> *If we confess our sins, He is faithful and righteous to forgive us our sins and to cleanse us from all unrighteousness.*

In other words if I confess to God—or in the Greek, *homologeo*, "to say the same thing about my sin as God does"— then God is the One who will forgive me and cleanse my heart. He can create a pure heart in me to be able to worship Him because He is a faithful and righteous God.

> 2 Corinthians 5:17 (NKJV): *Therefore, if anyone is in Christ, he is a new creation; old things have passed away; behold, all things have become new.*

Bethel Was a Time for Renewal and Rededication

We can learn from Jacob to keep building our walk of faith on the sure foundation that Messiah Yeshua will never leave us or forsake us. He will be with us always in every situation. We don't need to be afraid for the LORD is with us.

In Genesis 35:4, they brought all their foreign gods, including the earrings from their ears, to Jacob. The earrings were involved like charms as part of their idol worship. This does not mean there is something wrong with wearing earrings today! The idols consisted of those brought from Haran, including the ones that Rachel stole from her dad, and any idols the family servants (and captives taken from Shechem, Gen 34:29) possessed as part of their idol worship. It was to be a new start.

The Journey Continues

El Shaddai Blesses Israel with Wonderful Promises

Genesis 35:9–15: *Then God appeared to Jacob again when he came from Paddan-aram, and He blessed him. God said to him, "Your name is Jacob; you shall no longer be called Jacob, but Israel shall be your name." Thus He called him Israel. God also said to him, "I am God Almighty; be fruitful and multiply; a nation and a company of nations shall come from you, and kings shall come forth from you. The land which I gave to Abraham and Isaac, I will give it to you, and I will give the land to your descendants after you." Then God went up from him in the place where He had spoken with him. Jacob set up a pillar in the place where He had spoken with him, a pillar of stone, and he poured out a drink offering on it; he also poured oil on it. So Jacob named the place where God had spoken with him, Bethel.*

God appeared to Jacob at Bethel and as He blessed Jacob, He reminded him that his name was changed to Israel—

struggle with God. He also revealed that He is *El Shaddai*—God Almighty (as He said to Abraham in Genesis 17:1). He commanded Jacob to be fruitful and multiply, promising him that he would birth not just one nation, but a company of nations and kings.

EL SHADDAI

Note the promise that God made to Abraham. It echoes the truth of what He told Jacob at Bethel. *El Shaddai*—God Almighty—always keeps His covenant promises.

Genesis 17:1, 4–6: *Now when Abram was ninety-nine years old, the LORD appeared to Abram and said to him, "I am God Almighty; walk before Me, and be blameless. ... As for Me, behold, My covenant is with you, and you will be the father of a multitude of nations. No longer shall your name be called Abram, but your name shall be Abraham; for I have made you the father of a multitude of nations. I will make you exceedingly fruitful, and I will make nations of you, and kings will come forth from you."*

What Does the Name *El Shaddai* Mean?

God revealed His name, *El Shaddai*, first to Abraham and then to Jacob. This is an astounding, wonderful name that is made up of three Hebrew words.

El*: El* means "God," and in and of itself carries the idea of One mighty, strong, and prominent. The Lord—*yud, hey, vav, hey* (יהוה)—is already the Mighty God without *Shaddai*. So, what is God revealing about Himself to Abraham, to Jacob, and to us with the word *Shaddai*?

Shad*:* In modern Hebrew, *shad* is the word for a woman's breast. In the Scriptures, breast or breasts *(shadayim)* occurs twenty-four times as *Shaddai*. It can be interpreted as "the One who is mighty to nourish, supply, and satisfy." In Isaiah 66:10–13, there is a beautiful passage about praising the LORD for the future of Jerusalem. The prophet likened the abundance of peace and glory to an overflowing stream, as well as being nursed at the breasts of a comforting mother.

Isaiah 66:10–13: *Be joyful with Jerusalem and rejoice for her, all you who love her; be exceedingly glad with her, all you who mourn over her, that you may nurse and be satisfied with her comforting breasts, that you may suck and be delighted with her bountiful bosom." For thus says the LORD, "Behold, I extend peace to her like a river, and the glory of the nations like an overflowing stream; and you will be nursed, you will be carried on the hip and fondled on the knees. As one whom his mother comforts, so I will comfort you; and you will be comforted in Jerusalem."*

Dai: Think of the song "*Dayenu*" that we sing at Passover. *Dai* means "it's enough" *Dayenu* means, "It would have been enough for us" or "Our God is sufficient." This word carries the idea of provision, sustenance, and

blessings (see Genesis 49:24–25, Jacob's blessing for Joseph).

Therefore, to say *El Shaddai* is to identify the One who mightily nourishes and satisfies, pouring forth His abundance. *El Shaddai* is the all-sufficient and all bountiful God.

WHAT DOES THIS MEAN FOR YOU AND ME?

Yeshua is *El Shaddai*— Scripture tells us that Yeshua the Messiah is completely sufficient for all our matters of life and godliness.

2 Peter 1:2–4 (emphasis added)—*Grace and peace be multiplied to you in the knowledge of God and of [Yeshua] our Lord; seeing that **His divine power** has granted to us everything pertaining to life and godliness, through the true knowledge of Him who called us by His own glory and excellence. For by these He has granted to us His precious and magnificent promises, so that by them you may become partakers of the divine nature, having*

155

escaped the corruption that is in the world by lust.

Colossians 2:9–10—*For in Him all the fullness of Deity dwells in bodily form, and in Him you have been made complete, and He is the* head over all rule and authority.

Praise *El Shaddai*! He is the mighty God we serve! He is mighty to save, always providing bountifully in our walk of faith.

Back to Jacob

After the wonderful communion with God as He poured out His promises to Jacob and his descendants, Jacob worshipped God and memorialized Bethel—the House of God.

> Genesis 35:14–15: *Jacob set up a pillar in the place where He had spoken with him, a pillar of stone, and he poured out a drink offering on it; he also poured oil on it. So Jacob named the place where God had spoken with him, Bethel.*

Benjamin, the Twelfth Son, and Rachel's Death

Apparently, Rachel was great with child in their travels and gave birth to a son.

> Genesis 35:16–20: *Then they journeyed from Bethel; and when there was still some distance to go to Ephrath, Rachel began to give birth and she suffered severe labor. When she was in severe labor the midwife said to her, "Do not fear, for now you have another son." It came about as her soul was departing (for she died), that she named him Ben-oni; but his father called him Benjamin. So Rachel died and was buried on the way to Ephrath (that is, Bethlehem). Jacob set up a pillar over her grave; that is the pillar of Rachel's grave to this day.*

As she was dying, she named the baby *Ben-oni* or "son of my sorrows," reflecting perhaps on the severe pain of this

156

childbirth or the deeper pain that she carried in her life. Jacob stepped in and renamed him Benjamin or "son of my right hand." This was the only son that he named, turning his name into a promise for the future instead of a reminder of the past.

Avot: The Fathers in The Amidah

In this chapter we met Leah and Rachel and their twelve sons, who would be the future of the nation of Israel, as their descendants make up the tribes of Israel. As you read about them, remember that we women are essential in God's redemptive program for both Israel and the world.

There are many prayers in Judaism that begin with the *Avot*— "the Fathers"—and the *Amidah* is perhaps the most well-known. It is at the core of every traditional Jewish worship service: "The Prayer." *Amidah*, which literally means, "standing," refers to a series of blessings recited while standing.

The First Three Blessings of the Traditional Prayer

The first three blessings of praise of the Amidah in every worship service are always the same, with only minor variations for weekdays, Shabbat, and holidays. The first blessing is called *Avot*, Hebrew for "Fathers" or "ancestors," and serves as an introduction to the God of our biblical heritage, connecting us to the Divine. Immediately before reciting the Amidah, the tradition developed of taking three steps backward and then forward again to symbolize entering into God presence. This blessing praises God for remembering the good actions of the patriarchs Abraham, Isaac, and Jacob—and in more liberal congregations, the matriarchs, Sarah, Rebecca, Leah, and Rachel—and by implication, asks God to hear our prayer favorably because of their merit. The

157

blessing begins and ends with a formal bow at the knees and hips, symbolically demonstrating our subservience to God.[2]

Sarah, Rebekah, Leah, and Rachel were women in many ways like you and me. What made them unique is that they were chosen for God's purposes in His plan of redemption for Israel during the formation of His nation, the nation that would bless the world.

We Too Are Chosen for His Purposes!

Ephesians 1:9–10: *He made known to us the mystery of His will, according to His kind intention which He purposed in Him with a view to an administration suitable to the fullness of the times, that is, the summing up of all things in Messiah, things in the heavens and things on the earth.*

Israel was God's choice not because of anything special in the lives of the people themselves, but because God chose to pour His love out on them and use them.

God Chose Us Because He Loves Us!

Ephesians 1:3–6: *Blessed be the God and Father of our Lord Yeshua the Messiah, who has blessed us with every spiritual blessing in the heavenly places in Messiah, just as He chose us in Him before the foundation of the world, that we would be holy and blameless before Him. In love He predestined us to adoption as [daughters] through Yeshua the Messiah to Himself, according to the kind intention of His will, to the praise of the glory of His grace, which He freely bestowed on us in the Beloved.*

Let's continue to learn and grow in our study of their lives because these women are the mothers of Israel. Like me, you may have some questions about the lives and choices of Sarah,

---

[2] Rabbi Daniel Kohn, "The Amidah," taken from *My Jewish Learning,* https://www.myjewishlearning.com/article/the-amidah

Rebekah, Leah, and even Rachel. Perhaps when we meet them in heaven, after we give them hugs, we can ask our questions. However, I think I will have forgotten the unanswered mysteries of their lives and just be in awe of meeting this amazing group of women!

What then shall
we say
to these things?
If God is for us,
who is against us?

Romans 8:31

Five

A Detour for Judah: Tamar

THE PROMISE

It Included a Detour for Israel

In the time between the life stories of Rachel and Tamar, the family of Israel took a couple of turns.

Jacob's Favoritism of Joseph Led to Hatred, Depravity, and Grief

Genesis 37:1: *Now Jacob lived in the land where his father had sojourned, in the land of Canaan.*

Jacob settled down with his family. The next time the Scriptures focused in on the story of his life, Joseph was seventeen years old and pasturing the flocks with his brothers. A picture is given to us of what the family dynamic was like:

Genesis 37:3–4: *Now Israel loved Joseph more than all his sons, because he was the son of his old age; and he made him a varicolored tunic. His brothers saw that their father loved him more than all his brothers; and so they hated him and could not speak to him on friendly terms.*

This tunic given to Joseph was a status symbol that spoke loudly to all his older brothers. It meant that Jacob was elevating the importance of Joseph in the family. This meant that Joseph expected to inherit more than his older brothers. So his brothers already hated him because of this special tunic, but when Joseph told them about his dreams—which featured his brothers bowing down to him—they became outraged. When the opportunity presented itself for the brothers to kill him, they put him in a pit and discussed what to do. Judah suggested that instead of killing him, they sell him to a caravan of Ishmaelites who were on their way to Egypt. After selling him, they took Joseph's robe and dipped it in the blood of a slaughtered goat. When they showed the coat to their father, his response was heartbreaking:

> Genesis 37:33–35: *Then he examined it and said, "It is my son's tunic. A wild beast has devoured him; Joseph has surely been torn to pieces!" So Jacob tore his clothes, and put sackcloth on his loins and mourned for his son many days. Then all his sons and all his daughters arose to comfort him, but he refused to be comforted. And he said, "Surely I will go down to Sheol in mourning for my son." So his father wept for him.*

In fact, Jacob would spend the next twenty-five years mourning. During that time, there is no record that he sought the Lord for comfort or guidance. His mourning would end only when he was reunited with Joseph twenty-five years later in Egypt.

Do You Find this Account Sad and Discouraging?

Jacob was not being wise or fair-minded in his favoritism toward Joseph, which engendered deep hostility and hatred from the older brothers. Why didn't Jacob seek the Lord for wisdom and guidance to lead his family?

What can we learn from this dark time of grief for Jacob? If he had sought the Lord in his time of grief, do you think the

Lord would have answered him? Hadn't God spoken regularly to him and surrounded him with angels during his journeys? Yeshua appeared to him and interacted with him. Nevertheless, for the next twenty-five years, he lived with his broken heart, without the comfort of the God who loved him and always desired for Jacob to draw near to Him.

How Do I Respond to Unexpected Crushing Grief that I Encounter?

Do I rely on God's promises to assure me? God does not look with disdain upon me when my heart is broken. On the contrary, He desires for me to realize that He is right there with me in my sufferings. I want to rely on His promises, and I find Psalm 34 especially meaningful.

> Psalm 34:18–19: *The LORD is near to the brokenhearted and saves those who are crushed in spirit. Many are the afflictions of the righteous, but the LORD delivers him out of them all.*

The Hebrew word for "near" is *karov* and means that His presence is right there with me. In verse eighteen, it states the Lord saves all who are *crushed in spirit*. "Saves" in Hebrew is *yashav*, which comes from the same root word as Yeshua—the Savior. And the word "crushed"—*dakah*—is the same word used in Isaiah 53:5 to describe the suffering our Messiah endured for our sins.

> Isaiah 53:5 (definition added): *But He was pierced through for our transgressions, He was crushed (dakah) for our iniquities; the chastening for our well-being fell upon Him, and by His scourging we are healed.*

Consider the invitation we have in Hebrews 4:16: we are encouraged to draw near and come close to God with confidence because our Great High Priest—*Cohen HaGadol*—knows everything we go through and can understand and empathize with us. He desires to give us His abundant grace and mercy in our desperate situations and difficulties.

Hebrews 4:14–16: *Therefore, since we have a great high priest who has passed through the heavens, Yeshua the Son of God, let us hold fast our confession. For we do not have a high priest who cannot sympathize with our weaknesses, but One who has been tempted in all things as we are, yet without sin. Therefore let us draw near with confidence to the throne of grace, so that we may receive mercy and find grace to help in time of need.*

God had not forsaken Jacob during his long mourning period. We can say this with confidence because we know at the end of the story, he would be reunited with Joseph. What Joseph's brothers meant for evil; God meant for good. God was preparing Joseph during those twenty-five years to be able to bring Jacob and his family to Egypt. The study of the life of Joseph is found in Genesis 39–50. In his life story, we learn how vital Joseph was in God's plan of redemption as we see the move of Jacob and his family to Egypt and then the development of Israel as a nation.

The Move and the Promise Repeated

Genesis 46:1–5: *So Israel set out with all that he had, and came to Beersheba, and offered sacrifices to the God of his father Isaac. God spoke to Israel in visions of the night and said, "Jacob, Jacob." And he said, "Here I am." He said, "I am God, the God of your father;* **do not be afraid to go down to Egypt, for I will make you a great nation there. I will go down with you to Egypt, and I will also surely bring you up again; and Joseph will close your eyes.***" Then Jacob arose from Beersheba; and the sons of Israel carried their father Jacob and their little ones and their wives in the wagons which Pharaoh had sent to carry him* (emphasis added).

Genesis 46:8–27 lists the names of the seventy descendants of Jacob who moved to Egypt. God assured Jacob that He was with him and that He would bring them back to their own land.

Nevertheless, after Jacob's death, the brothers were afraid that Joseph had hidden bitterness towards them, but Joseph assured them God was in charge. In God's providential plan, He had worked all things together for the good of His people Israel.

> Genesis 50:18–22 (emphasis added): *Then his brothers also came and fell down before him and said, "Behold, we are your servants."* **But Joseph said to them, "Do not be afraid, for am I in God's place? As for you, you meant evil against me, but God meant it for good in order to bring about this present result, to preserve many people alive.** *So therefore, do not be afraid; I will provide for you and your little ones." So he comforted them and spoke kindly to them. Now Joseph stayed in Egypt, he and his father's household, and Joseph lived one hundred and ten years.*

Why Egypt, Lord?

Why was it essential for God to move His people to Goshen, which was a very fertile area of Egypt? If the seventy people in the family of Jacob had remained in Canaan, they would have continued to intermarry and be drawn into horrifying idol worship of the Canaanite nations. They would have assimilated to the point that they would not have been a recognizable people of Israel.

In God's plan, they moved to Egypt where they remained together, isolated from the Egyptians, and grew as a nation. The Pharaoh who knew Joseph gave them the fertile area of Goshen, and because they were farmers and shepherds, the Egyptians were not interested in intermarrying with them.

Why Slaves, Lord?

They were slaves for four hundred years, a span which gave the Israelites the opportunity to become a *great nation.* Being slaves ensured they were looking forward to a redemption day and reciting the promises and miracles of their fathers Abraham, Isaac, and Jacob. This slavery was actually part of the promise God gave Abraham in Genesis 15:13:

> Genesis 15:13–14: *God said to Abram, "Know for certain that your descendants will be strangers in a land that is not theirs, where they will be enslaved and oppressed four hundred years. But I will also judge the nation whom they will serve, and afterward they will come out with many possessions."*

Therefore, it was according to God's providential timing that He called Moses to deliver the nation of Israel out of the land of Egypt.

The Promise to Judah

Remember the blessing that Jacob gave Judah that we discussed in the last chapter?

The Scriptures prophesy that it will be through Judah's line that the Messiah of Israel would be born of a woman. At the end of his life, Jacob prophetically told all his sons what would take place for them in the days to come. When Jacob spoke to Judah in Genesis 49:8–10, we learn important truths that point us to Yeshua the Messiah.

Jacob prophesies that Judah will live up to his name, which means "One who praises God." Judah became the head of the royal tribe that gave Israel their kings, culminating in the coming of the King of kings, Yeshua the Messiah. The tribe of Judah remained faithful to the Davidic line even when Israel became a divided kingdom. Judah was described as a lion, first a young cub, and then a mature lion who would protect and defend his people. This description calls to mind the heavenly scene in Revelation 5, where John was distraught when no one was found worthy to break the seals and open the book. An elder comforted John, stepped in to speak to John, and said,

> *Stop weeping; behold, the Lion that is from the tribe of Judah, the Root of David, has overcome so as to open the book and its seven seals* (Revelation 5:5).

Yeshua is the Lion of Judah from the tribe of Judah.

The prophecy in Genesis 49 proclaimed that the ruling scepter would continue to be part of the line of Judah until *Shiloh* comes.

> Genesis 49:10: *"The scepter shall not depart from Judah, nor the ruler's staff from between his feet, until Shiloh comes, and to him shall be the obedience of the peoples."*

The Hebrew translation for *Shiloh* is simply "the one whose it is." That verse really says, "until He comes whose right it is," meaning whose right it is to have the scepter, the right to rule. In ancient rabbinical writings, *Shiloh* was always considered to be the name for Messiah—the One who would rule and reign forever and command the obedience of all people. This prophesied rule and reign is fulfilled in Messiah Yeshua even as Isaiah and Philippians declare.

> *I have sworn by Myself, the word has gone forth from My mouth in righteousness and will not turn back, that to Me every knee will bow, every tongue will swear allegiance* (Isaiah 45:23).

> *For this reason also, God highly exalted Him, and bestowed on Him the name which is above every name, so that at the name of Yeshua every knee will bow, of those who are in heaven and on earth and under the earth, and that every tongue should confess that Yeshua the Messiah*

is Lord, to the glory of God the Father (Philippians 2:9–11).

THE PROBLEM

Children from Judah

In this book, we are highlighting the way God used women in His redemptive program to fulfill the prophecy of "her seed" given in Genesis 3:15. Thus far we have studied the lives of Eve, Sarah, Rebekah, Leah, and Rachel.

As we just saw, the promised redemption of mankind, the promised Messiah, would come through the line of Judah. This required Judah to have descendants. Hmm. This is starting to sound familiar.

How Did Judah's Lineage Develop?

To understand how Judah's redemptive line developed, we need to study Genesis 38. Before the move to Egypt, while his father Jacob was engulfed with grief at the loss of Joseph, Judah decided to leave home. Do you think he was drowning in guilt for lying to his father and couldn't stand watching him mourn so bitterly? Whatever his reasons, Judah went to visit Hirah, who lived in the Canaanite town of Adullam. This was quite a distance from his family and not just around the corner. He took a woman named Shua to be his wife and had three sons named Er, Onan, and Shelah (see Gen 38:1–5).

He picked a wife for his oldest son, Er. Her name was Tamar. Genesis 38:7 explains what happened to Er:

> *But Er, Judah's firstborn, was evil in the sight of the Lord, so the Lord took his life.*

We don't have any other information about Er than that, but Judah then told his second-born son, Onan, to fulfill his brotherly duty and marry Tamar. This was done in order to honor his dead brother's memory by having a child who would share in his older brother's inheritance. We read what happened in Genesis 38:9–10:

> *Onan knew that the offspring would not be his; so when he went in to his brother's wife, he wasted his seed on the ground in order not to give offspring to his brother. But what he did was displeasing in the sight of the LORD; so He took his life also.*

We don't know what kind of evil the older brother committed to incur God's judgment, but we do know that Onan disrespected his father's instructions, and dishonored his brother and Tamar by spilling his seed on the ground. Every time he would have sex with Tamar, he would ejaculate his seed on the ground so she would not get pregnant. His selfishness and disregard for life was evil in the sight of God. God took Onan's life also.

Two Down, One to Go?

With two dead sons, Judah suspected that Tamar must be the problem. He was not going to give her his third son, Shelah.

> Genesis 38:11: *Then Judah said to his daughter-in-law Tamar, "Remain a widow in your father's house until my son Shelah grows up"; for he thought, "I am afraid that he too may die like his brothers." So Tamar went and lived in her father's house.*

Does it surprise you to realize that Judah had no intention of having Tamar marry his third son? This became evident as the years passed by and Judah's wife died. Judah was overcome with grief, losing his two sons and his wife as well. He wanted to protect his third son from Tamar, who still wore her widow's clothes, still lived in her father's house. Consider her dilemma! Tamar had been married and widowed by two men whom Scriptures say, *"did evil in the sight of God."* She had been lied to and betrayed by her own father-in-law—stuck as a widow in her father's pagan home. How do you think she felt? How would you feel? Unloved, rejected, humiliated, betrayed, grief stricken, trapped?

Another Woman Takes Matters into Her Own Hands

Tamar devised a plan. She decided to "take matters into her own hands." Does this remind you of Sarah? Or Rebekah? Tamar, unlike Sarah and Rebekah, did not have a husband who followed the God of Israel. She was a pagan Canaanite and it's doubtful that Judah or his sons had taught her about the One true God. Certainly, Tamar desired to remove her clothes of mourning and have a family of her own. As we read about her plan, we cannot justify her trickery, but we can feel her sense of desperation and powerlessness.

> There is an expression that seems appropriate at this point. "There but for the grace of God go I." Without His grace, I could become just like Tamar, operating in my flesh and not walking in the Spirit of God, not seeking God but devising my own way out of tough situations. I have lied, been deceitful, and tried to manipulate people and circumstance for my desired outcomes. But when I repent of my actions, God's grace always brings me back to His loving arms by granting me forgiveness as I look to Yeshua, the author and finisher of my faith—Hebrews 12:1–2 (Miriam Nadler, *Compassion and Redemption*, p. 27).

Take time to thank God for His love, His grace, and His total forgiveness that He pours out to you through Yeshua the Messiah.

Just What Did Tamar Do?

She sought her own solution to the problem of her childlessness and forced Judah to fulfill his promise. You see, besides the custom of the "next-in-line brother" raising up seed to provide for a widow, there was another tradition: for the father of the deceased man to provide a child for the widow.

Tamar knew it was sheep-shearing time, which would include lots of celebrations Judah would not want to miss. On his way to the sheep shearing, his route would take him past a pagan temple. Knowing that he was lonely since his wife had died, Tamar took off her mourning clothes and disguised herself as a temple prostitute. It all went according to her plan. Judah passed by, saw her, and wanted to have sex with her, not knowing who she was. They negotiated payment. Judah offered to send her a goat after he got home from the sheep shearing. Tamar used this payment offer to demand three items for a security deposit. She asked for his signet ring, which represented his authority; his jewelry, which was a sign of his wealth; and his staff, which identified him in the community. Judah willingly turned over these items. After their interlude was over, Judah did try to locate her to give her the goat and retrieve his identifying "security deposit" items but, of course, she could not be found.

Let Her Burn!

Three months later, it was reported to Judah that Tamar was pregnant by harlotry. This is how Judah reacted:

> Genesis 38:24–26 (emphasis added): *Now it was about three months later that Judah was informed, "Your daughter-in-law Tamar has played the harlot, and behold, she is also with child by harlotry." Then Judah said, **"Bring her out and let her be burned!"** It was while she was being brought out that she sent to her father-in-law, saying, **"I am with child by the man to whom these things belong." And she said, "Please examine and see, whose signet ring and cords and staff are these?"** Judah recognized them, and said, "She is more righteous than I, inasmuch as I did not give her to my son Shelah." And he did not have relations with her again.*

After Judah overreacted with "burn her," he was then deeply convicted when Tamar showed him his three identifying items. Judah realized that he had lied to Tamar about his third son and deceived her for many years, leaving her without hope in her father's house. At the end of Genesis 38:26, we learn that he never had sex with her again.

THE RESTORATION

Perhaps Tamar had been crying out to the God of Judah to understand how her life could be redeemed. Remember, she was living in the midst of a wicked Canaanite society, which included their depraved religious practices. She had been waiting for years to once again be part of Judah's family. She was reminded daily of her dire situation by the widow's garments she was forced to wear in her father's house. God does not justify Tamar's actions, nevertheless, in His abundant merciful compassion, He restored her life. Her clothes of mourning became garments of praise. Can you praise God along with Tamar from Psalm 30?

> Psalm 30:10–12 (NIV): *Hear, LORD, and be merciful to me; LORD, be my help." You turned my wailing into dancing; you removed my sackcloth and clothed me with joy, that my heart may sing your praises and not be silent. LORD my God, I will praise you forever.*

God saw Tamar's grief, despair, and disappointment, and He turned her life around and gave her dignity, hope, and a future. Widowed twice, God nevertheless allowed her to be pregnant. He answered the need of her heart.

Application for Us

This is what God desires to do for you and me. Do you believe that God will turn your sorrow into rejoicing? In Psalm 30:10–12, King David was crying out to God for mercy and help. God not only heard his prayer, but He turned the situation around. He went from crying to dancing, from sorrow to rejoicing, from no praise to eternal praise to the Lord God.

Just as He did for Tamar and David, God will pour out His mercy upon you.

Take time to read all of Psalm 30 and praise Him for what He alone can do in your life.

More Twins!

> Genesis 38:27–30 (NIV, definitions added): *When the time came for her to give birth, there were twin boys in her womb. As she was giving birth, one of them put out his hand; so the midwife took a scarlet thread and tied it on his wrist and said, "This one came out first." But when he drew back his hand, his brother came out, and she said, "So this is how you have broken out!" And he was named Perez. Then his brother, who had the scarlet thread on his wrist, came out. And he was named Zerah* (scarlet).

The midwife knew twins were coming so she tied a scarlet thread to the first tiny wrist that she saw! But suddenly the scarlet thread vanished as his tiny hand went back up the birth canal and his brother "broke out" first. The name Perez means "breakthrough." In God's providential care, Perez not only broke out of Tamar's womb first, but he also broke through the barrenness of her life. God gave her twin sons who were named Perez, meaning "breakthrough;" and Zerah, meaning "scarlet." Tamar and her sons became a blessed family and are forever remembered in the Scriptures as a blessing to Israel.

Tamar and both her sons Perez and Zerah are mentioned in the genealogy list of the Messiah Yeshua.

> Matthew 1:1–3 (emphasis added): *This is the genealogy of Yeshua the Messiah the son of David, the son of Abraham: Abraham was the father of Isaac, Isaac the father of Jacob, Jacob the father of Judah and his brothers,* ***Judah the father of Perez and Zerah, whose mother was Tamar*** (NIV).

In Ruth chapter four, the elders and all those gathered at the gate of Bethlehem were witnesses for the wedding of Boaz and Ruth. As the elders blessed them, they prayed that Ruth would be like Rachel and Leah who built up the family of Israel. Then they prayed that their baby would be like the family of Perez, whom Tamar bore to Judah.

> Ruth 4:11–12 (NIV, emphasis added): *Then the elders and all the people at the gate said, "We are witnesses. May the LORD make the woman who is coming into your home like Rachel and Leah, who together built up the family of Israel. May you have standing in Ephrathah and be famous in Bethlehem.* **Through the offspring the LORD gives you by this young woman, may your family be like that of Perez, whom Tamar bore to Judah."**

How amazing is this to read? In God's providence, He is causing "*all things to work together for good to those who love [Him, and] ... are called according to His purpose*" (Romans 8:28).

What encouragement can you find from the life of Tamar? Think of how her life was redeemed through God's gracious love and forgiveness. Tamar was a Canaanite woman who was completely accepted in the family of Israel. This was truly miraculous, as the Canaanites, because of their debased and wicked society, were to be utterly destroyed by the Israelites according to Deuteronomy 20:17–18.

If I were to elaborate on the evil of the Canaanites, I would need to put a warning label on this book, but suffice to say that God knew they needed to be wiped out because of their perversions and debauchery.

That said, God's heart and love for the world and more specifically, each individual, is pictured in the life of Tamar who went from darkness to light, from death to life, and from mourning to dancing. If you have accepted Messiah Yeshua—

who is the Lord of the breakthrough—as your Savior, He will turn your life around, as He did for Tamar.

Restoration for Judah

We have discussed a brief overview of the life of Joseph and how God orchestrated events to bring the family of Jacob to Egypt where they developed as a nation over the next four hundred years. It's always encouraging to note God's providential hand moving His people for His redemptive purposes. In Genesis 50, Joseph reiterated promises and assurances to his brothers. He let them know that he held no animosity or unforgiveness toward them. After the death of their father Jacob, they were uncertain about Joseph's motives and intentions toward them. I briefly discussed this passage earlier in this chapter. That said, these truths need to be remembered and emblazoned on our hearts and minds.

> Genesis 50:18–22: *Then his brothers also came and fell down before him and said, "Behold, we are your servants." But Joseph said to them, "Do not be afraid, for am I in God's place? As for you, you meant evil against me, but God meant it for good in order to bring about this present result, to preserve many people alive. So therefore, do not be afraid; I will provide for you and your little ones." So he comforted them and spoke kindly to them. Now Joseph stayed in Egypt, he and his father's household, and Joseph lived one hundred and ten years.*

A Brief Review

When we state that God is sovereign, it means that He is in charge because He is King over all. His providential care is sometimes characterized as "God's Hand in the Glove of History." Another definition from *Baker's Evangelical Dictionary of Biblical Theology* states:

Providence is the sovereign superintendence of all things, guiding them toward their divinely predetermined end in a way that is consistent with their created nature. This divine, sovereign, and benevolent control of all things by God is the underlying premise of everything that is taught in the Scriptures.

God is our sovereign King, and He oversees all, *working all things together for good to those who love God and are called according to His purposes* (Romans 8:28). This truth is echoed throughout Scripture and, in retrospect, we can see this promise working in the lives of individuals like Tamar and Joseph, as well as the nation of Israel. He is in charge of history which is HIS STORY for the nation of Israel and for each of us.

APPLICATION: MESSIAH YESHUA IS THE LORD OF THE BREAKTHROUGH

In the fullness of time, the LORD of the breakthrough broke into our world and opened for each of us a new and living way on the basis of His blood atonement and full pardon. Now each of us can walk boldly into God's presence because of the Breaker's finished work. Is there anything in your life that is too difficult for Yeshua the Breaker to break through and give you His healing, comfort, and victory?

1. Yeshua broke the power of sin to set us free from the prison of bondage to sin—and He continues to break the power of sin as we trust in Him each day.

   Galatians 5:1 (CJB): *What the Messiah has freed us for is freedom! Therefore, stand firm, and don't let yourselves be tied up again to a yoke of slavery.*

2. Yeshua is the path breaker, leading us into the divine presence of God and, as our King, He continues to lead us each step of the way.

   John 14:6 (CJB): *Yeshua said, "I AM the Way—and the Truth and the Life; no one comes to the Father except through me"* (see also Hebrews 4:14–16; 6:20; 10:19–25).

3. Yeshua can break open our stony hearts and give us a heart to love Him.

   Ezekiel 11:19–20: *And I will give them one heart, and put a new spirit within them. And I will take the heart of stone out of their flesh and give them a heart of flesh, that they may walk in My statutes and keep My ordinances and do them. Then they will be My people, and I shall be their God.*

4. Yeshua breaks down the walls between all people. Yeshua broke down the barrier separating us from God and from one another.

Ephesians 2:13–14 (CJB): *But now, you who were once far off have been brought near through the shedding of the Messiah's blood. For he himself is our shalom—he has made us both one and has broken down the barrier which divided us.*

5. We remember Yeshua, our Breaker, each time we take *Zikkaron* (Communion).

   1 Corinthians 11:23–24 (CJB): *For what I received from the Lord is just what I passed on to you—that the Lord Yeshua, on the night he was betrayed, took bread; and after he had made the* b'rakhah *he broke it and said, "This is my body, which is for you. Do this as a memorial to me."*

6. Yeshua, the Lion that is from the tribe of Judah, the Root of David, has overcome and He alone is worthy to break the seals of judgment.

   Revelation 5:1–5 (CJB): *Next I saw in the right hand of the One sitting on the throne a scroll with writing on both sides and sealed with seven seals; and I saw a mighty angel proclaiming in a loud voice, "Who is worthy to open the scroll and break its seals?" But no one in heaven, on earth or under the earth was able to open the scroll or look inside it. I cried and cried, because no one was found worthy to open the scroll or look inside it. One of the elders said to me, "Don't cry. Look, the Lion of the tribe of Y'hudah, the Root of David, has won the right to open the scroll and its seven seals."*

All of these promises are available to us by God's grace as we place our faith in Yeshua as our Messiah and the Lord of our breakthrough. But first, we must be broken before Him—for only when we are broken and yielded to Yeshua our King, will He heal our brokenness and restore us. The prophet Isaiah gives us insight into what happens after we are broken before God.

Isaiah 58:8-9: *Then your light will break out like the dawn, and your recovery will speedily spring forth; and your righteousness will go before you; the glory of the LORD will be your rear guard. Then you will call, and the LORD will answer; you will cry, and He will say, "Here I am."*

Let's remind each other that God is providentially in charge of our lives. The Holy Spirit is interceding for you, God is working all things together for good for those of us who love Him and are called for His purposes. He foreknew you, predestined you to be conformed to the image of Yeshua. He called you, justified you, and glorifies you. God is your defender and your strength. He gives you your value and your purpose to serve Him.

A Life-Changing Passage to Memorize

Romans 8:26-31: *In the same way the Spirit also helps our weakness; for we do not know how to pray as we should, but the Spirit Himself intercedes for us with groanings too deep for words; and He who searches the hearts knows what the mind of the Spirit is, because He intercedes for the saints according to the will of God. And we know that God causes all things to work together for good to those who love God, to those who are called according to His purpose. For whom He foreknew, He also predestined to become conformed to the image of His Son, so that He would be the firstborn among many brethren; and these whom He predestined, He also called; and these whom He called, He also justified; and these whom He justified, He also glorified. What then shall we say to these things? If God is for us, who is against us?*

Indeed, I brought you
up from the land
of Egypt And
ransomed you from the
house of slavery. And
I sent before you
Moses, Aaron, and
Miriam.

Micah 6:4

Six

The Sister Prophetess: Miriam

The redemptive plan of God required a nation of people. The children of Israel had been living in Egypt for about three hundred years. They had been exceedingly fruitful and had become mighty.

> Exodus 1:7: *But the sons of Israel were fruitful and increased greatly, and multiplied, and became exceedingly mighty, so that the land was filled with them.*

THE PROMISE

Remember, they were in Egypt and they were slaves according to the will of God. Their sojourn in Egypt was part of the promise God gave to Abraham in Genesis 15:13-14:

> *God said to Abram, "Know for certain that your descendants will be strangers in a land that is not theirs, where they will be enslaved and oppressed four hundred years. But I will also judge the nation whom they will*

serve, and afterward they will come out with many possessions."

God reiterated this promise to Jacob after the reunion with Joseph:

> Genesis 46:2–5: *God spoke to Israel in visions of the night and said, "Jacob, Jacob." And he said, "Here I am." He said, "I am God, the God of your father;* **do not be afraid to go down to Egypt, for I will make you a great nation there. I will go down with you to Egypt, and I will also surely bring you up again; and Joseph will close your eyes."**

Do you think the children of Israel had spent the intervening years reminding each other of the promises of God to *"bring [them] up again"* with *"many possessions?"* Do you think they had kept track of the years and knew the time was getting close?

One Courageous Girl

The exodus story is familiar to many of us because every year we celebrate Passover to remember our redemption by God through the blood of the Passover Lamb. In this chapter, we will take a closer look at the life of Miriam, the sister of Moses. Miriam was greatly used by God as she was honored as a prophetess and a worship leader. Her courageous and inspiring leadership of the tens of thousands of women in praise as they came through the Red Sea is an example to women of all ages.

That said, I wonder if I was a slave in Egypt and each day brought another horrible edict from an evil monarch, if I would even think about being courageous. When we are first introduced to Miriam in the book of exodus, she was a young girl of eight or ten years of age. As I thought about her, I wondered if her thinking could have gone something like this:

"Here I am, a young girl, living as a slave. Until a few years ago we were prosperous and favored in this foreign land, but now this new Pharaoh has taken over and he is so mean and cruel. Even though we live in Goshen away from the palace, how can we survive in the most powerful nation in the world, with an unstoppable army? With a religion of so many gods I lost count? And these Egyptians are not only physically beautiful, but they seem to be really smart with so much education. I guess if you're born an Egyptian you automatically have everything you could desire: wealth, power, education, religion, beauty, and pleasure. By contrast I am Hebrew slave, the daughter of Amram and Jochebed, who are both from the house of Levi. And I'm taking care of my three-year-old brother Aaron (Exodus 7:7), who is quite a handful. And now my mother is pregnant and about to give birth. I can't understand it. The new edict demands all Hebrew baby boys be thrown immediately at birth into the Nile River, but she and dad somehow believe that our God, the God of Israel, is blessing our family by giving us another child. I wonder if this new baby will be a sister or another brother. I hope it's a girl so she can live, but even so, we will still be slaves, still exiled from our own country under what seems to be crueler bondage day by day. I know my parents believe in the One true God of Israel. They have told me about my ancestors and the promises God made to them. They say He will deliver us. It's hard to have faith in a God when I can't see Him working."

Could Miriam Have Prayed this Kind of Prayer?

"Lord, help me to believe and see Your deliverance in my lifetime. If You can use me Lord, I want to make a difference in this world. Please give me courage to face each day."

If we look at Miriam's point of view, there is a very slim chance that she thought that her young life would make a difference. How could she possibly live victoriously and become a woman of destiny? Her life can encourage each of us as we affirm that with God all things are possible. Miriam was about to find out that God measures our lives differently. We can learn from her that as we entrust our lives into His hands, the Lord gives us what we need to have His strength and courage each day.

THE PROBLEM

An Overview: Where Are the Children of Israel?

The children of Israel had moved to Egypt while Joseph was second in command there. But years had passed. Egypt had a new ruler. The new pharaoh did not remember the blessings that Joseph brought nor recognize how Joseph had saved them in the time of famine. Instead, the new pharaoh only saw the vast numbers of God's *great nation.*

> Exodus 1:8–10: *Now a new king arose over Egypt, who did not know Joseph. He said to his people, "Behold, the people of the sons of Israel are more and mightier than we. Come, let us deal wisely with them, or else they will multiply and in the event of war, they will also join themselves to those who hate us, and fight against us and depart from the land."*

This paranoid Pharaoh had a plan to destroy the Israelites. He appointed taskmasters over them to make their labor more difficult and bitter as they built His storage cities. Yet it seemed the more Pharaoh tried to afflict them, the more the children of Israel multiplied. Exodus 1:12 puts it this way:

> *But the more they afflicted them, the more they multiplied and the more they spread out, so that they [the Egyptians] were in dread of the sons of Israel.*

This Hebrew word for "dread" means "to feel a loathing, abhorrence, or sickening terror."

First, the Tale of Two Righteous Women

Not only did the new Pharaoh make the lives of the Israelites bitter with hard labor, but then he spoke to the Hebrew midwives with a horrific, murderous request:

> Exodus 1:15–16: *Then the king of Egypt spoke to the Hebrew midwives, one of whom was named Shiphrah and the other was named Puah; and he said, "When you are helping the Hebrew women to give birth and see them upon the birthstool, if it is a son, then you shall put him to death; but if it is a daughter, then she shall live."*

Because these courageous midwives were in reverential awe of the God of Israel, they did not follow Pharaoh's plan to murder the infants:

> *But the midwives feared God, and did not do as the king of Egypt had commanded them, but let the boys live* (Exod 1: 17).

The King Questioned These Midwives

> *So the king of Egypt called for the midwives and said to them, "Why have you done this thing, and let the boys live"* (Exod 1:18)?

The Midwives Answer

> *The midwives said to Pharaoh, "Because the Hebrew women are not as the Egyptian women; for they are vigorous and give birth before the midwife can get to them"* (Exod 1:19).

God's Blessings on These Courageous Women

> *So God was good to the midwives, and the people multiplied, and became very mighty. Because the midwives feared God, He established households for them* (Exod 1:20–21).

APPLICATION: WHAT LESSONS CAN WE LEARN FROM THE LIVES OF SHIPHRAH AND PUAH?

1. When Peter and the apostles were questioned about why they didn't obey the order to not preach the Gospel they replied, *"We must obey God rather than men"* (Acts 5:29). We always have a choice to disobey and not comply when the authorities order us to do something against God and His Word. Pharaoh was an evil and powerful man, yet Shiphrah and Puah risked their lives to do the right thing. The courageous actions of these two obscure women, who put their lives on the line to *"obey God rather than men,"* teach us that a single act of faith and obedience can change the lives of countless others for generations to come.

2. Godly women will always choose to protect life. These women were not protecting their own children, yet they realized the importance and value of all life. Whether it is abortion, infanticide, child abuse, or the way we treat the disabled or the elderly, we need to stand up and protect those who cannot defend themselves.

   > Proverbs 31:8–9 (NIV): *Speak up for those who cannot speak for themselves, for the rights of all who are destitute. Speak up and judge fairly; defend the rights of the poor and needy.*

3. When we place God and His righteousness first, He will bless us. Some scholars say that midwives in Israel were sometimes barren themselves. If that's the case, it makes Shiphrah and Puah especially blessed by God for their actions because He gave them families, as it states in Exodus 1:20–21: *So God was good to the midwives, and the people multiplied, and became very mighty. Because the midwives feared God, He established households for them.* When we seek to honor God and build up His kingdom, God will take care of us and we lack nothing. He promises us in

Matthew 6:33: *"But seek first His kingdom and His righteousness, and all these things will be added to you."*

4. The influence of a righteous person can impact generations. We know Moses as the great 'deliverer' of God's people, but Shiphrah and Puah may have been the ones who 'delivered the deliverer!' With Moses' life spared, how many other lives were saved from Egyptian bondage? Our obedience to God can change the lives of those around us for years to come.

> Romans 14:7–8 (NIV): *For none of us lives for ourselves alone, and none of us dies for ourselves alone. If we live, we live for the Lord; and if we die, we die for the Lord. So, whether we live or die, we belong to the Lord.*

THE RESTORATION

There Is Something About this Baby!

In Exodus 2:2, we read that Miriam's mother did have a son: *The woman* (Jochebed) *conceived and bore a son; and when she saw that he was beautiful* (tov), *she hid him for three months* (definitions added).

In the New Covenant, we gain further insight into who Moses was at birth. The Greek phrase *asterios* to *theo* is parallel for "good/beautiful" or tov. In Steven's defense of his faith in Yeshua before the Jewish Council, he recited the history of Israel beginning with the call of Abraham. When he got to the part of the history about Moses, Steven described:

> Acts 7:20 (definition added): *It was at this time that Moses was born; and he was lovely in the sight of God* (asterios *to* theo), *and he was nurtured three months in his father's home.*

Righteous People Making Arks

His parents saw something extraordinary about baby Moses, and God gave them His wisdom to deal with this situation. No doubt they would have been familiar with the story of Noah and how God had told Noah to prepare an ark *(tavah)* of safety and refuge.

> Genesis 6:14 (definition added): *Make for yourself an ark* (tavah) *of gopher wood; you shall make the ark with rooms, and shall cover it inside and out with pitch.*

The exact same Hebrew word used for Noah's ark is also used to describe the basket for baby Moses in Exodus 2:3:

> But when she could no longer hide him, she took an ark (tavah) *of bulrushes for him, daubed it with asphalt and pitch, put the child in it, and laid it in the reeds by the river's bank* (NKJV).

As her mother prepared the ark of safety, Miriam probably helped with the preparations. Perhaps she gathered materials for the ark, watched her toddler brother Aaron, and even cared for three-month-old baby Moses to give her mother a much-needed break. And as the basket was being built with confidence and faith in the God of Israel, Amram and Jochebed would have retold the story of Noah and God saving his family through his faith in the one true God.

> Hebrews 11:7: *By faith Noah, being warned by God about things not yet seen, in reverence prepared an ark for the salvation of his household.*

God Keeps His Promises Using Unlikely Vessels

Noah lived by faith. Likewise, Moses's parents, by faith, would have reiterated the account of Abraham to their children. Miriam and Aaron would have been told of God's promise that Israel would be redeemed from their enslavement after four hundred years.

> Genesis 15:13 (definition added): God *said to Abram, "Know for certain* (yadah) *that your descendants will be strangers in a land that is not theirs, where they will be enslaved and oppressed four hundred years.*

Perhaps Miriam's parents were doing the math and God gave them the faith of their forefather Abraham to know *(yadah)* that their redemption was drawing near. In Exodus 2:4, Miriam was drawn directly into the life-and-death drama of her baby brother. She was wonderfully used by God to make an eternal difference. Moses was placed in the Nile River in his ark and Miriam waited.

> Exodus 2:4 (definition added): *His sister stood at a distance to find out* (yadah) *what would happen to him.*

Miriam positioned herself to see and understand what was happening. The phrase "to find out" is the Hebrew word *yadah,* which carries the meaning of not only knowing but

189

perceiving and discerning how to respond in the immediate circumstances. This "knowing" was from God as His Spirit moved in her heart and life. Do you believe the Lord will give you this same ability "to know" as you face difficult situations? God's wisdom will give you what you need to perceive and discern as you yield yourself to the power of the Holy Spirit who dwells in you (Romans 8:26–28).

Baby's Tears and a Young Girl's Suggestion!

The Egyptian princess who came to bathe in the Nile saw the ark. Out of curiosity she told one of her maids to get the basket. When the ark was opened, she saw Moses crying and at that very moment she was approached by Miriam. God moved the heart of this influential princess to not only be compassionate toward Moses, but to also listen to this young girl as she suggested that she could find a Hebrew woman to nurse the infant. We see Miriam's bravery and daring in the face of an unknown situation. God used the tears of baby Moses and the winsome words of Miriam to connect with this powerful Egyptian princess. As a result, Moses's life was saved. He was nursed by his own mother and raised in his own home for the first five or six years of his young life. Don't ever discount what God can use. He uses the foolish things of this world to confound the mighty. In this case, God used a baby's tears and a young girl's suggestion to lead this powerful princess to shelter Moses, so he could be cared for by his own family, and then raised in the palace for forty years.

> 1 Corinthians 1:26–3: *For consider your calling, brethren, that there were not many wise according to the flesh, not many mighty, not many noble; but God has chosen the foolish things of the world to shame the wise, and God has chosen the weak things of the world to shame the things which are strong, and the base things of the world and the despised God has chosen, the things that are not, so that He may nullify the things that are, so that no man may*

boast before God. But by His doing you are in Messiah Yeshua, who became to us wisdom from God, and righteousness and sanctification, and redemption, so that, just as it is written, "Let him who boasts, boast in the Lord."

Let him who boasts, boast in the Lord is a quote from Jeremiah 9:23. The word *boast* in Hebrew is *hallel* which means "praise." In other words, let him who gives praise, praise the Lord.

A Promise for Moses

God's love is revealed to Moses when He called him from the burning bush. The call of Moses to be the deliverer of the nation of Israel is found in the third and fourth chapters of Exodus. The Angel of the Lord, who is Yeshua, appeared to him in a burning bush that was not consumed. Moses understood that this was a great miraculous sight and he had to stop to see. "Marvelous sight" is *gadol* or "great;" *mareh*— vision, from the root word *roeh*—to see.

> Exodus 3:2–3 (definition added): *The angel of the LORD appeared to him in a blazing fire from the midst of a bush; and he looked, and behold, the bush was burning with fire, yet the bush was not consumed. So Moses said, "I must turn aside now and see this marvelous sight* (gadol mareh—big vision), *why the bush is not burned up."*

God described Himself to Moses as the God of his ancestors Abraham, Isaac, and Jacob. Considering the purpose of this book, I want to remind us of how important the matriarchs were in God's purpose of redemption. Without Sarah there would have been no Isaac, without Rebekah there would have been no Jacob, and without Jacob there would have been no Joseph from Rachel, and no Judah from Leah.

> Exodus 3:6–12 (emphasis added): *He said also, "I am the God of your father, the God of Abraham, the God of Isaac,*

*and the God of Jacob." Then Moses hid his face, for he was afraid to look at God. The LORD said, "I have surely seen the affliction of My people who are in Egypt, and have given heed to their cry because of their taskmasters, for I am aware of their sufferings. **So I have come down to deliver** them from the power of the Egyptians, and to bring them up from that land to a good and spacious land, to a land flowing with milk and honey, to the place of the Canaanite and the Hittite and the Amorite and the Perizzite and the Hivite and the Jebusite. Now, behold, the cry of the sons of Israel has come to Me; furthermore, I have seen the oppression with which the Egyptians are oppressing them. Therefore, come now, and I will send you to Pharaoh, so that you may bring My people, the sons of Israel, out of Egypt." But Moses said to God, "Who am I, that I should go to Pharaoh, and that I should bring the sons of Israel out of Egypt?" And He said, **"Certainly I will be with you, and this shall be the sign to you that it is I who have sent you: when you have brought the people out of Egypt, you shall worship God at this mountain."***

God assured Moses that He Himself had come down to deliver them and He would be with him. When the Lord called Moses to deliver Israel, He not only assured Moses of His presence and but also told him what the miracle sign would be. This sign *(ot)* would be that His people would worship the one true God at Mount Sinai.

Redeemed People Worship

Read this verse again and consider your own walk with God and the purpose of your redemption:

Exodus 3:12 (definition added): *And He said, "Certainly I will be with you, and this shall be the sign* (ot) *to you that it is I who have sent you: when you have brought the people out of Egypt, you shall worship God at this mountain."*

Worship is from the verb *avad* and the noun *avodah*, which means worship, work, and service.

In other words, we need to remember that God's presence was with Moses and God's presence is with us as well. Why does He desire for us to come into His presence? He desires our fellowship as we worship Him in spirit and truth.

And this is truly a miraculous event that we have become His children of love and light. The Hebrew word for sign is *ot* and it is used to describe a miracle sign just as the blood on the door was a miracle sign in Exodus 12:13 (definition added):

> *The blood shall be a sign* (ot) *for you on the houses where you live; and when I see the blood I will pass over you, and no plague will befall you to destroy you when I strike the land of Egypt.*

Back to Miriam

We could wonder and speculate about what Miriam was doing during the forty years Moses was growing up in the palace and then the subsequent forty years when Moses was living in the desert. Since the Scriptures make no mention of Miriam being married or having children, we can suppose that she remained single and committed to God. When we read of Miriam again in Exodus 15:20–21, she was leading all the women of Israel in praise and dance. She was called a prophetess and was also named along with Moses and Aaron as having been sent *(shalach)* by God to lead the Israelites out of bondage. This is a high honor, to be called a *sent one* like Moses and Aaron (Micah 6:4):

> Micah 6:4 (definition added): *Indeed, I brought you up from the land of Egypt and ransomed you from the house*

of slavery, and I sent (shalach) *before you Moses, Aaron and Miriam."*

The apostles in the first century were called the *shalachim* or "sent ones" as they were messengers of the Good News of Messiah. Because Miriam was called the same by the prophet Micah, we see that she was held in high esteem and was regarded as a leader among her people. Over those eighty years, through the death of her parents, while Aaron married and had sons, it seems that Miriam remained faithful to the one true God of Israel. Eighty years is a long time; nevertheless she was recognized as a both a worship leader and a prophetess, which means she spoke forth the Word of God. The Lord had a destiny for Miriam, beginning in her very young years, and continuing as she grew in maturity.

For each of us as well, God has a purpose and destiny for our lives. Whatever season of life we are in, the Lord wants you to live for Him. He desires that in your abundant life you use every day to bring Him glory. Miriam's faithfulness to the God of Israel and her people is recorded for our example. Isn't it encouraging to consider that God used her as a young girl as well as a mature woman of eighty-plus years? As a young slave girl and then growing up as a single woman—still enslaved—she would have had to keep her focus on God and His faithfulness. If she had *not* kept her focus and faith upon the God of Israel and His promises, she would not have been recognized by all of Israel nor ready to lead in songs and dances of victory.

But Miriam did live for the Lord and led hundreds of thousands of women in praise to God for what He alone could do.

Exodus 15:20–21: *Miriam the prophetess, Aaron's sister, took the timbrel in her hand, and all the women went out after her with timbrels and with dancing. Miriam*

answered them, "Sing to the LORD, for He is highly exalted;
the horse and his rider He has hurled into the sea."

As you read that description of the song that Miriam led the women in singing, you see that verse twenty-one begins, *"Miriam answered them."* This song was in answer to the song Moses and the men were singing that began in verse one of that chapter.

The Hebrew word for "answer," *anah*, means "respond, testify, to respond as a witness." Not only the men but the women—and I suspect the children—were engaged in this glorious time of worshipping the LORD and praising Him for His redeeming power. It was an atmosphere of praise and jubilation as the women danced and echoed the song to testify of God's amazing deliverance. Let's take a closer look at the Song of Moses and understand for our own lives what Miriam and the other women were responding to and testifying of. We find in the Song of Moses and in Miriam's refrain hope and purpose for our lives—to understand the path of victory.

Consider with me what this scene would have looked like. There were between two and three million Israelites that had been delivered out of Egypt that day that were at the Red Sea with Pharaoh. His mighty chariots were in hot pursuit of the freed slaves. Where do you think Miriam was positioned in this multitude? It makes sense that she would have been close to the front—near to her brothers, Moses and Aaron. She would have clearly heard the words that God spoke to Moses, and heard Moses as he proclaimed to all of Israel,

> *"Do not fear! Stand by and see the salvation of the LORD*
> *which He will accomplish for you today; for the Egyptians*
> *whom you have seen today, you will never see them again*
> *forever"* (Exodus 14:13).

Two to three million people marched through the sea on completely dry land while the sea waters piled up like walls to their right and to their left (Exodus 14:22). During their journey of victory, Pharaoh's army closed in with the sole purpose of destroying them. God first put the soldiers into confusion and their chariots began to swerve and got stuck in the sand. Then God told Moses to stretch out his staff so that the waters returned to their normal state. We read in Exodus 14 the summary of what happened that night.

> Exodus 14:28–31: *The waters returned, and covered the chariots, and the horsemen, and all the host of Pharaoh that came into the sea after them; there remained not so much as one of them. But the children of Israel walked upon dry land in the midst of the sea; and the waters were a wall unto them on their right hand, and on their left. Thus the LORD saved Israel that day out of the hand of the Egyptians; and Israel saw the Egyptians dead upon the seashore. And Israel saw that great work which the LORD did upon the Egyptians: and the people feared the LORD, and believed the LORD, and his servant Moses.*

The Song of Moses: The First Song in Scripture

> Exodus 15:1: *Then Moses and the sons of Israel sang this song to the LORD, and said, "I will sing to the LORD, for He is highly exalted; The horse and its rider He has hurled into the sea."*

First of all, they proclaimed that the Lord is highly exalted—He alone is worthy of all honor and praise. The strength to fight their battles came from Him. And only in His strength can we have His song of victory to sing.

> Exodus 15:2: *"The LORD is my strength and song, And He has become my salvation; This is my God, and I will praise Him; My father's God, and I will extol Him."*

The children of Israel declared that He is *Elohim*, the Creator God, and worthy of praise. He was the God of their fathers, Abraham, Isaac, and Jacob, and highly exalted.

Exodus 15:3: *"The LORD is a warrior; The LORD is His name."*

The covenant name of God is used in verse three, when the LORD is described as a warrior—a man of war—and His covenant name is reiterated. In our battles, we must acknowledge the one true God who has accomplished our redemption and equips us to walk through this life in victory.

Exodus 15: 4–8: *"Pharaoh's chariots and his army He has cast into the sea; And the choicest of his officers are drowned in the Red Sea. ⁵ "The deeps cover them; They went down into the depths like a stone. ⁶ "Your right hand, O LORD, is majestic in power, Your right hand, O LORD, shatters the enemy. ⁷ "And in the greatness of Your excellence You overthrow those who rise up against You; You send forth Your burning anger, it consumes them as chaff. ⁸ "At the blast of Your nostrils the waters were piled up, The flowing waters stood up like a heap; The deeps were congealed in the heart of the sea."*

Next, the song focuses on what God did to destroy their enemy enslavers who only sought to destroy the Israelites and defame the name of the God of Israel.

Exodus 15: 9–10 (NIV, definition added): *"The enemy boasted, 'I will pursue, I will overtake them. I will divide the spoils; I will gorge myself on them. I will draw my sword and my hand will destroy them.' ¹⁰ But you blew with your breath (ruach), and the sea covered them. They sank like lead in the mighty waters."*

The imagery of God's *ruach*, spirit, or breath, is a powerful picture for when the Spirit of God blew the flowing waters upright to stand on either side of the people. Those walls of water became as walls of protection until the mixed multitude (see Exodus 12:38) made up of the Israelites and those neighbors who sought refuge behind the blood-stained

Passover doors were led safely through the sea. Then in verse ten, we see God's judgment come upon those who tried to destroy His people and defame His holy name. God's holy breath caused the sea to cover the Egyptians and they drowned, sinking like heavy stones into the sea.

Isn't this what God promises each of us? If we trust in the Lord with all our heart and do not lean on our own understanding, God will make our paths straight and we can walk through this life with His protection and direction (see Proverbs 3:5–6). This is the path of victory to walk where He is leading us even if it is through the seas of life with troubles on every side. Yeshua told us that "in the world you will have tribulations but take courage for I have overcome the world" (see John 16:33).

> Exodus 15:11: *Who is like You among the gods, O LORD? Who is like You, majestic in holiness, awesome in praises, working wonders?*
>
> *Mi kamocha ba'elim Adonai? Mi Kamocha ne'dar baKodesh, Nora tehillot, oseh pheleh?*

The next verse is a mighty chorus of praise which includes two rhetorical questions about God: This verse is often included in our Hebrew liturgical prayers of praise to the Lord The first question asks if there is anyone equal to the Lord God of Israel. The Israelites were acknowledging the Lord their God to be the supreme God. Egyptians worshipped hundreds of gods but none of their false deities could compare to God Almighty. The next question has us consider the unique character of the God of Israel. He is holy. His magnificence is revealed in His holiness. He is astounding. God alone is worthy of our praise and adoration. And He performs wonders. In the life of Sarah we studied this word *pheleh* or *palay* (see p. 60). The Lord Himself spoke and asked,

Is anything too difficult for the LORD? At the appointed time I will return to you, at this time next year, and Sarah will have a son (Genesis 18:14).

Remember, the word "difficult" can also be translated: surpassingly, extraordinarily wonderful. The same Hebrew word *palay* is found in Exodus 15:11, and referred to miracles that only God can perform—working wonders; *oseh*—He does; and *palay*—amazing miracles for His people.

The first song in Scripture was sung by newly redeemed slaves. The Israelites, under the influence of the Holy Spirit, were in midst of a miracle so wondrous, so amazing, so remarkable, that they could only ask, "Who could possibly be like You, Lord?"

I invite us today to ponder these rhetorical questions for ourselves.

Then at the end of this glorious song of the redeemed, hundreds of thousands of women, led by Miriam, echoed these truths in joyful refrains. With their tambourines and dances of praise, these ladies affirmed that there is no one like our God. Their echoes throughout the song reverberated the magnificent truths about God and further strengthened the community of Israel as they joined their voices together. Adding the dance and instruments heighted the thanksgiving and praise in celebration to the Lord.

Before We Leave the Song, One More Thing to Note

The first song in Scripture exalted the Triune God.

In the first six verses, "the LORD," the covenant name of God, is used. In verse two, the name *Elohim*, Creator God, is extolled. The reference to *Your right hand* in verse six is prophetically speaking of Yeshua the Messiah and His power, which is declared throughout this song (see also Exodus 15:12; 16–17; Psalm 118:113–16, 22; and Isaiah 53:1). In verses eight and ten, they praise the power of God's Spirit. The Hebrew word for "spirit" is *ruach*. This word *ruach* is used to describe the breath from God's nostrils. It is used again for the wind that moved the waters, first moving them into a pile to make a sure path to freedom and then moving them to cover and destroy the pursuing enemies.

Victorious Ones Sing the Song of Moses

Consider for your own life how this Song of Moses can give you courage to live each day in victory. As His redeemed people, we are called to be both diligent and courageous, but only as we "abide in Yeshua." Don't think of this abiding as a 'let's hang out together sometime' idea. Rather, *abiding* means a sustained, conscious communion with the Lord, whereby we are in fellowship with Him. It refers to looking to Him for all our resources, acknowledging total dependence on Him—not as an automatic process, but a deliberate choice that we followers make daily.

Yeshua instructs us,

> John 15:4–5: *Abide in Me, and I in you. As the branch cannot bear fruit of itself unless it abides in the vine, so neither can you unless you abide in Me. I am the vine, you are the branches; he who abides in Me and I in him, he bears much fruit, for apart from Me you can do nothing.*

Redemption Requires God's Healing Power

The Lord God of Israel brought His people through the Red Sea in complete victory. As newly freed slaves, they experienced a powerful time of praise and worship as they reached the other side of the Red Sea and all of Israel rejoiced together singing God's praises. We noted that there were hundreds of thousands of women who were an integral part of this time of rejoicing, and it was Miriam who led them in echoing the praises with dancing and song.

There on the shores of the Red Sea, with the enemy army of Egypt destroyed, the children of Israel naturally desired to keep the celebration going with more praising and dancing and joy. However, God had a different plan. As their Redeemer and source of their freedom, He knew what was needed for His children to be truly liberated in spirit, soul, and body.

Instead of directing Moses to lead them to the Springs of Elim where they would find plenty of fresh water, God had a different travel route that included the wilderness. Miriam and Aaron were there with Moses, who led the people out. In the wilderness, they began to learn that God had a purpose for their journey there, which He designed for them in love.

What Did the Newly Redeemed Need to Learn About Their Redeemer?

> Exodus 15:22: *Then Moses led Israel from the Red Sea, and they went out into the wilderness of Shur; and they went three days in the wilderness and found no water.*

The verb "led" is *nasa* in Hebrew and carries the meaning of a forceful pulling up camp and setting out on a journey. The same verb is used in Psalm 78:52 where it states that God led them:

> *"But He led* (nasa) *forth His own people like sheep and guided them in the wilderness like a flock"* (definition added).

The Israelites were freed from slavery, they needed to learn to worship God. The Lord knew exactly what they needed to learn about Him in order to truly worship and have an intimate relationship with Him. They had been slaves for hundreds of years and their labor was bitter. This bitterness caused anger, resentment, hatred, cynicism, and distrust to consume their hearts and minds. They needed to be healed. This healing was not just about physical restoration; no, there was a more profound lesson they needed to learn. They needed to be healed from the inside out.

What happened after their victorious deliverance through the Red Sea gives us the key as to why God revealed Himself in these desperate circumstances as their Healer.

Moses led them out from the Red Sea. That's a picture of strong and purposeful leadership. There on the shores of the Red Sea, it might have been tempting to remain in that place of victory, maybe even plunder the Egyptian valuables that washed ashore. However, God knew exactly what they needed. He knew it was necessary for them to face the wilderness in order to learn to trust Him. The Israelites had been freed from physical slavery, but now they needed to be restored from the bitterness of heart and soul.

What Shall We Drink?

As their wilderness walk progressed, they went for three days without finding water. How long have you gone without water? Most health experts tell us to drink lots of it. A single day in the wilderness without water might have been bearable, two days would have been challenging, but three days would have been impossible, especially for the small children and animals. With their water supply nearly exhausted on the third day, they finally found water. They had heightened thirst and fatigue, so they were utterly disillusioned to find the water undrinkable.

> Exodus 15:23: *When they came to Marah, they could not drink the waters of Marah, for they were bitter; therefore it was named Marah.*

It is understandable by human standards that their response would be one of utter disappointment followed by complaints, accusations, and criticism. Why would God lead them into a waterless wilderness situation? Why does God allow us to encounter wilderness experiences in our own lives? Remember they were slaves for four hundred years under the Egyptians and in Exodus 1:14, it states that *"the [Egyptians] made their lives bitter with hard labor."* Think about your life before you accepted Yeshua's redemption. Like a slave in Egypt, you were a slave to sin and under the sentence of daily condemnation and eternal judgment.

Those newly freed slaves had much to learn about their awesome God who had just delivered them with signs and wonders. The place where they found the bitter water was called *Marah*, which is based on the Hebrew root *mar*, which means bitter. The word "rebellious" *(mamriim)* is based on this same root and is found in a number of Scriptures, including an exhortation to the Israelites as they were about to cross the Jordan River and enter the Promised Land:

> Deuteronomy 9:7 (definition added): *Remember, do not forget how you provoked the* LORD *your God to wrath in the wilderness; from the day that you left the land of Egypt until you arrived at this place, you have been rebellious* (mamriim) *against the* LORD.

From the very beginning of their wilderness journey to their entrance into the land of promise, it was essential for the children of Israel to understand their own hearts and the need for the Lord to heal them from the bondage of their rebelliousness. The Prophet Jeremiah puts it this way:

> *The heart is more deceitful than all else and is desperately sick; who can understand it? I, the* LORD, *search the heart, I test the mind, even to give to each man according to his ways, according to the results of his deeds* (Jeremiah 17:9–10).

The rebelliousness and bitterness of their hearts was exposed very quickly at this first test from the Lord. Just three days had passed since the nation of Israel had experienced God's miraculous deliverance through the Red Sea. In light of their recent, miraculous liberation, would it not have been appropriate for them to have acknowledged that they had a faithful God, and then to humbly and thankfully have asked Moses to intercede? Instead of an acknowledgement of God's redeeming power, their response revealed why their bitter hearts needed to be healed. They grumbled and murmured to Moses, saying, *"What shall we drink?"* (Exodus 15:24). This might sound like an innocent question, but we know from the context that the attitude behind the grumbling reflected a dissatisfied and complaining spirit which ultimately leads to rebellion.

Here at this bitter place called Marah, God took the opportunity to respond mercifully to Moses' prayer while teaching His children a valuable lesson.

In Exodus 15:25, it states that Moses called out in his distress:

> *Then he cried out to the Lord, and the Lord showed him a tree; and he threw it into the waters, and the waters became sweet. There He made for them a statute and regulation, and there He tested them.*

It seems like an unusual way to make anything sweet. The Hebrew for "showed" is from the root *yarah*, which means to instruct or teach. In fact, the word Torah is based on this root, *yarah*.

The wood from this tree that Moses tossed into the water did not have a magical effect on the water; it was simply a symbolic act of obedience in anticipation of God working a miracle. In fact, some commentators note this tree could have been a bitter tree that grew in this region and, if so, the miracle of the waters becoming sweet is that much more mysterious. At the end of verse twenty-five it states, "*... there He tested them.*"

An Open Book Test

I would venture to say that most of us do not look forward to tests in school, however we understand tests are a necessary way to measure what we have learned.

This was not a test meant to trick them, but rather teach them. The test that God was giving the children of Israel was really an open book test. God was not asking them to guess or be uncertain as to how to pass the test, but rather He gave them clear instructions about how to please Him and be blessed.

We read both the answer and the application for the test written down in His book, the Hebrew Scriptures. This very book is our resource as we face the tests and temptations of life. Let's understand together the application and the lesson He wanted them to learn.

> Exodus 15:26: *And He said, "If you will give earnest heed to the voice of the LORD your God, and do what is right in His sight, and give ear to His commandments, and keep all His statutes, I will put none of the diseases on you which I have put on the Egyptians; for I, the LORD, am your healer."*

If... Then

In this conditional promise, God was teaching them that if they would listen and obey Him, then they would have His blessing and answer to their prayers. Furthermore, if they would only be obedient, then they would not be judged like the Egyptians were with the horrible plagues that came upon them. Finally, God revealed His name to them: *"I, the LORD, am your healer."* God wants each Israelite to understand that He is their personal Healer.

Let's take a closer look at these verses. After they were delivered from bondage, the bitter-water test was their initiation into what it meant to have the Lord as their healer. When God called Himself, *the Lord... your healer*, He was not referring to the healing of a sickness, but to the transforming of the undrinkable, bitter water to sweet life-giving liquid.

When God promised them that He would *put none of the diseases on you which I have put on the Egyptians,* this promise was about the fact that the plagues the Egyptians suffered were judgments against their false gods. God wants His people to worship Him alone. He was teaching them that if they would revere Him and obey His words, they would not come into such a judgment on sin.

According to the historian Herodotus, the Egyptians were the healthiest of the nations of antiquity; nevertheless the Egyptians' defiance of God made their diseases and plagues legendary. The blessings of the Egyptians were turned into plagues by their disobedience. The sweet, life-giving waters of the Nile were turned into blood. This was a judgment against the worship of Hopi, the god of the annual flooding of the Nile in ancient Egyptian religion. The flood deposited rich silt (fertile soil) on the river's banks, allowing the Egyptians to grow crops. The Egyptians worshipped Hopi and this false god was celebrated among the Egyptians.

By contrast, if the children of Israel would trust and worship the one true God and follow His Word, He would transform their bitterness into blessedness. If they put away false worship and followed their Redeemer, then He would be their personal Healer. Their bitterness could be healed. Not a physical restoration; the spiritual inside-out healing would begin.

The Lord Your Healer

In Hebrew, to heal, *rapha,* is to restore something to its original wholeness. *Rapha* is used for far more than just physical, bodily hurts. Psalm 147:3 says the Lord *"heals the brokenhearted and binds up their wounds."*

The verb is often used of the whole relationship with God being restored:

> Jeremiah 33:6-7: *Behold, I will bring to it health and healing, and I will heal them; and I will reveal to them an abundance of peace and truth. I will restore the fortunes*

*of Judah and the fortunes of Israel and will rebuild them
as they were at first.*

In Isaiah 57:18, God specified bringing peace, restoring comfort, and forgiving sin as part of healing: *"I have seen his ways, but I will heal him; I will lead him and restore comfort to him and to his mourners."* God heals their backsliding, according to Hosea 14:4:

I will heal their apostasy, I will love them freely, for My anger has turned away from them.

Psalm 107:20 describes God rescuing Israel from judgment on sin as healing: *He sent His word and healed them, and delivered them from their destructions* (Psalm 107:20).

This is just a partial list for the uses of healing in the Tanakh. In fact, the Lord's entire history of ministering to Israel pictured as a father healing the hurts of his son, especially the son's waywardness.

Hosea 11:1–3: When Israel was a youth I loved him, and out of Egypt I called My son. The more they called them, the more they went from them; they kept sacrificing to the Baals and burning incense to idols. Yet it is I who taught Ephraim to walk, I took them in My arms; but they did not know that I healed them.

Isaiah 53:5, which contains the phrase *"by His stripes we are healed,"* refers to Messiah, who in His atoning death and resurrection, provided for the healing of the whole person. It refers to the relationship with God and every aspect of a person's life, because every aspect is affected by sin, and all are interrelated.

Isaiah 53:5: But He was pierced through for our transgressions, He was crushed for our iniquities; the chastening for our well-being fell upon Him, and by His stripes we are healed.

Healing, in the Scriptures, involves restoration of every aspect of a person's life to the condition God intended for it. We can look forward to this total restoration and healing when we get to heaven, but God provides glimpses of it now through Yeshua the Messiah. Yeshua came to heal each of us back to a whole person. He makes us a new creation who can enter the presence of the living God.

APPLICATION: WHAT CAN WE LEARN FOR OURSELVES?

What about us? Even as a believer for many years, I acknowledge I'm in desperate need of God's healing power to transform my mind and my heart each day. It surprises me that I'm still overwhelmed with layers of disappointment, bitterness, and pain that surface with a new offense or a past betrayal that comes to mind. I realize that I desperately need to be healed through the blood of my Messiah, my Healer. Can you relate to this in your own life? Do the fiery darts of the evil one, as well as weakness of your own flesh pound upon your mind and heart to condemn you and render you ineffective?

If so remember what Romans 8:1–2 teaches us:

> *Therefore there is now no condemnation for those who are in Messiah Yeshua. For the law of the Spirit of life in Messiah Yeshua has set you free from the law of sin and of death.*

As new creations in Messiah, we are liberated to walk in the freedom of Yeshua's love and grace. We are no longer slaves to sin but children of God. We continually need to learn what it means to be forgiven to worship our King and to have our paths directed by His loving hands. The Lord needed the Israelites—and us as well—to know that He is the source of all our needs, both physical and spiritual, and He is with us in every step of our wilderness walk.

How's Miriam Doing in the Wilderness?

We met Miriam when she was a child of maybe nine years old. She was strategically used by God to help save her baby brother Moses. She grew up to be a prophetess and worship leader. At the age of eighty-nine, Miriam led the women in praise as they came through the Red Sea. She was a chosen servant of the Lord in her leadership position, but like all of us, she was in constant need of God's healing power and His grace in her life. She too needed God's forgiveness and mercy.

> Numbers 12:1–4: *Then Miriam and Aaron spoke against Moses because of the Cushite woman whom he had married (for he had married a Cushite woman); and they said, "Has the LORD indeed spoken only through Moses? Has He not spoken through us as well?" And the LORD heard it. (Now the man Moses was very humble, more than any man who was on the face of the earth.) Suddenly the LORD said to Moses and Aaron and to Miriam, "You three come out to the tent of meeting." So the three of them came out.*

For some reason, Miriam led her younger brother Aaron to speak against Moses. They complained about his wife. By this time, most commentators agree that Zipporah, Moses's first wife, would have died. Moses took another wife who was an Ethiopian woman. Do you think that Miriam was feeling set aside, replaced by another woman? Whatever the reason, Miriam didn't approve of his choice, and it caused her to complain aloud!

Hey! What About Me?

I can reinterpret the questions she asked, *"Has the Lord indeed spoken only through Moses? Has He not spoken through us as well?"* into this one: "What am I—chopped liver?" This response is actually a cliché. It is a semi-serious expression of frustration, anger, or indignation at having been overlooked and/or regarded as inferior. The phrase likely originated as a part of Jewish humor, referring to the serving of chopped liver that was a common side dish (thus overlooked in favor of the main course), the taste of which many do not find appealing. But we can hear Miriam's disappointment, sarcasm, and anger.

What happens next is terrifying! The Lord said to Moses, Aaron, and Miriam, *"You three come out to the tent of meeting."* God then lets them know His displeasure:

> Numbers 12:6–9: *He said, "Hear now My words: If there is a prophet among you, I, the LORD, shall make Myself known to him in a vision. I shall speak with him in a dream. Not so, with My servant Moses, he is faithful in all My household; with him I speak mouth to mouth, even openly, and not in dark sayings, and he beholds the form of the LORD. Why then were you not afraid to speak against My servant, against Moses?" So the anger of the LORD burned against them and He departed.*

What was God saying to them? First of all, Moses was not just an ordinary man, but he was God's chosen deliverer. God revealed Himself to His servant Moses as they spoke mouth to mouth. God is reminding Miriam and Aaron that their presumptuous and arrogant attitude against Moses is in fact arrogance against Him and His choice of Moses.

Only Miriam Was Judged by God, So She Was the "Ringleader"

Miriam was immediately struck with leprosy:

> Numbers 12:10: *But when the cloud had withdrawn from over the tent, behold, Miriam was leprous, as white as snow. As Aaron turned toward Miriam, behold, she was leprous.*

Aaron's Plea to Moses—He Takes Responsibility Along with His Sister

> Numbers 12:11–12: *Then Aaron said to Moses, "Oh, my lord, I beg you, do not account this sin to us, in which we have acted foolishly and in which we have sinned. Oh, do not let her be like one dead, whose flesh is half eaten away when he comes from his mother's womb!"*

Moses' Prayer to God on Behalf of His Sister

> Numbers 12:13: *Moses cried out to the LORD, saying, "O God, heal her, I pray!"*

God Answers Moses and Renders His Judgment

Numbers 12:14–16 *"Let her be shut up for seven days outside the camp, and afterward she may be received again." So Miriam was shut up outside the camp for seven days, and the people did not move on until Miriam was received again. Afterward, however, the people moved out from Hazeroth and camped in the wilderness of Paran.*

The Significance of Leprosy

This disease illustrates the destructive influence of our sin nature and the need for God's healing power to redeem us. In Luke 17:11–13, the lepers "stood afar off" because leprosy was a dreaded, loathsome disease. In order to deal with it, God gave Moses many, detailed instructions. This was an incurable disease that would eventually disfigure and rot away the body. It was widely known that only God could heal it. So, when Messiah healed the leper in Matthew 8:1–4, His divine nature was revealed to many. In the Scriptures, leprosy illustrates the work of sin. Like leprosy, sin is a vile, contaminating, mortifying, unclean thing. It starts out as a spot that grows and festers until it takes in the whole person, condemning that person to death. It is a reminder that we are separated from God by our sin and reminds us that all people are alike in sin:

Romans 3:22–23: *For there is no [difference]; for all have sinned and fall short of the glory of God.*

Yes, Miriam was a powerful leader who God used throughout her life, yet she was also a sinner in need of God's grace and forgiveness. The judgment of leprosy upon her and then her complete healing is a powerful picture of God's forgiving love and grace for Miriam.

Why was Miriam Placed Outside the Camp?

This place outside the camp or gate was a place where the refuse was thrown, a terrible place of separation from her people. For those seven days when Miriam was "outside the camp," she had time to repent of her utter sinfulness and be renewed in God's love and His purposes for her life. Seven is the number of completion, so her days of punishment and healing symbolized that she was completely healed and forgiven.

Outside the Camp or Gate:

> Hebrews 13:11–14: *For the bodies of those animals whose blood is brought into the holy place by the high priest as an offering for sin, are burned outside the camp. Therefore Yeshua also, that He might sanctify the people through His own blood, suffered outside the gate. So, let us go out to Him outside the camp, bearing His reproach. For here we do not have a lasting city, but we are seeking the city which is to come.*

When God revealed Himself, "*I, the LORD, am your healer*" (Exodus 15:26), He was including Moses, Miriam, and Aaron. Perhaps Miriam had been going over her life and thinking of her role in the redemptive process with pride. Do you think she was feeling overlooked and underappreciated? Her heart and mind needed to be continually healed from her past life of slavery, and, when she grew lax in her worship of God, she allowed the resentment and bitterness to surface in her heart. She was loved and respected by the community of Israel because they chose to not move while she was suffering "outside the camp."

What WAS So Special About Moses, Anyway?

Moses was a picture of the Deliverer who was to come.

Yeshua's Coming is Prophesied

> Deuteronomy 18:15: *The LORD your God will raise up for you a prophet like me from among you, from your countrymen, you shall listen to him.*

Yeshua's Coming Is Acknowledged

Hebrews 3:1–2: *Therefore, holy brethren, partakers of a heavenly calling, consider Yeshua, the Apostle and High Priest of our confession; He was faithful to Him who appointed Him, as Moses also was in all His house.*

John 1:17 (KJV): *For the law was given by Moses, but grace and truth came by Yeshua the Messiah.*

Moses delivered the nation of Israel from the bondage of physical slavery. Yeshua delivered the world from the bondage of slavery to sin and made a way of salvation for all who would believe.

Yeshua is our Great Deliverer—He is the fulfillment of all the Scriptures

Yeshua told the two disciples on the road to Emmaus:

"How foolish you are, and how slow to believe all that the prophets have spoken! Did not the Messiah have to suffer these things and then enter his glory?" And beginning with Moses and all the Prophets, he explained to them what was said in all the Scriptures concerning himself (Luke 24:25–27, NIV).

The writer of Hebrews contrasted the ministry of Moses and Yeshua:

Hebrews 3:5–6 (NIV): *"Moses was faithful as a servant in all God's house," bearing witness to what would be spoken by God in the future. But Messiah is faithful as the Son over God's house. And we are his house, if indeed we hold firmly to our confidence and the hope in which we glory.*

Yeshua Is Our Eternal Great High Priest

Hebrews 4:14–16: *Therefore, since we have a great high priest who has passed through the heavens, Yeshua the Son of God, let us hold fast our confession. For we do not have a high priest who cannot sympathize with our weaknesses, but One who has been tempted in all things as we are, yet without sin. Therefore let us draw near with confidence to the throne of grace, so that we may receive mercy and find grace to help in time of need.*

Yeshua Is Even Now Making Intercession on Our Behalf

Romans 8:33–34 (NIV): *Who will bring any charge against those whom God has chosen? It is God who justifies. Who then is the one who condemns? No one. Messiah Yeshua who died—more than that, who was raised to life—is at the right hand of God and is also interceding for us.*

Yeshua suffered and died "outside the camp" so I can dwell in the house of the Lord forever—worshiping in His presence (see Hebrews 13:11–14). And He has taken my sin away—completely away—*"As far as the east is from the west, so far has He removed our transgressions from us"* (Psalm 103:12).

Miriam, Aaron, and Moses all Died Before They Could Enter the Promised Land

In Numbers 20:27–29, there is a description of Aaron's death and then in Deuteronomy 34, God gives details about how He took Moses to Mount Nebo. There on the mountain God showed Moses the Promised Land before he died. After his death, God buried him so that no man would know where he was buried (Deuteronomy 34:6). Sadly, instead of having the victory of taking his people into the Promised Land, Moses could only view the land from the mountaintop.

APPLICATION: WHAT CAN WE LEARN FROM THE MISTAKES OF THESE CHOSEN LEADERS?

Both Moses and Aaron were kept from entering the Promised Land. Numbers 20 recounts the story. Instead of speaking to the rock at Meribah, as God had explicitly instructed, Moses in his anger struck the rock twice. Aaron was included in God's judgment against them.

Remember, Israel got water from a rock on two occasions that are recorded by the Tanakh. The first is in Exodus 17.

> Exodus 17: 5-6, (emphasis added): *Then the Lord said to Moses, "Pass before the people and take with you some of the elders of Israel; and take in your hand your staff with which you struck the Nile, and go. Behold, **I will stand** before you there on the rock at Horeb; and you shall strike the rock, and water will come out of it, that the people may drink." And Moses did so in the sight of the elders of Israel.*

Note that in verse six, God Himself says that He will stand on the rock that Moses will strike.

In Numbers 20, the children of Israel started quarreling again about water. In anger, Moses hit the rock two times, despite having gotten different instructions from the Lord this time.

> Numbers 20:8: *Take the rod; and you and your brother Aaron assemble the congregation and speak to the rock before their eyes, that it may yield its water. You shall thus bring forth water for them out of the rock and let the congregation and their beasts drink.*

The Lord pronounced His judgment in Numbers 20:12–13:

> *But the LORD said to Moses and Aaron, "Because you have not believed Me, to treat Me as holy in the sight of the sons of Israel, therefore you shall not bring this assembly into*

the land which I have given them." Those were the waters of Meribah, because the sons of Israel contended with the LORD, and He proved Himself holy among them.

Why was God so angry at Moses and Aaron when Moses struck the rock instead of speaking to it? Because the **Rock** was **Yeshua the Messiah** who was struck, and then this Rock followed the children of Israel in their wilderness journey providing everything they needed. Paul taught us about this Rock in 1 Corinthians 10:4:

And all (the children of Israel) *drank the same spiritual drink, for they were drinking from a spiritual rock which followed them; and the rock was Messiah* (definition added).

What Is the Application for Us?

We are to believe God and treat Him as holy. Yeshua died once for all for our sins to complete our redemption, so when Moses in anger struck the rock a second time, he in a sense crucified Yeshua again. He spurned the source of Living Water that God had been providing to them throughout their wilderness journey. He disobeyed God's specific command to speak to the rock, therefore he dishonored the Lord before the people. Remember the word "honor" in Hebrew is *kavod*, which means "heavy" or "weighty." In other words, we must take what God says seriously and give His Word its due weight of glory. When I don't take His Word seriously by trusting and depending on Yeshua, I am saying that Yeshua didn't do enough for me. We need to be careful to seek Yeshua first and His righteousness (Matthew 6:33).

Take time to praise Yeshua!

Revelation 22:12–13 (NIV): *For He says: "Look, I am coming soon! My reward is with me, and I will give to each person according to what they have done. I am the Alpha*

*and the Omega, the First and the Last, the Beginning and
the End."*

Why Are We Here?

Why is it important for us to consider these leaders since
they displeased God? In 1 Corinthians 10:11–13, the Apostle
Paul said that what happened to the Israelites during those
forty years of wilderness wandering was written down to teach
us. We can learn from their mistakes about how to please the
Lord during the tests we face during our earthly wilderness
walk.

Paul told us that in our "wilderness walk," we will be
tested, but the good news is that we have the examples like
Miriam, Aaron, and Moses to teach us how to live.

> 1 Corinthians 10:11–12: *Now these things happened to
> them as an example, and they were written for our
> instruction, upon whom the ends of the ages have come.
> Therefore, let him who thinks he stands take heed that he
> does not fall.*

Those verses explain that we need to walk in humility. We
are not to depend on our own wisdom and strength, or we will
fall.

In my "wilderness walk" with the Lord I will be tested, and
these tests will reveal what is really in my heart. The next
verse in 1 Corinthians 10 teaches us three things about our
tests and how God is involved:

> *No temptation has overtaken you but such as is common
> to man; and God is faithful, who will not allow you to be
> tempted beyond what you are able, but with the
> temptation will provide the way of escape also, so that you
> will be able to endure it* (1 Cor 10:13).

So, we must realize that His tests are:

1. Common for all of us—everyone is going through tests.
2. Controlled by God. He is faithful and will not allow us to be tested beyond what we are able to endure.
3. Conquerable—God will make a way of escape. We can get through in His strength and power.

Can We Learn from Miriam?

As the firstborn, she most likely had a strong-willed personality, which would have been a great gift as she navigated the perils of speaking to the Egyptian princess and living as a slave all those years, yet remaining faithful to the Lord. Her personality may have gotten in her way when Miriam spoke out against the wife that Moses chose, and she forgot to honor God's choice of Moses as her leader. Miriam disregarded the fact that it was God who placed Moses in the position of leadership when she spoke out against her youngest brother. This was a grievous offense to God when she disrespected and dishonored God's choice. We discussed the judgment of leprosy and God's healing of her. When discussing the issue of leprosy, this incident is spoken of in Deuteronomy 24:9: *Remember what the LORD your God did to Miriam on the way as you came out of Egypt.*

Miriam's death is recorded in Numbers 20:1:

> Then the sons of Israel, the whole congregation, came to the wilderness of Zin in the first month; and the people stayed at Kadesh. Now Miriam died there and was buried there.

Application

For each of us, we need to be careful to recognize that God has put authority in place. Therefore, we are to honor this authority even if we sometimes disagree or feel we can do a better job than the person in charge. Another aspect to think about would be the fact that God created Miriam as He wove her in her mother's womb giving her the personality He knew she would need to be His tool in His redemptive story. God has woven each of us in our mother's womb so we are exactly as He planned and He desires to use each of us for His glory as we yield ourselves to Him.

In Conclusion

Miriam, Aaron, Moses. They all died before Israel entered the Promised Land. Each of them dishonored the Lord. Each one had a significant role in God's plan of redemption. They were in fact ordinary and flawed individuals called by our extraordinary God to serve Him, *sent ones* (Micah 6:4) instrumental in God's plan. I believe we will meet them in Heaven, and I especially look forward to meeting Miriam. I wonder if she'll be leading in worship dance with a tambourine in her hand!

Be encouraged to think about them. God used them with all their flaws and God will use us too as we keep entrusting our lives into His hands.

Seek the Lord while He
may be found; call upon
Him while He is near.
Let the wicked forsake
his way, and the
unrighteous man his
thoughts; and let him
return to the Lord, and
He will have compassion
on him; and to our
God, for He will
abundantly pardon.

Isaiah 55:6-7

Seven

An Improbable Heroine: *Rahab*

THE PROMISE

From Genesis to Exodus to Joshua

God's redemptive plan requiring woman continued in the book of Joshua. The Children of Israel were preparing to enter the Promised Land, where the battle for the impenetrable city of Jericho loomed before Joshua and his men. This is where we get to know our unlikely heroine, Rahab the harlot.

In Joshua 2:1 we meet her:

> *Then Joshua the son of Nun sent two men as spies secretly from Shittim, saying, "Go, view the land, especially Jericho." So, they went and came into the house of a harlot whose name was Rahab, and lodged there.*

This miracle of God's victory over the mighty city of Jericho emphasizes how our powerful God can overcome any obstacle in our lives if we trust in His way of doing things. In our glimpse of the historical setting, we should remember the children of Israel's entrance to the land flowing with milk and honey had been on hold for thirty-eight additional years, following their rebellion against God. Remember that they had refused to enter the Promised Land at first, out of fear and unbelief, saying,

> *"Why is the LORD bringing us into this land, to fall by the sword? Our wives and our little ones will become plunder; would it not be better for us to return to Egypt?" So they said to one another, "Let us appoint a leader and return to Egypt"* (Numbers 14:3-4).

God's answer to this rebellion was,

> *"Surely all the men who have seen My glory and My signs which I performed in Egypt and in the wilderness, yet have put Me to the test these ten times and have not listened to My voice, shall by no means see the land which I swore to their fathers, nor shall any of those who spurned Me see it. But My servant Caleb, because he has had a different spirit and has followed Me fully, I will bring into the land which he entered, and his descendants shall take possession of it"* (Numbers 14:22-24).

Finally, the generation who disbelieved God's promises at Masah and Meribah had died. The time had arrived to enter the Promised Land.

A Promise for Joshua

After the death of Moses, God chose Joshua, the son of Nun, to be the leader of the Israelite people. The Lord commissioned Joshua with the task of conquering the land of Canaan under His guidance. God gave Joshua continual assurances of His presence throughout the whole process. The verses that God gave to Joshua are applicable for us as well.

Joshua 1:9: *God said to Joshua, "Have I not commanded you? Be strong and courageous! Do not tremble or be dismayed, for the LORD your God is with you wherever you go."*

In Matthew 28:18–20, are we not commanded to go into all the world and preach the Good News by Yeshua? And are we not assured that God's presence is with us wherever He sends us?

And a Renewed Promise for the New Generation of Israel

The response of the children of Israel to the new leadership of Joshua confirmed their continued loyalty to God and to Joshua. When Joshua took the place of Moses to lead them, all the children of Israel gave their promise of obedience and loyalty.

Joshua 1:17: *Just as we obeyed Moses in all things, so we will obey you; only may the LORD your God be with you, as He was with Moses.*

What a dramatic change from the generation past, when all of Israel (except for Joshua and Caleb) rebelled against not only their leaders but also the Lord God Almighty.

The plan of Joshua was to have two spies sneak into the walled city of Jericho and gather intelligence as they viewed the land. In Hebrew the word "view" or "spy out" is the common Hebrew word for "see"—*raah. Raah* carries the idea of accessing and advising, taking into consideration what was seen. Because Joshua trusted that God would deliver the land into their hands, he knew the spies would be under God's protection and guidance. Consequently, as a good leader, he wanted to be wise in his planning as he approached the city.

We have mentioned before that God's providence is always working on behalf of His plan of redemption. He is in charge. His hand is in the glove of history for His redemptive purposes.

Go Back to Joshua 2:1

> *So they went and came into the house of a harlot whose name was Rahab, and lodged there.*

This sounds strange, doesn't it? How did the two spies make their way into the city without being immediately recognized as strangers? How did they meet Rahab? Why did they go into her house of prostitution? These questions can be answered in one statement: All that was happening was part of God's providential plan because God was involved, and God had already seen that Rahab's heart had turned to Him.

THE PROBLEM

The problem was Jericho. That's oversimplifying the problem, really, but Jericho is a good picture of it. The Children of Israel were facing the same test they had failed a generation ago. The previous generation, faced with city of Jericho and the Canaanite people, had said this:

> Numbers 13:31-33: *But the men who had gone up with [Caleb and Joshua] said, "We are not able to go up against the people, for they are too strong for us." So they gave out to the sons of Israel a bad report of the land which they had spied out, saying, "The land through which we have gone, in spying it out, is a land that devours its inhabitants; and all the people whom we saw in it are men of great size. There also we saw the Nephilim (the sons of Anak are part of the Nephilim); and we became like grasshoppers in our own sight, and so we were in their sight."*

The new generation of Israel had been warned about the scope of what they were facing.

Deuteronomy 9:1-2: *Hear, O Israel! You are crossing over the Jordan today to go in to dispossess nations greater and mightier than you, great cities fortified to heaven, a people great and tall, the sons of the Anakim, whom you know and of whom you have heard it said, "Who can stand before the sons of Anak?"*

The Canaanite cities the Israelites had been afraid to attack forty years before were still strong. The Canaanite giants were still there.

But the promise God made to Abraham was still there, too:

Deuteronomy 9:3–5 (emphasis added): *Know therefore today that it is the LORD your God who is crossing over before you as a consuming fire. He will destroy them and He will subdue them before you, so that you may drive them out and destroy them quickly, just as the LORD has spoken to you. Do not say in your heart when the LORD your God has driven them out before you, 'Because of my righteousness the LORD has brought me in to possess this land,' but it is because of the wickedness of these nations that the LORD is dispossessing them before you. It is not for your righteousness or for the uprightness of your heart that you are going to possess their land, but it is because of the wickedness of these nations that the LORD your God is driving them out before you, in order to confirm the oath which the LORD swore to your fathers, to Abraham, Isaac and Jacob."*

So It Should Have Been Easy, Right?

Unfortunately, Joshua's spies were recognized to be strangers because the king of Jericho immediately sent his men to confront Rahab. This unfolding drama gives us an amazing demonstration of the providence of God, because the Lord God of Israel had led the two spies to the only believing home in all of Jericho.

THE RESTORATION

Rahab, who had come to trust in the God of Israel, knew that the spies would lose their lives if she revealed that they were in her home. And this was war! The Canaanites were the enemies of Israel and sought to defeat them and their God. Now that she was on the side of the God of Israel, Rahab used her wisdom and bravery as God gave her His grace. She hid the spies on her rooftop, gave the king's men false intel and successfully diverted their attention away from the safety of her home.

Did Rahab Really Have Faith?

In her conversation with the spies, Rahab said,

> "I know that the LORD has given you the land, and that the terror of you has fallen on us, and that all the inhabitants of the land have melted away before you. For we have heard how the LORD dried up the water of the Red Sea before you when you came out of Egypt, and what you did to the two kings of the Amorites who were beyond the Jordan, to Sihon and Og, whom you utterly destroyed" (Joshua 2:9–10).

She begins her statement with the fact that she knew their God was a victorious God who would keep His promises to His people. She also understood that pagan Jericho was a doomed city. Somehow, when she heard of the miracle of the Red Sea and the defeat of the two powerful kings on the other side of the Jordan, her knowledge of God became a faith and trust in Him. Everyone else in Jericho, Rahab said, heard these same accounts of the exploits of the people of Israel and their God, and responded in terror.

> "When we heard it, our hearts melted and no courage remained in any man any longer because of you; for the LORD your God, He is God in heaven above and on earth beneath" (Joshua 2:11).

She said they had *"courage"* which in Hebrew is no *ruach*, no "breath," no "wind," or no "spirit." However, for Rahab, this same fear or terror of the Lord translated into her reverence and awe for the One true God.

She stated *the Lord your God is in charge both in heaven and on earth.* This statement, along with her affirmation in verses nine and ten above, reveal that Rahab had already trusted in the God of Israel.

I think it bears repeating: God's providence is totally miraculous. For when Joshua told the spies to go view the land, Joshua knew these spies were not alone in their recognizance mission. Joshua knew that the same God who saw the need and provided the ram for Abraham's sacrifice would see and provide a way for His children at Jericho as well. The name *Jehovah Yireh*—The God Who Provides, from Genesis 22:14—literally means "The LORD Who Sees," which is based on the Hebrew word *raah*, to see. In other words, God sees the need and situation and provides accordingly for our every necessity. God saw ahead in the life of Rahab and provided a home on the walls of Jericho that became a safe haven not only for the spies, but also for her family in the midst of wartime and terror. Rahab was the only person in Jericho who trusted the God of Israel, and God brought the spies to her.

Who Was Rahab: Harlot or Heroine?

Or Maybe an Innkeeper?

I want to note there is a difference of opinion among teachers of Scripture, which include some traditional Jewish scholars and some Christian teachers, who conclude that Rahab the harlot was not really a harlot. They assert that she could have been a woman who kept an inn rather than one who ran a house of prostitution. However when Rahab is introduced in Joshua 2:1—and later in Joshua 6:25—both times she is described by Hebrew word *zanah*, which means "one who practices prostitution." It is the same word Judah used to accuse his daughter-in-law Tamar of becoming pregnant by harlotry when he wanted to have her burned (Gen 38:24).

The New Covenant confirms this label for, in both James 2:25 and Hebrews 11:31, the writers use the Greek word *porne* to describe Rahab, which is also translated "prostitute." Could it be that by the time the spies came to her home, because of her faith in the God of Israel, she had been using her location as an inn rather than a house of prostitution? There is no way to know. One thing we are certain of is that Rahab's label as a harlot did not define her, for the Lord chose to use her in an extraordinary way for His purposes. By her courageous faith and deeds, she is forever recorded in the Hall of Faith in Hebrews 11. She is named along with other heroes of the faith such as Noah, Abraham, Moses, and Joseph. There are only three women mentioned in Hebrews 11: Sarah (11:11); Moses's parents, which included his mother Jochebed (11:23); and Rahab the harlot (11:31).

> Hebrews 11:31: *By faith Rahab the harlot did not perish along with those who were disobedient, after she had welcomed the spies in peace.*

James, or *Yacov*, the half-brother of Yeshua, uses Rahab as an example of a person who didn't just say she believed, but she took actions on behalf of the spies, which demonstrated that she did trust in the God of Israel. She had given her heart to Him and then acted on her new faith. James puts it this way:

> James 2:25: *In the same way, was not Rahab the harlot also justified by works when she received the messengers and sent them out by another way?*

Do We Have to Keep Calling Her a Harlot?

Some have asked the question, "Why does the New Covenant keep the label of 'harlot?'" According to 2 Corinthians 5:17, any person who accepts Messiah Yeshua as Lord and Savior is a new creation. Could this former label be another way that God is showing us His unending grace in the life of Rahab? In Messiah, we are no longer defined by our old labels. Yet, those old labels can be a cause for rejoicing when we use them to note with thanksgiving how far God has brought us. God changed Rahab and used her mightily in giving Israel the victory. She was no longer Rahab the harlot, but rather she was Rahab—a daughter of the one true God of Israel. She's a heroine of our faith who serves as an example to women throughout the ages of God's abundant mercy and grace to change and redeem her life and the lives of her entire household.

A Deeper Look at Rahab's Faith

God gave Rahab His favor and His wisdom for He knew her heart. In fact, God had His plans for her, just as He worked out all things for good in the life of Tamar, here again we see God revealing Himself to Rahab's longing heart. As we take a closer look at the words Rahab used in her plea to the two Israeli spies, I hope you will be encouraged to see how God was revealing Himself to her. God loved Rahab and even though she lived in one of the most notoriously pagan and well-fortified cities in the land, nothing could stop the eternal love of God from reaching her.

In Joshua 2:12–13, we find Rahab's request to the spies and there are four words that will take us deeper into Rahab's faith:

> *"Now therefore, please swear to me by the LORD, since I have dealt kindly with you, that you also will deal kindly with my father's household, and give me a pledge of truth,*

and spare my father and my mother and my brothers and my sisters, with all who belong to them, and deliver our lives from death."

Let's take a closer look at her request.

Word One

The word "swear" is *shava* and means "to swear by an oath." *Shava* comes from the same root word as *shavuah* or "week," which is comprised of seven days. This number seven in Hebrew carries the meaning of complete faithfulness.

Furthermore Rahab told the spies to swear the oath using the name of the LORD, which is the covenant name for God, the Great I AM (*yud, hey, vav, hey*). This is same name that God revealed to His servant Moses when the Lord appeared to Him in the burning bush. Moses told God that he was not qualified to bring the children of Israel out of Egypt. Moses gave God his first reason:

> Exodus 3:13–14: *Then Moses said to God, "Behold, I am going to the sons of Israel, and I will say to them, 'The God of your fathers has sent me to you.' Now they may say to me, 'What is His name?' What shall I say to them?" In the next verse, God reveals His covenant name to Moses—God said to Moses, "I AM WHO I AM"; and He said, "Thus you shall say to the sons of Israel, 'I AM has sent me to you.'"*

Word Two

Rahab used the word "kindly" two times in her request. "Kindly" is *chesed*, which usually refers to God's covenant love for us. She asked for *chesed* on behalf of her entire family specifically mentioning her father, her mother, her sisters, her brothers, and *all who belong* to them.

One of my favorite verses that describes God's *chesed*—His covenant love—is found in Jeremiah 31:3,

"The Lord appeared to him from afar, saying, 'I have loved you with an everlasting love; therefore I have drawn you with lovingkindness (chesed)'" (definition added).

Word Three

Rahab also asks for a pledge or sign. This Hebrew word is *ot* and is usually translated as "a miracle sign." We noted this in Exodus where the word "sign" is used for the blood of the Lamb on the doors in Egypt.

Exodus 12:13 (definition added): *'The blood shall be a sign* (ot) *for you on the houses where you live; and when I see the blood I will pass over you, and no plague will befall you to destroy you when I strike the land of Egypt.'*

How could Rahab possibly have had this knowledge of the one true God of Israel? I think the clue to help us understand is in Joshua 2:11 when she told the spies, *"When we heard it, our hearts melted and no courage remained in any man any longer because of you; for the LORD your God, He is God in heaven above and on earth beneath."*

Word Four

The Hebrew word for "heard" is *shema*, which we have mentioned before because God told His people to *"Hear (shema) O Israel that the Lord your God is one God"* (see Deut 6:4, definition added). This word "hear" means "to listen with understanding with the intent of obeying what the LORD is saying." Everyone in Jericho *heard* of the same miracles of the God of Israel. Only Rahab opened her heart to truly listen and believe in the one true God as opposed to the many false gods in her native land of Canaan.

The Sign of the Scarlet Cord

As we work our way through this passage, another incredible foreshadowing of the redemption of Yeshua is the scarlet cord. This was the *ot*, the sign or pledge provided for

Rahab. She was to hang it from her window in her home on the outside wall of Jericho. This was a miracle sign which would be flaming red or scarlet in color. However, not only is this color significant, but the word for "cord" is also reassuring for this word is "hope" in Hebrew—*tikvah*. In Jeremiah 29:11, God is promising His children a future and a hope using this same Hebrew word, *tikvah*. What a miraculous sign for Rahab! The cord of confident expectation or hope is colored deep red. This color reminds us of that blood that was shed for each of us. In Isaiah 1:18, God invites to understand His redemption:

> *"Come now, and let us reason together," says the* LORD, *"though your sins are as scarlet, they will be as white as snow; though they are red like crimson, they will be like wool."*

In the New Covenant, we have the fulfillment of the hope of our redemption through the Lamb of God who takes away the sin of the world.

> Ephesians 1:7: *In Him we have redemption through His blood, the forgiveness of our trespasses, according to the riches of His grace.*

She Had Faith in God and Showed Faith in His Servants

Rahab followed the instructions given by the spies as she waited to be delivered.

> Joshua 2:21: *She said, "According to your words, so be it." So she sent them away, and they departed; and she tied the scarlet cord in the window.*

Why Does God Use Such a Strange Plan for Victory?

Marching and Trumpets?

God had a seemingly bizarre plan for the battle of Jericho. He told Joshua to have the armed men march around the city once each day, for six days. In front of them, the priests were to carry the ark, blow trumpets, but the soldiers were to keep silent. On the seventh day, the assembly marched around the walls of Jericho seven times. Joshua told them that by God's order, every living thing in the city must be destroyed, except Rahab and her family. All articles of silver, gold, bronze, and iron were to go into the Lord's treasury. At Joshua's command, the men gave a great shout, and Jericho's walls fell down flat! The Israelite army rushed in and conquered the city.

What Happened to Rahab After the Battle?

Rahab, who was once an outcast, became part of God's family. Only Rahab's home was left untouched by the devastation and only she and her family were spared. We read in Joshua 6:25:

> Rahab the harlot and her father's household and all she had, Joshua spared; and she has lived in the midst of Israel to this day, for she hid the messengers whom Joshua sent to spy out Jericho.

Don't miss the phrase that tells us Rahab *lived in the midst of Israel*. She married Salmon, who many scholars speculate was one of the two spies that she had hidden on her rooftop. From verses at the end of the book of Ruth, we know that Rahab and Salmon were not only part of the family of Israel, but also in the Messianic line!

Ruth 4:21: *And to Salmon was born Boaz.*

God's amazing grace was poured out into the life of Rahab the harlot. Think about Rahab's declaration of her faith in the Lord. That can challenge each of us! First consider that Rahab had no Scripture, no personal witness, a degrading profession in a wicked, idol-worshipping society—just to name a few of the obstacles in her life that might have kept her from becoming a believer in the God of Israel. Yet when she heard of the miracle-working God of Israel, she sought to know the Lord. Praise the Lord that we understand from Scripture the assurance for us that God will always have compassion on the one who is seeking Him. It says in Isaiah 55:6–7,

"Seek the LORD while He may be found; call upon Him while He is near. Let the wicked forsake his way, and the unrighteous man his thoughts; and let him return to the LORD, and He will have compassion on him; and to our God, for He will abundantly pardon."

APPLICATION FOR US

1. Are you praying for someone, perhaps a co-worker or a family member, who seems unreachable, living a completely pagan lifestyle? Don't give up. Keep praying. God reached Rahab with His love and forgiveness and in His miracle-working power, He can reach that person that you may think is unreachable. Let's keep on asking, seeking, and knocking on behalf of those who God has put in our lives.

Yeshua encourages us in Matthew 7:7–8,

"Keep asking, and it will be given to you; keep seeking, and you will find; keep knocking, and the door will be opened to you. For everyone who keeps asking receives; he who keeps seeking finds; and to him who keeps knocking, the door will be opened" (CJB).

2. Consider the battle of Jericho that God told Joshua how to win. How does God fight our battles? The examples from the life of David and Jehoshaphat teach us that when we are fighting battles for His honor and glory, then the LORD is the One who fights our battles.

One very well-known example is from the life of David when he was a teenage shepherd. At his father Jesse's request, David took some provisions to his brothers who were on the front lines of a Philistine battle and where the entire army of

Israel was being "held hostage" by a nine-foot arrogant giant of a man. When Goliath taunted the armies of Israel David responded:

> 1 Samuel 17:45–47: *Then David said to the Philistine, "You come to me with a sword, a spear, and a javelin, but I come to you in the name of the LORD of hosts, the God of the armies of Israel, whom you have taunted. This day the LORD will deliver you up into my hands, and I will strike you down and remove your head from you. And I will give the dead bodies of the army of the Philistines this day to the birds of the sky and the wild beasts of the earth, that all the earth may know that there is a God in Israel, and that all this assembly may know that the LORD does not deliver by sword or by spear; for the battle is the LORD's and He will give you into our hands."*

Adonai Tzva'ot —The Lord of the Heavenly Armies—is the One who fought not only David's battles, but also is the same God who is the One who will fight our battles. When we honor the Lord and give Him first place, He will come to our defense.

Another example of how He fights our battles is when The Lord of the Heavenly Armies came to the aid of King Jehoshaphat when he was about to be attacked. The prophet told the troubled king:

> 2 Chronicles 20:15–18, 21–22 (NIV, emphasis added): *He said: "Listen, King Jehoshaphat and all who live in Judah and Jerusalem! This is what the LORD says to you: 'Do not be afraid or discouraged because of this vast army. For the battle is not yours, but God's. Tomorrow march down against them. They will be climbing up by the Pass of Ziz, and you will find them at the end of the gorge in the Desert of Jeruel. You will not have to fight this battle. Take up your positions; stand firm and see the deliverance the LORD will give you, Judah and Jerusalem. Do not be afraid; do not be discouraged. Go out to face them tomorrow, and*

the LORD will be with you.'" Jehoshaphat bowed down with his face to the ground, and all the people of Judah and Jerusalem fell down in worship before the LORD. ... After consulting the people, Jehoshaphat appointed men to sing to the LORD and to praise him for the splendor of his holiness as they went out at the head of the army, saying: **"Give thanks to the LORD, for his love endures forever."** *As they began to sing and praise, the LORD set ambushes against the men of Ammon and Moab and Mount Seir who were invading Judah, and they were defeated.*

Paul taught us:

2 Corinthians 10:3–5: *For though we walk in the flesh, we do not war according to the flesh, for the weapons of our warfare are not of the flesh, but divinely powerful for the destruction of fortresses. We are destroying speculations and every lofty thing raised up against the knowledge of God, and we are taking every thought captive to the obedience of Messiah.*

And he instructed us in Ephesians 6 to clothe ourselves in God's armor to stand *"strong **in the Lord** and in the strength of His might,"* against the enemy of our souls.

Ephesians 6:10–13: *Finally, be strong in the Lord and in the strength of His might. Put on the full armor of God, so that you may be able to stand firm against the schemes of the devil. For our struggle is not against flesh and blood, but against the rulers, against the powers, against the world forces of this darkness, against the spiritual forces of wickedness in the heavenly places. Therefore, take up the full armor of God, so that you may be able to resist in the evil day, and having done everything, to stand firm.*

Colossians 1:13–14: *For He rescued us from the domain of darkness, and transferred us to the kingdom of His beloved Son, in whom we have redemption, the forgiveness of sins.*

Thank You, Lord, that just as You saved Rahab and her family from destruction and delivered them into Your family, You have redeemed me from the domain of darkness and placed me into the kingdom of Your beloved Son. Thank You *Adonai Tzva'ot*—The LORD of the Heavenly Armies—for enabling me to stand firm in You and take every thought captive to the obedience of Messiah Yeshua. Amen

"

For I know the plans
that I have for you,"
declares the Lord, "plans
for welfare and not for
calamity to give you a
future and a hope. Then
you will call upon Me and
come and pray to Me, and
I will listen to you. You
will seek Me and find Me
when you search for Me
with all your heart."

Jeremiah 29:11-13

Eight

An Exceptional Moabitess:
Ruth

From the book of Joshua and his conquering the land of Canaan we move into the time of the judges to meet our next woman who was central in God's redemptive program. In fact, she might be one of your favorite women of Scripture. Her name was Ruth, and she was born into the accursed nation of Moab and is often identified as Ruth the Moabitess throughout the Scriptures.

THE PROMISE

What does a Moabite woman have to do with the redemption plan of God?

Remember, in Genesis 3:14, God said that the seed of a woman would defeat the serpent, pointing to the coming Messiah's sacrifice for sins. In Genesis 12:1-3, speaking to Abraham, God identified the family from whom the promised Messiah would come. He reiterated the promise to Abraham's son and grandson. Then in the blessing of Jacob to Judah, he identified the tribe from which the Messiah would come.

Genesis 49:10: *The scepter shall not depart from Judah, nor the ruler's staff from between his feet, until Shiloh comes, and to him shall be the obedience of the peoples.*

Let's see where this Moabitess, Ruth, fits into God's ultimate redemption plan, and how God's redemption for her individually worked.

The Time of the Judges

As we said, the historical setting for the book of Ruth took place during the period of the judges. We met Rahab during the conquering of the land that God had given the twelve tribes of Israel. After they conquered the land, Joshua assigned the tribes their various portions of the land of Israel. Unfortunately, the time of the judges—which lasted for more than three hundred years—was period of anarchy and idolatry in the life of Israel. It was a cycle that was repeated over and over again. First, the Israelites turned to idols instead of worshipping the one true God. Next, their surrounding enemies oppressed them and persecuted them. When the people of Israel became desperate enough, they cried out in distress to the Lord. In answer to their prayers, God raised up a judge who redeemed them from the time of oppression by their enemies. Then the fear of their enemies would wane and the lure of idolatry would grow, and the cycle would begin again.

These judges were put in place by God to govern. They decided private and public issues which gave the Israelites guidance and direction in their everyday lives. However, it's important to note that there was no Israeli Defense Force to make sure the policies of the judges were followed. God Himself wanted to be the King to reign over them, however the people for the most part did not give God His true place of worship. They rejected His rule over them. Instead of following the true King of Israel, they turned to their own ways and did not follow God's Word. In fact, the final verse of Judges gives an accurate snapshot of the situation:

> *In those days there was no king in Israel; everyone did what was right in his own eyes* (Judges 21:25).

Ruth and Her Book

Many scholars believe that Samuel, the great prophet of Israel, was the author of this four-chapter account of God's amazing grace. Ruth stands alongside Esther as the only women to have their names listed in the books of the Hebrew Scriptures. Another proof of God's love for the whole world is that Ruth was a Gentile, and not just a Gentile, a Moabite.

A Promise?

We learned how the Lord feels about the nation of Moab in Deuteronomy 23:3–6:

> *No Ammonite or Moabite shall enter the assembly of the LORD; none of their descendants, even to the tenth generation, shall ever enter the assembly of the LORD, because they did not meet you with food and water on the way when you came out of Egypt, and because they hired against you Balaam the son of Beor from Pethor of Mesopotamia, to curse you. Nevertheless, the LORD your God was not willing to listen to Balaam, but the LORD your God turned the curse into a blessing for you because the LORD your God loves you. You shall never seek their peace or their prosperity all your days.*

Even though the Lord had cursed the nation of Moab, the Lord included Ruth the Moabite in the royal line of the Messiah of Israel.

THE PROBLEM

Everyone is Doing What's Right in His Own Sight!

The book of Ruth is one of my favorite books of Scripture. I'm always encouraged to study this book and see how the Lord used an ordinary Moabite woman to lovingly win her embittered mother-in-law back to faith in the God of Israel. There is a wonderful love story that develops in this book as well as a loving friendship that changed the course of Ruth and Naomi's lives. We don't know the exact timing for this book, but we're told it is during the time of the judges.

> Ruth 1:1 (definition added): *Now it came about in the days when the judges governed, that there was a famine in the land. And a certain man of Bethlehem in Judah* (Elimelech) *went to sojourn in the land of Moab with his wife and his two sons.*

Why Not Move?

If there was a famine in your hometown, wouldn't it seem reasonable to temporarily move just forty miles away to a place where bread was plentiful? The Hebrew word for sojourn (*ger*) indicates that as strangers, *this certain man of Bethlehem* did not intend to be in Moab permanently, but rather after the famine passed, would move back to the land of promise. Nevertheless, a question must be raised.

Why Move?

Why would Elimelech, whose name means "my God is King," move his family from his ancestral home of Bethlehem to the accursed nation of Moab? The Scriptures do not indicate that Elimelech sought the Lord's guidance or provision during this time. It seems that, doing what was *right in his own eyes*, he decided to move with his wife and his yet unmarried sons. The Scriptures teach over and over again that if we seek God first, He will provide for all our needs. How ironic that Elimelech left Bethlehem, which means House of Bread—*Beit*

Lechem in Hebrew—to live in an accursed land just to find physical food. Had he sought the Lord and what God wanted to teach him through this famine, the outcome for his legacy would surely have been quite different.

The Story of Ruth: A Very Rough Beginning

The end of Ruth 1:2 states, *"Now they entered the land of Moab and remained there."* This seems to indicate that Elimelech's plans changed somewhere. He and his family were no longer just sojourners living as strangers; they had settled in. But then tragedy struck.

> Ruth 1:3–4: *Then Elimelech, Naomi's husband, died; and she was left with her two sons. They took for themselves Moabite women as wives; the name of the one was Orpah and the name of the other Ruth. And they lived there about ten years.*

What was Naomi to do? They were already settled in Moab and even though her husband died, instead of moving back to Bethlehem, she decided to remain in Moab and find Moabite wives for her two sons. Despite the disobedience of Elimelech, and then Naomi, to the Lord God, He was overseeing their situation. In His providential power, He was working all things together for good. However, before things got better, there was more unfortunate news. After living in Moab for ten years, both of Naomi's sons died.

> Ruth 1:4–5 (TLV): *They married Moabite women—one was named Orpah and the second was named Ruth, and they dwelt there about ten years. Then those two, Mahlon and Chilion, also died. So the woman was left without her children and her husband.*

How About You?

Some of you can readily relate to Naomi's heartbreaking situation. Perhaps you have lost your husband and after ten years you are still grieving and missing him every day. Can you imagine, on top of that grief, losing both of your children as well? This immense heartbreak for Naomi is almost unbearable to think about. For Naomi, this is not just about physical death, but also the death of her hopes and dreams. These hopes would have surely included having a legacy from her sons to give her grandchildren who would carry on their family name. Now where could Naomi go to find comfort for her situation? Where can any of us go when our dreams are shattered and we find ourselves virtually alone in tearful anguish?

This was a critical time for Naomi as she needed to make a choice about her future. What should a daughter of the God of Israel do when faced with desperation and unbearable sorrow? The Scriptures reveal to us from Naomi's responses to her daughters-in-law, Orpah and Ruth, that she had already turned away from the only source of true comfort. Naomi chose to do what she thought right in her own eyes. Instead of looking to the God of Israel for comfort, she chose to accuse God of not only not caring, but actually plotting harm against her.

However, before judging Naomi too harshly, I must ask myself: what do I do when I am overcome with grief and pain? Do I ever accuse the Lord of not caring? Blame Him for doing evil against me? The Scriptures are so clear to let us know that God's Word must be the resource for our lives at these critical times. We are taught that we can absolutely trust the Lord in every circumstance. Paul told those in the congregation in Corinth where to find ultimate comfort in their situations of sorrow:

> 2 Corinthians 1:3–5: *Blessed be the God and Father of our Lord Yeshua the Messiah, the Father of mercies and God of all comfort, who comforts us in all our affliction so that we will be able to comfort those who are in any affliction with the comfort with which we ourselves are comforted*

by God. For just as the sufferings of Messiah are ours in abundance, so also our comfort is abundant through Messiah.

In this section, God is called the "Father of mercies," which in Hebrew is *Av HaRachmiim*. Father of Mercies is based on two Hebrew words: "Father" is *Av* and "mercy" is *rachamiim*, which is in the plural form. He's not called the Father of Mercy, because God doesn't just give us a single drop of mercy at a time. Rather, His lavish mercies are new every morning and in abundance whenever we look to Him. When I learned that the word "mercy" is based on the root word *rachem*, which means a woman's womb, I was amazed. In other words, this comfort from *Av HaRachmiim*—the Father of Mercies—is likened to the safety and comfort of a baby in its mother's womb. I love to discover how the full character of God is displayed in His creation of women.

Consider what overwhelming grief and affliction of our souls does to us without the One who can bring us His merciful compassion. God wants us to bring our anguish and our tears to Him because He loves us, and only He can bring the comfort to our hearts that we really need. We don't want to overlook the fact that Ruth and Orpah would have been in mourning as well because both of them had lost her husbands. As this story unfolds, we learn that Ruth did not become bitter and estranged from God; rather, she became a woman of great determination and faith who placed her trust in the God of Israel.

News from Her Hometown: the House of Bread

Naomi's story continues in Ruth 1:6:

Then she arose with her daughters-in-law that she might return from the land of Moab, for she had heard in the land of Moab that the LORD had visited His people in giving them food.

Here Naomi uses the covenant name of God when it states that *"she heard ... that the LORD had visited His people in giving them food."* Naomi probably received this news from Jewish travelers or merchants passing through Moab. She heard the famine was over and Bethlehem, the house of Bread, sounded good to her once more. So, she decided to return to her hometown. Moab had turned out to be a place of death and devastation for her and she had no other option but to go back. As Naomi and her two daughters-in-law prepared to return, we begin to see inside Naomi's heart:

> Ruth 1:8–9: *And Naomi said to her two daughters-in-law, "Go, return each of you to her mother's house. May the LORD deal kindly with you as you have dealt with the dead and with me. May the LORD grant that you may find rest, each in the house of her husband." Then she kissed them, and they lifted up their voices and wept.*

Both Ruth and Orpah protested: Ruth 1:10: *And they said to her, "No, but we will surely return with you to your people."* In the next section, we can feel the pent-up grief and anguish pouring out of Naomi. She explained through her bitterness that she was too old to have any more sons for them to marry. And even if she could have more sons, would they wait until the sons were of marrying age? Listen to her cynicism and doubt about God's goodness as she continued to clarify the situation for them. Naomi slandered the God of Israel.

> Ruth 1:13: *"Would you therefore wait until they were grown? Would you therefore refrain from marrying? No, my daughters; for it is harder for me than for you, for the hand of the LORD has gone forth against me."*

With this clarification from her mother-in-law, Orpah is convinced through tears to return to her own people and her own pagan gods. By the way, the pagan gods of the Moabite religion were many. The chief demonic god was named Chemosh, which had various meanings like "destroyer," "subduer," or "fish god." With the departure of Orpah, Noami made one more attempt to dissuade Ruth from coming with her.

> Ruth 1:14–15: *And they lifted up their voices and wept again; and Orpah kissed her mother-in-law, but Ruth clung to her. Then she said, "Behold, your sister-in-law has gone back to her people and her gods; return after your sister-in-law."*

THE RESTORATION

Courage to Follow and to Care

Ruth was not going back to her own people or her false gods because we understand, from her famous declaration to Naomi, that she had come to faith in the one true God of Israel. These promises of trust and support are found in Ruth 1:16–17:

> But Ruth said, "Do not urge me to leave you or turn back from following you; for where you go, I will go, and where you lodge, I will lodge. Your people shall be my people, and your God, my God. Where you die, I will die, and there I will be buried. Thus may the LORD do to me, and worse, if anything but death parts you and me."

Remind yourself of Ruth's circumstances: for ten years she had a childless marriage. Naomi wanted to leave her in Moab. Now we see Ruth's heart and discover that she desired to follow Naomi but more importantly, she desired to follow the God of Israel. When Ruth had this strong push from Naomi to return to her people and her own gods, she chose to follow Naomi, to live where she lived, to identify with Naomi's people, and to follow Naomi's God until she died. There were no promises of security for Ruth. There was no assurance of her ever having a husband or children of her own, yet she was "all in" to follow Naomi, and more importantly, the God of Naomi.

She completely gave herself to the God of Israel despite the bitter witness of her mother-in-law. Do you find this astonishing? How can Ruth have had such faith, such commitment, and the strength to even speak much less follow through these promises of faithfulness?

Look into this determination that Naomi couldn't argue with:

> Ruth 1:18 (definitions, emphasis added): *When she* (Naomi) *saw that she* (Ruth) *was **determined** to go with her, she said no more to her.*

The word "determined" in Hebrew is *ametz* and it means "resolute," "courageous," and "to strengthen." When Joshua was about to enter into the Promised Land, God exhorted him in Joshua 1:9,

> *Have I not commanded you? Be strong and courageous! Do not tremble or be dismayed, for the LORD your God is with you wherever you go.*

This command to *be strong and courageous* was repeated four times in the first chapter of Joshua and again in Joshua 10:25. Each time this command was given, it was a reference to God's strength and courage that He would supply during the challenges both Joshua and the nation of Israel would face.

When Naomi saw this courage or determination (*ametz*) in Ruth, it prevented Naomi from trying to persuade Ruth to return to her false gods. Where did Ruth receive such courage when she had no strength or courage of her own? Where but from the Lord God of Israel? The Lord knew the plans He had for Ruth and Naomi. As Ruth was seeking the Lord with all her heart, she found Him. God directed her paths and continued to give her the courage she needed each step of the way. Ruth found her courage and determination to follow Naomi from the LORD God of Israel. She had no guarantees of acceptance and provision from Naomi; in fact, it was just the opposite. But Ruth's heart followed after God.

Is This Naomi?

When Ruth and Naomi got back to Bethlehem, the entire city was stirred. A noisy crowd gathered to receive Naomi and Ruth when they arrived back in the House of Bread.

> Ruth 1:19: *So they both went until they came to Bethlehem. And when they had come to Bethlehem, all the city was stirred because of them, and the women said, "Is this Naomi?"*

Why were the women who knew Naomi in such disbelief? People might have expected Naomi to have a few more grey hairs, but when she came home, Naomi looked more like a beggar than the wealthy wife of Elimelech who left a little over ten years ago. She had nothing to show for all those years.

What was Naomi's response to such a question?

> Ruth 1:20-21: *She said to them, "Do not call me Naomi; call me Mara, for the Almighty has dealt very bitterly with me. I went out full, but the LORD has brought me back empty. Why do you call me Naomi, since the LORD has witnessed against me and the Almighty has afflicted me?"*

The name *Naomi* is based on the Hebrew word for "pleasant" (*naiim*). One familiar place this word is used is in Psalm 133:1: *Behold, how good and how pleasant it is for brothers to dwell together in unity!* Naomi is truly a beautiful name, however here she revealed the innermost bitterness of her heart. Naomi wanted them to call her Mara, which means "bitter." At Passover, we eat bitter herbs or *moror* to remember the bitterness of bondage and here Naomi asked to be reminded of her bitter life as she told the women to call her Mara.

Notice that she told them *the Almighty has dealt very bitterly* with her and, furthermore, she accused this same Almighty of testifying against her and afflicting her.

Who is this Almighty One? In Hebrew "Almighty" is *Shaddai* and it is a word that describes not only power, but also power that is all bountiful. The LORD God revealed Himself to Abram as *El Shaddai* in Genesis 17:1:

> *When Abram was ninety-nine years old, the LORD appeared to Abram and said to him, "I am Almighty God (El Shaddai); walk before Me and be blameless"* (NKJV).

Job's advice about the Almighty could have helped Naomi understand how she should have responded to the LORD:

> Job 5:17: *Behold, how happy is the man whom God reproves, so do not despise the discipline of the Almighty* (Shaddai).

When Naomi accused the Almighty of afflicting her, I wonder if she had entirely overlooked how she and her family left Bethlehem. Even in her own words she told the women that she "*went out full*," meaning when they left there was an abundance of food and supplies but she had returned "*empty*." In other words, in Naomi's mind, even though she left with plenty, she is now returning empty, without any resources. What a false perception a bitter heart can give. Who was standing next to her? Naomi completely disregarded Ruth, who had totally committed herself to her and was her constant encourager. Because of her bitterness toward the Lord, Naomi did not see Ruth, her most valuable blessing, standing next to her.

Application: Has This Ever Happened to You?

Take time to examine your heart and mind to see if bitterness has clouded your perception of the blessings God is providing for you and the answers to prayer He has given you. Ask the Lord to reveal to you if there is hidden unforgiveness that is leading to bitterness. Confess this unforgiveness and bitterness to God and take time to praise Him. (Read Psalm 103 or Psalm 51 or another meaningful passage.)

Redemption for Naomi

There was good news in this narrative. Naomi's life changed as she discovered the blessings God was providing her in Ruth. Through Ruth's love and willingness to follow Naomi's instructions, the Lord used her to powerfully draw her mother-in-law back into the arms of *El Shaddai*, the Almighty God who became her *Av HaRachmiim*—the Father of Mercies.

Ruth Takes Center Stage

At last, Ruth was about to become a main character in her love story. And every love story needs a hero, to whom we are introduced in Ruth 2:1:

> *Now Naomi had a kinsman of her husband, a man of great wealth, of the family of Elimelech, whose name was Boaz.*

We concluded our study of Rahab with the joyful news that she and her husband had a son named Boaz. This same Boaz was the man we're told here was a very close relative of Naomi's husband. We were also told that Boaz was "*a man of great wealth*" in Hebrew is *chayil gibbor* which literally means "a man of powerful might." In this short verse, we are given important information about our hero: Boaz was not only a very close relative to Naomi, but he was also a man of valor and strength with resources that could make a difference in the poverty-stricken situation of Naomi and Ruth. Even his name "Boaz" means "one who is a pillar of strength."

Not Afraid of Back-Breaking Work

Their love story started at the beginning of the barley harvest, which takes place in the early part of May. The timing was ideal for Ruth to find work as a gleaner in the fields of Bethlehem.

In order to help the poor and the strangers, Israel was warned by God not to reap the corners of their fields or gather the gleanings of the harvest. The gleaners were the poor and the strangers who welcomed the chance to provide sustenance for themselves, even if it meant back-breaking labor of picking up the small pieces of grain which had fallen around the corners of the field (Leviticus 19:9–10). This was not easy work, but for a person without money or land, it was a way to feed yourself.

Ruth asked permission from Naomi to glean in order that they might have food to eat. But notice how she phrases her request.

> Ruth 2:2 (emphasis added): *And Ruth the Moabitess said to Naomi, "Please let me go to the field and glean among the ears of grain after one **in whose sight I may find favor**." And she said to her, "Go, my daughter."*

Ruth used an expression found throughout the Scriptures: to find "*one in whose sight I may find favor*." This expression was used by a person of inferior status to refer to someone who is of higher authority. This was clearly seen in the conversation that Moses was having with God. It is obvious that God is in a position of higher authority than Moses.

> Exodus 33:12–14 (CJB): *Moshe said to ADONAI, "Look, you say to me, 'Make these people move on!' But you haven't let me know whom you will be sending with me. Nevertheless, you have said, 'I know you by name,' and also, 'You have found favor in my sight.' Now, please, if it is really the case **that I have found favor in your sight**, show me your ways; so that I will understand you and continue finding favor in your sight. Moreover, keep on seeing this nation as your people." He answered, "Set your mind at rest—my presence will go with you, after all."*

Moses sought favor in the sight of God, because he knew he could not lead without God's favor in his life. Ruth understood that as a stranger, she needed to find grace or favor in the eyes of those who managed the fields for harvesting.

Ruth's statement was also an acknowledgment to Naomi that she was willing to work hard but that God would have to give her the open door of grace. Ruth 2:3 pictures for us the absolute providential care that was at work in Ruth's life:

> Ruth 2:3: *So she departed and went and gleaned in the field after the reapers; and she happened to come to the portion of the field belonging to Boaz, who was of the family of Elimelech.*

In the next verse Boaz, who owned the field, appeared— and had a very interesting conversation with his head reaper:

> Ruth 2:5–7: *Then Boaz said to his servant who was in charge of the reapers, "Whose young woman is this?" The servant in charge of the reapers replied, "She is the young Moabite woman who returned with Naomi from the land of Moab. And she said, 'Please let me glean and gather after the reapers among the sheaves.' Thus she came and has remained from the morning until now; she has been sitting in the house for a little while."*

Ruth Finds Favor in the Sight of Boaz

Boaz didn't waste any time but immediately went to Ruth and said:

> Ruth 2:8–9: *"Listen carefully, my daughter. Do not go to glean in another field; furthermore, do not go on from this one, but stay here with my maids. Let your eyes be on the field which they reap, and go after them. Indeed, I have commanded the servants not to touch you. When you are*

thirsty, go to the water jars and drink from what the servants draw."

Here Boaz gave Ruth his protection from those who would seek to do harm or prey upon the gleaners who were at the edges of the fields. Boaz put Ruth among his women who were working in the fields so she would be safe and cared for while reaping.

Ruth's answer revealed her surprise at his gracious behavior to her:

Ruth 2:10: *Then she fell on her face, bowing to the ground and said to him, "Why have I found favor in your sight that you should take notice of me, since I am a foreigner?"*

And Boaz replied to her,

Ruth 2:11-12*: "All that you have done for your mother-in-law after the death of your husband has been fully reported to me, and how you left your father and your mother and the land of your birth, and came to a people that you did not previously know. May the LORD reward your work, and your wages be full from the LORD, the God of Israel, under whose wings you have come to seek refuge."*

Ruth was a stranger no more. Her faith in the God of Israel made her part of the family of God. Boaz pronounced a blessing for her, wherein he asked God to reward her fully for all she had done. He asked God to help her know His peace, His protection, and His provision because she chose to find her safe haven in the God of Israel.

What Does it Mean for the Lord to Reward Her Work?

Let's take a closer look at Ruth 2:12 and this blessing from Boaz:

> *May the LORD reward your work, and your wages be full from the LORD, the God of Israel, under whose wings you have come to seek refuge.*

Do you think that Ruth was looking for a reward for her work? As a lowly gleaner, she was just hoping to pick up enough pieces of grain to provide food for Naomi and herself. This labor was a matter of survival in this new land. What kind of a blessing was Boaz giving to Ruth? The word "reward" is based on the Hebrew word *shalem* which means "complete." *Shalem* is from the well-known Hebrew word *shalom* which means "peace, wholeness, completeness." The form that is used in Ruth 2:12 is found elsewhere with the meaning of "restitution, restoration, or pay back." As found in Psalm 62:12 (CJB, definition added):

> *Also to you, Adonai, belongs grace, for you reward* (shalem) *all as their deeds deserve.*

Boaz blessed Ruth as the Lord's daughter who would find her completeness and wholeness in serving the God of Israel.

Do We Get Rewards for Our Work?

God wants the same blessing for all His daughters. When we serve the LORD out of a heart of love, the reward we seek is to know that our labor is not in vain in the Lord, and our ways are pleasing to Him. The imperfect tense of the verb *shalem* indicates that what God was doing, right then,—in the present tense for Ruth—He will continue to do in and through her life. For us as well, all that we are able to do for His glory is accomplished by His grace. God recognizes and rewards the faith of all who serve Him by relying on His strength. He continually gives us His shalom as we serve in His power.

> Philippians 1:6: *For I am confident of this very thing, that He who began a good work in you will perfect it until the day of Messiah Yeshua.*

Philippians 4:13: *I can do all things through Him who strengthens me.*

Ephesians 2:8–10: *For by grace you have been saved through faith; and that not of yourselves, it is the gift of God; not as a result of works, so that no one may boast. For we are His workmanship, created in Messiah Yeshua for good works, which God prepared beforehand so that we would walk in them.*

What were the works that God had prepared for Ruth to walk in? As she yielded herself to the God of Israel and was strengthened by Him, she became a blessing to not only her mother-in-law but to the whole house of Israel. Officially her job was "gleaner," but her work for the Lord was to be His instrument of blessing through her work.

Depending on the various seasons of our lives, we all have had different jobs and varied roles. I love my new role of being a grandmother of two wonderful grandsons. Many of you reading this book may have at least two full-time jobs, which could include motherhood, and another vocation, such as teacher or lawyer. In whatever season of life, we are in we are encouraged by Paul to understand that we are serving the Messiah and our labor is never in vain in the Lord.

Colossians 3:23–24: *Whatever you do, do your work heartily, as for the Lord rather than for men, knowing that from the Lord you will receive the reward of the inheritance. It is the Lord Messiah whom you serve.*

1 Corinthians 15:58: *Therefore, my beloved brethren, be steadfast, immovable, always abounding in the work of the Lord, knowing that your toil is not in vain in the Lord.*

The Lord is My Reward

Let's dig a little deeper and look at the second phrase of Ruth 2:12: "... *and your wages be full from the LORD.*" Not only did the reward from the Lord give Ruth recognition for her faithfulness to God, but this reward also acknowledged God's faithfulness to Ruth.

The word that Boaz uses in this phrase, "wages," is *maskoret* in Hebrew from the root *sacar*. This word is first used in Genesis 15:1 when the Lord spoke to Abram:

> After this, the word of the LORD came to Abram in a vision: "Do not be afraid, Abram. I am your shield, your very great reward" (NIV).

The *"great reward"* (*sacar*) for Abram is the same reward for all who have the faith of Abraham. The great reward is God Himself. For Abram, and for ourselves as well, it's only through Yeshua that our lives can be complete and fulfilled. He is our reward, the recompense that makes our life worth living. As the Messiah declares to His followers in John 10:10:

> "The thief comes only to steal and kill and destroy; I came that they may have life, and have it abundantly."

It's such a privilege to be given Yeshua's abundant, eternal life as my own! Oh, how He desires to bless us! We can have such hope each day, because God assures us—as Yeshua said to Paul—*"My grace is sufficient for you, for power is perfected in weakness"* (2 Cor 12:9).

> Ephesians 3:20-21: Now to Him who is able to do far more abundantly beyond all that we ask or think, according to the power that works within us, to Him be the glory...

The Ultimate Protection and Refuge

The conclusion of his blessing in Ruth 12:2 is a beautiful picture of God's protection: *"... the God of Israel, under whose wings you have come to seek refuge."*

The word "refuge" means "to seek shelter," and implies having trust, confidence, and dependence upon. Just like Ruth whose hope in God was her place of refuge, we find this same shelter as we seek the Lord, acknowledging our need for His protection and security.

> Psalm 2:12: *Do homage to the Son, that He not become angry, and you perish in the way, for His wrath may soon be kindled. How blessed are all who take refuge in Him.*

A Love Story Orchestrated by the God of Israel

The rest of the book of Ruth weaves in the beautiful love theme of Naomi's restoration from her bitterness. Once more Naomi came to believe in the goodness of God. Under Naomi's guidance, Ruth approached Boaz at the end of the harvest and requested that he become her kinsman redeemer. Boaz was more than happy to redeem her and the property of Naomi. He just had to ask another closer relative first, who, as it turns out, was unable to marry Ruth. This redemption transaction was a public affair witnessed by all the elders and community of Bethlehem as recorded in Ruth chapter four.

> Ruth 4:9–12: *Then Boaz said to the elders and all the people, "You are witnesses today that I have bought from the hand of Naomi all that belonged to Elimelech and all that belonged to Chilion and Mahlon. Moreover, I have acquired Ruth the Moabitess, the widow of Mahlon, to be my wife in order to raise up the name of the deceased on his inheritance, so that the name of the deceased will not be cut off from his brothers or from the court of his birth place; you are witnesses today." All the people who were in the court, and the elders, said, "We are witnesses. May the Lord make the woman who is coming into your home like Rachel and Leah, both of whom built the house of Israel; and may you achieve wealth in Ephrathah and become famous in Bethlehem. Moreover, may your house be like the house of Perez whom Tamar bore to Judah, through the offspring which the Lord will give you by this young woman."*

Wow! What a blessing the elders gave to Boaz—that his wife Ruth would build up the House of Israel. And in verse twelve, our genealogy of grace was merged together with the house of Perez, the breaker. Do you get the idea that this love story was full of blessings and surprising grace at every turn?

Wedding Bells and a New Baby

Ruth 4:13: So Boaz took Ruth, and she became his wife, and he went in to her. And the LORD *enabled her to conceive, and she gave birth to a son.*

Note that it was the covenant God of Israel, the Lord, who made it possible for Ruth to get pregnant and give birth. Remember how the women of Bethlehem responded to Naomi when she first arrived? They were incredulous as they looked on her poverty and bitterness. However, the faith of just one Moabite woman and her willing kinsman redeemer changed everything! Then those same women gave their own blessing to Naomi.

Ruth 4:14–16: Then the women said to Naomi, "Blessed is the LORD *who has not left you without a redeemer today, and may his name become famous in Israel. May he also be to you a restorer of life and a sustainer of your old age; for your daughter-in-law, who loves you and is better to you than seven sons, has given birth to him." Then Naomi took the child and laid him in her lap, and became his nurse.*

Talk about a turnaround! Naomi heard those women proclaim that God had redeemed her. God became her *Goel*, her Redeemer, by providing Boaz. The women proclaimed that the child born to Ruth will be to Naomi "*a restorer of life.*" In Hebrew "restore" is *shuv* or "return back." Life is expressed in the word *nefesh*, which means one's soul, the inner person that includes our desires. And don't miss the last verse in the portion above, where Naomi was intimately involved with raising her grandson!

It seems that these same women who gave the blessing to Naomi, also gave Ruth's son his name.

> Ruth 4:17: *The neighbor women gave him a name, saying, "A son has been born to Naomi!" So they named him Oved (Obed). He is the father of Jesse, the father of David.*

What a beautiful way to conclude this love story of redemption! God's grace was lavishly poured out on Ruth, enabling her in turn to show God's mercy and lovingkindness to her mother-in-law. This was a twofold love story that exhibited much more than a romance and marriage. This story exhibited the deep sacrificial love of Ruth to Naomi and also the redeeming love of Boaz to both Ruth and Naomi.

The Servant of the Lord: Another Title for Messiah Yeshua

The women of Bethlehem gave the name of Oved (Obed) to Ruth and Boaz's baby. This name is from the Hebrew *oved*, which means "one who serves" or "one who worships." *Oved* or *avodah*, depending on the context, can mean either worship or service.

The Hebrew name, Oved, points us to the ultimate Servant who came to seek and to save us from our sins. Yeshua is called the Servant of the LORD in Isaiah. The prophet was telling us that God's salvation would reach both Israel and the whole world through His Servant. Isaiah prophesied that only the Servant of the Lord would bring both Israel and the nations back to God. God spoke through the prophet in Isaiah 49:6:

> He says, *"It is too small a thing that You should be My Servant to raise up the tribes of Jacob and to restore the preserved ones of Israel; I will also make You a light of the nations so that My salvation may reach to the end of the earth."*

When God proclaims, "... *So that My salvation may reach to the end of the earth,*" the phrase "my salvation" is *Yeshuati* in Hebrew and means "my Yeshua" or "my Salvation." Here it was clearly stated that God's Yeshua is the Servant who will save not only Israel but all the nations of the world who come to Him. In Isaiah 49:6, God also declared that His Servant would be a light to the nations. The New Covenant reiterates how Yeshua fulfilled His calling.

> John 1:1–5: *In the beginning was the Word, and the Word was with God, and the Word was God. He was in the beginning with God. All things came into being through Him, and apart from Him nothing came into being that has come into being. In Him was life, and the life was the Light of men. The Light shines in the darkness, and the darkness did not comprehend it.*

> John 8:12: *Then Yeshua again spoke to them, saying, "I am the Light of the world; he who follows Me will not walk in the darkness, but will have the Light of life."*

Paul testified that Messiah Yeshua did bring salvation to Israel and the nations. In Ephesians 2:12–14, Paul explained how Messiah became a servant to all of those who accepted His way of salvation. Only in Yeshua's shalom can both Jews and the nations be made one.

> Ephesians 2:12–14: *remember that you were at that time separate from Messiah, excluded from the commonwealth of Israel, and strangers to the covenants of promise, having no hope and without God in the world. But now in Messiah Yeshua you who formerly were far off have been brought near by the blood of Messiah. For He Himself is our peace, who made both groups into one and broke down the barrier of the dividing wall.*

We can be forever encouraged by the lives of Ruth the Moabite and Boaz the mighty Israelite from the tribe of Judah. They came together in God's covenant love forming another link in His redemptive chain. Ruth and Boaz were the great-grandparents of King David, building the royal line of the Messiah of Israel.

Be encouraged to know that God's promises will never fail you. Remember His promises for us through the prophet Jeremiah and mediate on one of your favorite promises that the LORD has made in your life.

> Jeremiah 29:11–13: *'For I know the plans that I have for you,' declares the LORD, 'plans for welfare and not for calamity to give you a future and a hope. Then you will call upon Me and come and pray to Me, and I will listen to you. You will seek Me and find Me when you search for Me with all your heart.*

APPLICATION: WHERE DO I LOOK FOR BREAD IN A FAMINE?

The cautionary tale of Elimelech and Naomi should make us reflect. How do we respond when we are in a season of famine? When I reflect on my own spiritual journey with the Lord, I confess to finding myself many times with a scarcity of resources—in a season of spiritual drought. But instead of seeking the Lord first, I allowed worry to take over my life, thus turning to alternative, unsatisfying sources for nourishment. Thankfully, over the years of my walk of faith, I have been growing little by little into the same truths that God desired to teach the children of Israel in their wilderness wanderings. God is clear about what He wants us to learn during our times of famine. It states in Deuteronomy 8:3:

> *He humbled you and let you be hungry, and fed you with manna which you did not know, nor did your fathers know, that He might make you understand that man does not live by bread alone, but man lives by everything that proceeds out of the mouth of the LORD.*

Learn from Yeshua

At the very beginning of His earthly ministry, after Yeshua had been fasting and praying for forty days, Yeshua repeats this same verse from Deuteronomy as a rebuke to Satan:

> *...being tempted by the devil. And He (Yeshua) ate nothing during those days, and when they had ended, He became hungry. And the devil said to Him, "If You are the Son of God, tell this stone to become bread." And Yeshua answered him, "It is written, 'Man shall not live on bread alone'"* (Luke 4:2–4, definition added).

In Yeshua's Sermon on the Mount, He also gave His followers divine teaching on the matter of food and our treasures found in Matthew 6:24–32. The section gave us the ultimate cure for anxiety and worry. At the end of His teaching, Yeshua provided us with His conclusion on all these matters.

> Matthew 6:33–34: *But seek first His kingdom and His righteousness, and all these things will be added to you. So do not worry about tomorrow; for tomorrow will care for itself. Each day has enough trouble of its own.*

Learn from King David

King David understood the absolute need to seek God first during times of famine. He eloquently expressed these truths in Psalm 37:16–19:

> *Better is the little of the righteous than the abundance of many wicked. For the arms of the wicked will be broken, but the LORD sustains the righteous. The LORD knows the days of the blameless, and their inheritance will be forever. They will not be ashamed in the time of evil, and in the days of famine they will have abundance.*

In Psalm 37, David promised that in days of famine, God's children will have an abundance. Yeshua taught us the same principle in Matthew 5:6:

> *Blessed are those who hunger and thirst for righteousness, for they shall be satisfied.*

In other words, if we as followers of Yeshua seek His righteousness and His Kingdom first, there will never be a lack. We always have complete satisfaction guaranteed!

David then reiterated that when we follow the Lord, He will order and direct our spiritual walk in Him. There is a beautiful assurance in Psalm 37:25. David looked back over his life and declared that God had never forsaken him nor allowed his family to beg for bread.

> Psalm 37:23–26: *The steps of a man are established by the LORD, and He delights in his way. When he falls, he will not be hurled headlong, because the LORD is the One who*

266

holds his hand. I have been young and now I am old, yet I have not seen the righteous forsaken or his descendants begging bread. All day long he is gracious and lends, and his descendants are a blessing.

But notice what David said in verse twenty-four: *"when he falls, God is still holding his hand."* I know that many times when I have fallen, I have turned aside in despair thinking that God did not care about my situation or my specific prayer need. During these times of famine, I would begin to stumble in unbelief. However, despite my unfaithfulness, I found that God was and is always faithful, never letting go of my hand. Even when I make mistakes—big or small—as soon as I turn back to God and confess to Him, He is always there to forgive and restore me to an intimate relationship with Himself. For you as well, when you turn back to God and confess your sins according to 1 John 1:9, God is always faithful to forgive and restore you to Himself:

> *If we confess our sins, He is faithful and righteous to forgive us our sins and to cleanse us from all unrighteousness..*

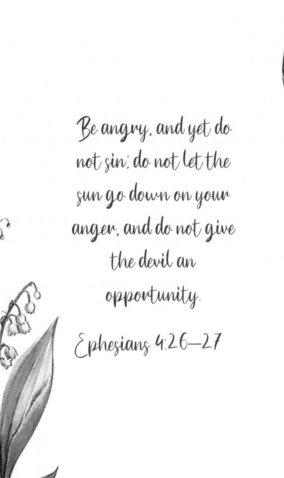

Be angry, and yet do
not sin; do not let the
sun go down on your
anger, and do not give
the devil an
opportunity.

Ephesians 4:26–27

Nine

Wisdom & Beauty: Abigail

In this chapter we will meet a wise Israeli woman named Abigail (*Avi Gayeel*—My Father is Joy). Her importance in the redemptive line of Messiah was crucial because God used her to prevent David from ruining his reputation while he was on the run from King Saul. Before David had a chance to establish his kingdom, he could have greatly damaged his standing. God provided Abigail, a woman of courage, humility, and wisdom to intercede and keep David from disgrace.

THE PROMISE

In the redemptive plan of God, the next milestone on the road to the Messiah was His covenant promise to His servant David. The promise was this:

> *Now therefore, thus you shall say to My servant David, "Thus says the LORD of hosts, 'I took you from the pasture, from following the sheep, to be ruler over My people Israel. I have been with you wherever you have gone and have cut off all your enemies from before you; and I will make you a great name, like the names of the great men who*

are on the earth. I will also appoint a place for My people Israel and will plant them, that they may live in their own place and not be disturbed again, nor will the wicked afflict them any more as formerly, even from the day that I commanded judges to be over My people Israel; and I will give you rest from all your enemies. The LORD also declares to you that the LORD will make a house for you. When your days are complete and you lie down with your fathers, I will raise up your descendant after you, who will come forth from you, and I will establish his kingdom. He shall build a house for My name, and I will establish the throne of his kingdom forever. I will be a father to him and he will be a son to Me; when he commits iniquity, I will correct him with the rod of men and the strokes of the sons of men, but My lovingkindness shall not depart from him, as I took it away from Saul, whom I removed from before you. Your house and your kingdom shall endure before Me forever; your throne shall be established forever'" (2 Sam 7:8-16).

Before this covenant promise was given, though, you could argue that David had already had an impressive career. He'd fought a giant, been anointed as the next king, and the current king had tried to assassinate him. We'll pick up the story with the death of Samuel, the prophet who anointed David and guided him. When Samuel died, it is unlikely that David could mourn properly—David was living on the run, constantly in fear of being killed by King Saul.

1 Samuel 25:1: *Then Samuel died; and all Israel gathered together and mourned for him, and buried him at his house in Ramah. And David arose and went down to the wilderness of Paran.*

Abigail and Nabal

In 1 Samuel 25:2–3, the Scriptures present Abigail and her husband Nabal:

Now there was a man in Maon whose business was in Carmel; and the man was very rich, and he had three thousand sheep and a thousand goats. And it came about while he was shearing his sheep in Carmel (now the man's name was Nabal, and his wife's name was Abigail. And the woman was intelligent and beautiful in appearance, but the man was harsh and evil in his dealings, and he was a Calebite).

What was the description of Abigail in that passage? It stated that she was *"intelligent and beautiful."* These single words in English are two-word Hebrew phrases: "Intelligent" is *tovah sekhel* or "good understanding." *Tovah* is the adjective of *tov* meaning "good" and modifies *sekhel. Sekhel* is well-known to Yiddish speakers. It is a word that means having wise judgment and common sense. When someone does something wise or discerning, you'd say: "She has real *sekhel!*" One can be intelligent but not necessarily display common sense, or *sekhel*, but as we will discover, Abigail was both wise and discerning.

Abigail was also described as *beautiful in appearance— yafat tohar*, which means beautiful of form and face. This was the same description is used in Genesis 29:17 for Rachel, who, we remember, was gorgeous too. *Yafat* is the adjective of *yaffa*, which means "pretty" and *tohar* is "form."

Abigail's husband Nabal was described as harsh, which is *kasha* in Hebrew. This same word *kasha* was used to describe the Jewish people in Exodus 33:5, where it was translated as obstinate.

For the Lord had said to Moses, "Say to the sons of Israel, 'You are an obstinate (kasha) people...'"

Nabal was also evil in his deeds; *raah* is the most common word translated as "evil," and so it is here. Nabal was a Calebite, from the line of Caleb, which means he was from the tribe of Judah.

THE PROBLEM

So What Exactly Happened Here?

David was in the wilderness, hiding from Saul In the next verse of the narrative there is a request from David's men to Nabal:

> It came about...that David heard in the wilderness that Nabal was shearing his sheep. So David sent ten young men; and David said to the young men, "Go up to Carmel, visit Nabal and greet him in my name; and thus you shall say, 'Have a long life, **peace** be to you, and **peace** be to your house, and **peace** be to all that you have. Now I have heard that you have shearers; now your shepherds have been with us and we have not insulted them, nor have they missed anything all the days they were in Carmel. Ask your young men and they will tell you. Therefore let my young men find favor in your eyes (motza chen b'eynaiim), for we have come on a festive (tov) day. Please give whatever you find at hand to your servants and to your son David'"
> (1 Samuel 25:2,4–8, emphasis, definitions added)

How Did That Cause a Problem?

Did you notice how courteous David's men were? David instructed them to explain that while Nabal's shepherds were working in the fields, they had treated them with respect and provided protection from robbers. Now that it was sheep-shearing time, which included celebrations with plenty of food for everyone, they desired to find favor in his eyes because of those men they had protected, Nabal's shepherds. It was a time to share in the plentiful provisions.

Nabal's Response Was a Problem

> 1 Samuel 25:10–11: But Nabal answered David's servants and said, "Who is David? And who is the son of Jesse? There are many servants today who are each breaking away from his master. Shall **I** then take **my** bread and **my** water

and **my** meat that **I** have slaughtered for **my** shearers, and give it to men whose origin **I** do not know" (emphasis added)?

Nabal's answer to David's servants was rude and demeaning to them and to their leader David. Of course Nabal would have known who David was: the mighty warrior who killed Goliath and gave Israel victory over many of their enemies! Nabal chose to reject David's anointing as the future king of Israel and then pretended to be poor and to not have enough food for his own men. Remember in 1 Samuel 25:2, Nabal was described as "*very rich, and he had three thousand sheep and a thousand goats.*" Nabal's name means "fool," so keep this in mind as we read this parable of Yeshua about the rich man whom Yeshua called a fool.

How did the response of Nabal resemble the rich man in Yeshua's parable?

> Luke 12:16–23 *And Yeshua told them a parable, saying, "The land of a rich man was very productive. And he began reasoning to himself, saying, 'What shall I do, since I have no place to store my crops?' Then he said, 'This is what I will do: I will tear down my barns and build larger ones, and there I will store all my grain and my goods. And I will say to my soul, "Soul, you have many goods laid up for many years to come; take your ease, eat, drink and be merry."' "But God said to him, 'You fool! This very night your soul is required of you; and now who will own what you have prepared?' So is the man who stores up treasure for himself, and is not rich toward God." And He said to His disciples, "For this reason I say to you, do not worry about your life, as to what you will eat; nor for your body, as to what you will put on. For life is more than food, and the body more than clothing."*

Notice that the fool Nabal and the rich fool in Yeshua's parable constantly speak of "me, myself and I," which reflects their self-centeredness. They completely disregarded the LORD. Nabal in his stinginess and arrogance responded like the "rich man" in the parable.

And It's Even Worse Than That

Nabal also emulated Satan in his prideful attitude. We have a description of the fall of Lucifer in Isaiah:

> Isaiah 14:12–14 (emphasis added): *"How you have fallen from heaven, O star of the morning, son of the dawn! You have been cut down to the earth, you who have weakened the nations!* ***But you said in your heart, 'I will ascend to heaven; I will raise my throne above the stars of God, and I will sit on the mount of assembly in the recesses of the north. I will ascend above the heights of the clouds; I will make myself like the Most High.'"***

Please note from this portion that Satan refers at least five times to himself with "I will" to describe how he would ascend above God and take God's place. The fool Nabal in his riches and pride deemed himself an invincible man who could do what he wanted.

Here Comes Trouble

How did David respond when his men came back to report to him?

> 1 Samuel 25:12–13: *So David's young men retraced their way and went back; and they came and told him according to all these words. David said to his men, "Each of you gird on his sword." So each man girded on his sword. And David also girded on his sword, and about four hundred men went up behind David while two hundred stayed with the baggage.*

Rage. He responded with rage. We read of David's true intent later:

1 Samuel 25:21–22: Now David had said, "Surely in vain I have guarded all that this man has in the wilderness, so that nothing was missed of all that belonged to him; and he has returned me evil for good. May God do so to the enemies of David, and more also, if by morning I leave as much as one male of any who belong to him."

And Explosive Overreaction

How can a seemingly small thing like Nabal's refusal to invite David's men to the party cause David to get so angry? From 1 Samuel 25:22, we understand that David's plan was to kill all the males in Nabal's household. This slaughter of these innocent males of all ages would have surely caused David to lose his testimony, first to his own men, and then to the greater community around them.

We should note that this is in stark contrast to the previous chapter in 1 Samuel, where we find the account of how David responded when he had the "perfect" opportunity to kill Saul. The Scriptures record this account:

1 Samuel 24:2–7: Then Saul took three thousand chosen men from all Israel and went to seek David and his men in front of the Rocks of the Wild Goats. He came to the sheepfolds on the way, where there was a cave; and Saul went in to relieve himself. Now David and his men were sitting in the inner recesses of the cave. The men of David said to him, "Behold, this is the day of which the LORD said to you, 'Behold; I am about to give your enemy into your hand, and you shall do to him as it seems good to you.'" Then David arose and cut off the edge of Saul's robe secretly. It came about afterward that David's conscience bothered him because he had cut off the edge of Saul's robe. So he said to his men, "Far be it from me because of the LORD that I should do this thing to my lord, the LORD's anointed, to stretch out my hand against him, since he is the LORD's anointed." David persuaded his men with these

*words and did not allow them to rise up against Saul. And
Saul arose, left the cave, and went on his way.*

David's men thought he should take Saul's life since Saul
was vulnerable and unguarded in the cave. They wanted
David to "take matters into his own hands" by having him kill
Saul and take the throne. By contrast, David's words and
actions were honoring to the Lord as David pointed his men to
God's choice and God's plan.

What had taken place in David's life between Saul's cave
and Nabal's field that led him to plan a murderous slaughter
of Nabal's men? Was he mourning the loss of his mentor
Samuel? The Scriptures don't reveal exactly why, but let's
consider our own lives. Are you ever surprised by an
overreaction of anger and rage in your life?

Application: On Guard Against Our Emotions

The Scriptures give us instructions as to how we can guard
against such an overreaction when an unexpected difficult
situation arises. We are exhorted in Hebrews 12:15:

> *See to it that no one comes short of the grace of God; that
> no root of bitterness springing up causes trouble, and by
> it many be defiled.*

There is also the teaching about the "little foxes spoiling
the vines" found in Song of Solomon 2:15–16:

> *Catch the foxes for us, the little foxes that are ruining the
> vineyards, while our vineyards are in blossom. My beloved
> is mine, and I am his; He pastures his flock among the
> lilies.*

Here the Shulamite woman said that those little foxes are
devious. When the vineyards were producing their best fruit,
the foxes would sneak into the vineyards and ruin the vines.
However instead of doubting her beloved's love, the Shulamite
woman affirmed his love and his presence in the pastures. She

declared the truth about her beloved when she said: *My beloved is mine, and I am his* (see Song of Solomon 6:3).

The evil one comes to steal and destroy our trust in the true promises of God. The false prophets of Israel are compared to the cunning foxes who disseminate ruin.

> Ezekiel 13:3-4: *Thus says the Lord GOD, "Woe to the foolish prophets who are following their own spirit and have seen nothing. O Israel, your prophets have been like foxes among ruins."*

When we are offended and ridiculed, we must remember what Paul taught us in Romans 12:18–19:

> *If possible, so far as it depends on you, be at peace with all men. Never take your own revenge, beloved, but leave room for the wrath of God, for it is written, "Vengeance is Mine, I will repay," says the Lord.*

In summary, we must always remember that it is *the little foxes* that ruin the vine (Song of Solomon 2:15), which can cause us to fall short of God's grace (Hebrews 12:15), to allow distrust to creep in, and to give ear to false teaching (Ezekiel 13:3).

David did not take time to pray or seek God! He disregarded the fact that vengeance belongs to the Lord (Romans 12:19). He also ignored the truth and responsibility that he was the Lord's anointed who would one day be king of Israel.

We must always remember that Yeshua is the True Vine and we are the branches. Unless we abide (*meno* in Greek means "to stick like glue") in Him, we cannot bear good fruit (see John 15:1–5). If you are not abiding in Yeshua the True Vine, then the "little foxes" that you allow to enter your life will destroy the good fruit that Yeshua desires for us to produce (see John 15:8, 16; Ephesians 2:10).

How does God want us to respond to a situation that causes us great anger?

> Ephesians 4:26–32: *Be angry, and yet do not sin; do not let the sun go down on your anger, and do not give the devil an opportunity. He who steals must steal no longer; but rather he must labor, performing with his own hands what is good, so that he will have something to share with one who has need. Let no unwholesome word proceed from your mouth, but only such a word as is good for edification according to the need of the moment, so that it will give grace to those who hear. Do not grieve the Holy Spirit of God, by whom you were sealed for the day of redemption. Let all bitterness and wrath and anger and clamor and slander be put away from you, along with all malice. Be kind to one another, tender-hearted, forgiving each other, just as God in Messiah also has forgiven you.*

THE RESTORATION

A Woman in an Emergency

Abigail was informed of the impending danger for all her household and took action:

> 1 Samuel 25:14–19: *But one of the young men told Abigail, Nabal's wife, saying, "Behold, David sent messengers from the wilderness to greet our master, and he scorned them. Yet the men were very good to us, and we were not insulted, nor did we miss anything as long as we went about with them, while we were in the fields. They were a wall to us both by night and by day, all the time we were with them tending the sheep. Now therefore, know and consider what you should do, for evil is plotted against our master and against all his household; and he is such a worthless man that no one can speak to him." Then Abigail hurried and took two hundred loaves of bread and two jugs of wine and five sheep already*

prepared and five measures of roasted grain and a hundred clusters of raisins and two hundred cakes of figs, and loaded them on donkeys. She said to her young men, "Go on before me; behold, I am coming after you." But she did not tell her husband Nabal.

Abigail lived up to her description. She used her God-given wisdom (*sekhel*) in this emergency mode to hurriedly prepare abundant provisions, without waiting to consult her husband. Abigail then went to meet David on his way to her home, and she wisely placed her men in front with the food.

Abigail's Speech

Abigail approached David in humbleness:

1 Samuel 25:20–23: It *came about as she was riding on her donkey and coming down by the hidden part of the mountain, that behold, David and his men were coming down toward her; so she met them. Now David had said, "Surely in vain I have guarded all that this man has in the wilderness, so that nothing was missed of all that belonged to him; and he has returned me evil for good. May God do so to the enemies of David, and more also, if by morning I leave as much as one male of any who belong to him." When Abigail saw David, she hurried and dismounted from her donkey, and fell on her face before David and bowed herself to the ground.*

The phrase "*fell on her face*" uses the Hebrew word *naphal*, which means to fall off her donkey, like Rebekah when she met Isaac. After this, Abigail "*bowed herself to the ground*," which uses the Hebrew word *shahach* for prostrating oneself flat on one's face to worship.

Her Appeal to David

Picture with me this beautiful woman (*yafat tohar*), who fell on her face to lay flat before him—displaying both humility and respect. Then Abigail clearly took the blame for what happened.

> She fell at his feet and said, "On me alone, my lord, be the blame. And please let your maidservant speak to you, and listen to the words of your maidservant. Please do not let my lord pay attention to this worthless man, Nabal, for as his name is, so is he. Nabal is his name and folly is with him; but I your maidservant did not see the young men of my lord whom you sent" (1 Sam 25:24–25).

Refocusing David's Attention

Abigail proceeded to direct David's attention away from herself, pointing David back to the Lord:

> "Now therefore, my lord, as the LORD lives, and as your soul lives, since the LORD has restrained you from shedding blood, and from avenging yourself by your own hand, now then let your enemies and those who seek evil against my lord, be as Nabal" (1 Sam 25:26).

Her Prophetic Words of Encouragement to David

> "Now let this gift which your maidservant has brought to my lord be given to the young men who accompany my lord. Please forgive the transgression of your maidservant; for the LORD will certainly make for my lord an enduring house, because my lord is fighting the battles of the LORD, and evil shall not be found in you all your days. Should anyone rise up to pursue you and to seek your life, then the life of my lord shall be bound in the bundle of the living with the LORD your God; but the lives of your enemies He will sling out as from the hollow of a sling. And when the LORD does for my lord according to all the good that He has spoken concerning you, and appoints you ruler over Israel, this will not cause grief or a troubled heart to my lord, both by having shed blood without cause and by my lord having avenged himself. When the LORD

deals well with my lord, then remember your maidservant" (1 Sam 25:27–31).

What amazing prophetic truths she gave to David. Abigail reminded him that the LORD is the One who was fighting his battles and defeating his enemies. We can wonder about David. How could David have forgotten the victory God gave him over Goliath? However, before I criticize David, I am reminded of my overreaction to insults which can fuel a burning desire to get back at the one who hurt me.

It's very likely that Abigail heard of David's restraint with King Saul in the cave and Saul's response to David. She is reminding David of God's faithfulness, protection, and timing in his life.

David Responds

David's response to Abigail's exhortation is rich with the realization of what she has done for him:

> Then David said to Abigail, "Blessed be the LORD God of Israel, who sent (shalach) you this day to meet me, and blessed be your discernment (taam), and blessed be you, who have kept me this day from bloodshed and from avenging myself by my own hand. Nevertheless, as the LORD God of Israel lives, who has restrained me from harming you, unless you had come quickly to meet me, surely there would not have been left to Nabal until the morning light as much as one male." So David received from her hand what she had brought him and said to her, "Go up to your house in shalom. See, I have listened to you and granted your request" (1 Sam 25:32–35, definitions added).

What Happened Next?

What happened when Abigail returns home is a picture of the LORD's judgment on those who reject and despise His anointed:

Then Abigail came to Nabal, and behold, he was holding a feast in his house, like the feast of a king. And Nabal's heart was merry within him, for he was very drunk; so she did not tell him anything at all until the morning light. But in the morning, when the wine had gone out of Nabal, that his wife told him these things, and his heart died within him so that he became as a stone. About ten days later, the LORD struck Nabal and he died (1 Sam 25:36–38).

And They All Lived Happily Ever After?

There is a happy ending to this narrative as God honors Abigail through David's proposal!

When David heard that Nabal was dead, he said, "Blessed be the LORD, who has pleaded the cause of my reproach from the hand of Nabal and has kept back His servant from evil. The LORD has also returned the evildoing of Nabal on his own head." Then David sent a proposal to Abigail, to take her as his wife. When the servants of David came to Abigail at Carmel, they spoke to her, saying, "David has sent us to you to take you as his wife." She arose and bowed with her face to the ground and said, "Behold, your maidservant is a maid to wash the feet of my lord's servants." Then Abigail quickly arose, and rode on a donkey, with her five maidens who attended her; and she followed the messengers of David, and became his wife. David had also taken Ahinoam of Jezreel, and they both became his wives. Now Saul had given Michal his daughter, David's wife, to Palti the son of Laish, who was from Gallim (1 Sam 25:39–44).

Indeed, the Lord blessed Abigail and she became David's wife. One of the outstanding qualities that Abigail demonstrated was her wisdom (*sehkel*), discernment (*taam*) and good judgment. We who are spiritually maturing (older women) are exhorted to teach the younger women (in age an in terms of spiritual growth) to be of a sound mind, sensible mind.

> *Older women likewise are to be reverent in their behavior, not malicious gossips nor enslaved to much wine, teaching what is good, so that they may encourage the young women to love their husbands, to love their children, to be sensible, pure, workers at home, kind, being subject to their own husbands, so that the word of God will not be dishonored* (Titus 2:3-5).

Both the verb "encourage" and the noun "sensible" are based on the compound Greek word *sofronizo* or *sofron soza*—saved (*frone*) mind—parallel to the Hebrew words *skehel*, *taam*, and *bin*.

APPLICATION: BE LIKE ABIGAIL:
AN EXAMPLE FOR US

1. How did Abigail view herself (self-perception)?

   She saw herself as a servant of the Most High God. She was not defined by her husband's terrible reputation or character. What her husband said about her or how he treated her did not define who she was. She was presented with a difficult situation, but by the grace of God and her undying trust in Him, she was able to be of sound mind and see herself as a daughter of the God of Israel (see Romans 12:3).

2. How was her state of mind (mental stability)?

   When the crisis came, she did not panic. She did not break down and become paralyzed with fear, rather she cast her anxiety on the Lord (see 1 Peter 5:7) and used discernment and good judgment in putting a plan together (see 2 Corinthians 10:3–5).

3. How did others view her (her appearance)?

   We have already noted that she was beautiful, but her beauty was more than skin deep. Her loveliness was part of her character that gave her the trust and respect of those around her (her servant who confided in her, members of her household who helped her prepare and traveled with her, and David, who responded to her request).

4. How was her spiritual life?

   Abigail did not have a spirit of timidity. She displayed God's power and love and her own sound mind as she pointed David to the Lord and to His plan and promises for David's life. 2 Timothy 1:7 (definition added): *For God has not given us a spirit of fear, but of power and of love and of a sound mind* (**saved mind**).

Recap:

Abigail's actions were rooted in her trust in what the Lord could do. She was confident that David was the Lord's anointed and should be honored. She could see that her husband's foolish response could bring death to her entire household and be a shameful reproach on David as well. She took the blame upon herself. In a sense, she said, "Take my life instead of those of my husband and my family." God used her to diffuse the situation, bring peace, and help David to be the man of God he desired to be. I pray that we would all seek to be in our right minds—our saved minds—so that we will live for the Lord and honor Him with our lives. Like Abigail, each of us can be a courageous, wise woman for Yeshua. Abigail—*Avi gayeel*—in Hebrew means "my Father is joy." Even though she was married to a rich fool, her life reflected her heavenly Father's pleasure in her life and her joy in being His daughter!

In Him we have
redemption through
His blood, the
forgiveness
of our trespasses,
according to the riches
of His grace, which
He lavished on us.

Ephesians 1:7–8

Ten

Death, Birth, & Shalom:
Bathsheba

In the previous chapter we met David as he was on the run from King Saul whose desire was to kill him. It was during this time of running from Saul that we met Abigail who was used by God to keep David from a murderous rampage upon all the males in her household. After her husband Nabal died, Abigail became David's wife.

We look into the life of King David again, a number of years later, and find him about 50 years old, in the middle of his very successful reign as king over all Israel. We will also meet a woman named Bathsheba who is crucial to our study as to how God used women to accomplish His redemptive plan.

THE PROMISE

Remember, God had promised David that his house and kingdom would endure forever, therefore he'd have a son to come after him to be king.

When your days are complete and you lie down with your fathers, I will raise up your descendant after you, who will come forth from you, and I will establish his kingdom. He shall build a house for My name, and I will establish the throne of his kingdom forever. I will be a father to him and he will be a son to Me; when he commits iniquity, I will correct him with the rod of men and the strokes of the sons of men, but My lovingkindness shall not depart from him, as I took it away from Saul, whom I removed from before you. Your house and your kingdom shall endure before Me forever; your throne shall be established forever (2 Sam 7:12-16).

By the time he met Bathsheba, the Scriptures tell us David already had at least six sons (1 Chron 3:1-9). So the covenant promise to David is well in hand, isn't it? But David's son of promise was yet to come.

THE PROBLEM

2 Samuel 11:1 informs us that it was springtime; the time when a king was expected to go to the battle front to encourage his faithful soldiers and lend his expertise to their military campaign. However David decided to stay in Jerusalem.

2 Samuel 11:1: *Then it happened in the spring, at the time when kings go out to battle, that David sent Joab and his servants with him and all Israel, and they destroyed the sons of Ammon and besieged Rabbah. But David stayed at Jerusalem.*

David sent the general Joab and his troops to lay siege to Rabbah, the key city of the enemy Ammonites (see 2 Samuel 11:1, 16–17; 1 Chronicles 20:1–3). The Ammonite army had fled to the walled city of Rabbah. Joab and the army of Israel besieged the city, giving the Ammonites time to run out of food and water before they attacked. All this army maneuvering would have taken place in the early spring. The winter rains were over. The weather was getting warmer.

In retrospect we know that his decision to stay behind would expose David to great temptation and eventual heartache. Did David forget his calling? Had he forgotten his humble beginnings? David was the youngest son of Jesse when God instructed the prophet Samuel to anoint him to be the king of Israel.

> 1 Samuel 16:11–13 (emphasis added): *And Samuel said to Jesse, "Are these all the children?" And he said, "There remains yet the youngest, and behold, he is tending the sheep." Then Samuel said to Jesse, "Send and bring him; for we will not sit down until he comes here." So he sent and brought him in. Now he was ruddy, with beautiful eyes and a handsome appearance. And the LORD said, "Arise, anoint him; for this is he."* **Then Samuel took the horn of oil and anointed him in the midst of his brothers; and the Spirit of the LORD came mightily upon David from that day forward.**

This anointing from God was evident immediately. When King Saul searched for a musician who could soothe his troubled mind, he received this report from one of his men:

> *Then one of the young men said, "Behold, I have seen a son of Jesse the Bethlehemite who is a skillful musician, a mighty man of valor, a warrior, one prudent in speech, and a handsome man; and the LORD is with him"* (1 Sam 16:18).

Why would David, a man after God's own heart, at the height of his successful reign, neglect his responsibility to his loyal army? Did he forget that God is the One who anointed him and chose him to be king? Had his heart grown cold and callous toward his calling from God? Was he tired and discouraged?

How About Us?

We can ask these same questions for our own lives to avoid David's cold heart, discouragement, and apathy. Each of us are in different seasons of our lives as we continue to walk with the Lord. We need to always remember God's anointing, His provisions, and His instructions about going to war.

1. Remember that you were chosen and anointed by God.

   Yeshua declares to us: "You did not choose Me but I chose you, and appointed you that you would go and bear fruit, and that your fruit should remain, so that whatever you ask of the Father in My name He may give to you" (John 15:16).

2. Remember that the LORD has given us everything we need for life and godliness.

   Grace and peace be multiplied to you in the knowledge of God and of Yeshua our Lord; seeing that His divine power has granted to us everything pertaining to life and godliness, through the true knowledge of Him who called us by His own glory and excellence. For by these He has granted to us His precious and magnificent promises, so that by them you may become partakers of the divine nature, having escaped the corruption that is in the world by lust (2 Peter 1:2–4).

3. Remember that we are in spiritual warfare and must never neglect this battle that we are waging each day.

   Finally, be strong in the Lord and in the strength of His might. Put on the full armor of God, so that you will be able to stand firm against the schemes of the devil. For our struggle is not against flesh and blood, but against the rulers, against the powers, against the world forces of this darkness, against the spiritual forces of wickedness in the heavenly places (Eph 6:10–12).

Meet Bathsheba:

> 2 Samuel 11:2–3: *Now when evening came David arose from his bed and walked around on the roof of the king's house, and from the roof he saw a woman bathing; and the woman was very beautiful in appearance. So David sent and inquired about the woman. And one said, "Is this not Bathsheba, the daughter of Eliam, the wife of Uriah the Hittite?"*

David had just taken an afternoon nap. He was outside on his rooftop enjoying the refreshing early evening breezes as the sun was setting. Perhaps he was looking for that perfect sunset. While walking on his roof and taking in his magnificent view, he saw the form of a beautiful woman. So, David asked about her. The reply came back to him, *"Is this not Bathsheba, the daughter of Eliam, the wife of Uriah the Hittite?"*

Warning Ahead:

Wait a minute! Stop right here! When David heard Bathsheba's name and the name of her husband, Uriah, warning sirens should have started ringing in David's heart and soul. Was he so full of arrogance and pride that he felt he could do whatever he wanted? David should have checked his lustful urges upon realizing that this woman was Bathsheba, who he had known since she was a child. If he had turned his heart toward heaven, the Lord could have brought to his mind Bathsheba's grandfather Ahithophel, who was one David's own most trusted advisors. In fact, Ahithophel was the chief counselor of David as recorded in 2 Samuel 16:23:

> *The advice of Ahithophel, which he gave in those days, was as if one inquired of the word of God; so was all the advice of Ahithophel regarded by both David and Absalom.*

Bathsheba's father, Eliam, was a member of David's elite guard, and her husband Uriah was a God-fearer who served him faithfully for many years. But, alas, David's heart had turned away from the Lord and he was concerned solely with satisfying his own desires.

David had already decided he'd rather stay home in his palace instead of carrying out his duty to go to war. Even though his responsibility was to be with his soldiers giving them encouragement and support, there he was on his palace rooftop in the late afternoon. If we could peek into David's rationale, it might go something like this:

> "Hey I'm the king! I'm feeling pretty energetic and vigorous after that nap. But I'm also feeling so bored and lonely. Poor me! If only there was something fun to do, someone to make me happy. Wait, who is that lovely lady I see in the distance? I can see her beautiful form and I want a closer look. In fact, I want to meet her. I'm the king and I can do as I please. For surely, she can give me some moments of happiness to spice up this monotonous day I've been having."

The Scriptures go on to tell us what David did:

> 2 Samuel 11:4–5: *Then David sent messengers and took her when she came to him and he lay with her. (She had purified herself from her uncleanness). Then she returned to her house. The woman conceived and sent word to David saying, "I'm pregnant"* (TLV).

The Tree of Life Version gives us a clearer picture, perhaps, about the timing of her menstrual period. There are other points of view from various commentators, but from the Tree of Life translation, it seems that Bathsheba was engaging in a ritual act of purification for holiness—bathing naked in the *mikveh* to cleanse herself from the uncleanness of menstruation. Some commentators write that Bathsheba was being immodest and seductive. In my opinion, these theories do a great disservice to Bathsheba. She did not choose her bathing location or even the timing of it. If she had just purified herself from her monthly period, the most logical explanation is that Bathsheba was at a mikveh, which is the ritual purification bath for women seven days after the end of their monthly menstruation. She was bathing according to the requirements of the purity customs of her day, after her menstrual period. The phrase "she had purified herself from her uncleanness" is in the past tense indicating that when she went to the palace, Bathsheba had already had her menstrual period and was ceremonially clean after being at the mikveh—the ritual bath according to the law of Moses.

David's palace rooftop would have been one of the highest buildings, if not the highest, in Jerusalem and from that height he saw her bathing in a *mikveh*. These places for ceremonial bathing would have been situated where Jewish women could go monthly. A *mikveh* had to have a source of running water, like a spring, or fresh water, such as rainwater. Therefore, they were constructed in the ground and the walls of a *mikveh* would not be tall enough to conceal Bathsheba from the prying eyes of David from his lofty, royal vantage point.

Bathsheba: an Israelite Trying to Honor the Purity Laws

Consider with me what this says about Bathsheba. As a woman of Israel, it tells us that she was trying to honor the God of Israel and the laws of Moses. Because her father was one of David's trusted men and her grandfather was David's most trusted counselor, we can assume that she grew up near the palace. Bathsheba would have heard the accounts of God's miracles and faithfulness to His people. All her life she would have known only one earthly king of Israel who loved the God of Israel with all his heart. During those twenty years of David's rule, she would have seen David's heart for God. Most certainly she would have recited many of David's psalms as she worshiped the God of Israel. When she was summoned by

King David, she would have been about twenty years old or possibly even younger.

A Kingly Summons

When David summoned her, it would have been an invitation that she could not refuse. After all, he was her king and the king of Israel. He was probably the most powerful man she had ever known, and he was more than twice her age. When David overpowered and seduced Bathsheba, he must have utilized his kingly charm and perhaps his physical power. We can surmise that she was overwhelmed, stunned, shocked, and terrified to displease him. He was the commanding king of Israel, whom she had probably idolized her whole life. The Scriptures do not give us additional insight into Bathsheba's emotional disposition or state of mind. The only words from Bathsheba that were recorded during this entire scenario are found in the message she sent to David in 2 Samuel 11:5: *"I am pregnant."*

From Manipulation to Murder

The announcement of her pregnancy set the king into motion maneuvering and manipulating the situation. David called Uriah from the battlefield to visit Bathsheba. The plan was to get Uriah to sleep with his wife in order to make it appear that the child in her womb was Uriah's. But much to David's consternation, his plan didn't work. Uriah was a man of integrity and such an honorable soldier of David's army that he did not want to have pleasure with his wife while his men were fighting the battles of David's kingdom.

When this first plan failed, David plotted murder to get rid of Uriah. He gave orders to Joab to make Uriah's death inevitable on the battlefield. Then, after David received confirmation that Uriah had been killed in battle and after a suitable mourning time for Bathsheba, David married her.

The Scriptures are clear regarding the LORD's response: 2 Samuel 11:26–27:

> *Now when the wife of Uriah heard that Uriah her husband was dead, she mourned for her husband. When the time of mourning was over, David sent and brought her to his house and she became his wife; then she bore him a son. But the thing that David had done was evil in the sight of the LORD.*

It's astonishing to consider what David must have been thinking when he plotted Uriah's death and claimed Bathsheba as his own. Meanwhile, the palace of the king of Israel became a place of intrigue with his sordid secrets for a number of months.

God's Mercy Through Nathan

In the LORD's mercy and grace toward David and Bathsheba, God sent the prophet Nathan to confront David regarding this evil that he had committed. He had sinned not only in the sight of Bathsheba and those in his kingdom but, more importantly, in the sight of Almighty God.

We continually need God's wisdom to help us communicate to our friends, our family members, and those in our congregation as Nathan the prophet also needed great wisdom from God to speak to a disobedient king. Nathan had a very difficult task, which was to confront David, who had been living in lies and denial for many months. The Scriptures state in 2 Samuel 12:1 that *"the LORD sent Nathan to David."* Instead of barging in with a "repent or perish" message, with God's guidance, Nathan told David a story of two men who lived in the same city. One of these men was very, very rich and the other was very, very poor. The rich man had abundant flocks in contrast to the poor man who had only one baby lamb. This baby lamb was beloved by his family so much so that his children would feed this lamb at the dinner table and even have this lamb sleep in their beds with them. Many of you animal lovers are relating to this poor man as you have your cute puppies and your snuggly kittens eating from your tables, sleeping in your beds, and being loved as a member of your family. It was the same for this poor man and his family, as Nathan explained to David that this little ewe lamb was like a daughter to them. Nathan understood that any interesting story needs a problem to solve. The conflict in Nathan's tale arose when a traveler came to the city to visit the rich man. Hospitality customs demanded that the rich man provide the traveler with a good meal. However, this wealthy man did not want to take any lambs from his well-stocked flocks.

Nathan's tale concluded in 2 Samuel 12:4:

> ...*Rather, he took the poor man's ewe lamb and prepared it for the man who had come to him.*

I find it intriguing that in this verse the same Hebrew word that was used for when David took Bathsheba is used twice. The rich man was unwilling to take (*lakach*) his own lamb, but rather took (*lakach*) the poor man's little ewe lamb.

David's response was immediate and full of indignation:

> *Then David's anger burned greatly against the man, and he said to Nathan, "As the LORD lives, surely the man who has done this deserves to die. He must make restitution for the lamb fourfold, because he did this thing and had no compassion"* (1 Sam 12:5–6).

Notice David's outrage at the rich man who had taken the one little lamb away from the poor man. In David's vulnerable state of rage, Nathan confronted David with God's message of judgment on him, his household, and his kingdom. This was Nathan's opening to confront David with the truth of God's displeasure and judgment upon him. After Nathan declared, *"You are the man!"* (1 Sam 12:7), he then gave David a list to help him remember and acknowledge that the LORD was the

One who anointed him and gave him all that he had. Nathan then added a phrase that strikes my heart, *"… if that had been too little, I would have added to you many more things like these!"* (1 Sam 12:8). In other words, David had forgotten that the God he served was a God of abundant blessings and lovingkindness. His God would not withhold any good thing from David whom He loved.

Also note that Nathan did not accuse Bathsheba in his story. He acknowledged her powerlessness in the situation by representing her as the "one ewe lamb" who was taken by the rich man.

"I Have Sinned Against the Lord."

After he heard the stern rebukes and consequential judgments from God, David's rage turned to repentance. He acknowledged his sin to Nathan and to God.

> 2 Samuel 12:13: *Then David said to Nathan, "I have sinned against the LORD."*

David appealed to God's lovingkindness and His great compassion. It was at this time, after his adultery with Bathsheba, the murder of Uriah, and being confronted by Nathan the prophet, that David wrote Psalm 51.

> Psalm 51:1–4: *Be gracious to me, O God, according to Your lovingkindness; according to the greatness of Your compassion blot out my transgressions. Wash me thoroughly from my iniquity and cleanse me from my sin. For I know my transgressions, and my sin is ever before me. Against You, You only, I have sinned and done what is evil in Your sight, so that You are justified when You speak and blameless when You judge.*

Even though he had hurt many around him, including Bathsheba, David recognized that his sin was against God who is his judge.

Psalm 32, which many scholars believe David wrote just after his confession in Psalm 51, is an essential teaching that David penned for all of us who have sinned against the Holy One of Israel. In verses three and four of Psalm 32, we have a glimpse as to what is was like for Bathsheba to be in the palace with David during those months when David was estranged from the LORD.

> Psalm 32:3–4: *When I kept silent about my sin, my body wasted away through my groaning all day long. For day and night Your hand was heavy upon me; my vitality was drained away as with the fever heat of summer. Selah.*

Bathsheba Expecting Her First Child

Bathsheba would have had the joy of being pregnant and expecting her first child, but according to this verse, the atmosphere around the palace bedroom and throne room must have been oppressive, with all David's moaning, groaning, and sickness.

And How About Us, Again?

It's easy to point a finger at David because he messed up so royally, but we need to ask ourselves: Have we grieved God's heart by sinning against Him? I can certainly answer yes to this question as I identify with King David in his prideful heart, telling lies, and even covering up his lies to stir up strife. Furthermore, when I do not confess my sins, I know I am grieving the Holy Spirit of God who dwells in me. The result of quenching the Holy Spirit also quenches my vitality and strength to live for the Lord. I am miserable and have no desire to honor God or to be His earthen vessel of grace into the lives of others.

Psalms 51 and 32 are contrite prayers for forgiveness and restoration back to God. But I want us to note what David promises to the Lord in Psalm 51:13. In Psalm 51:10, David is praying and acknowledging that the Creator God is the only

One who can create a pure heart in him. The word "clean" is *tahor* and means "ceremonially clean"—completely cleansed in order to worship the One true God. In addition to confessing his sins, David is giving God his assurance to teach others who have sinned about the joy of forgiveness. The purpose of his teaching would be to bring or turn many back to God.

> Psalm 51:10–13: *Create in me a clean heart, O God, and renew a steadfast spirit within me. Do not cast me away from Your presence, and do not take Your Holy Spirit from me. Restore to me the joy of Your salvation and sustain me with a willing spirit. Then I will teach transgressors Your ways, and sinners will be converted to You.*

Forgiveness, Consequences, and a Turning Point

In response to David's repentance, Nathan delivered another message from the Lord to David:

> *And Nathan said to David, "The LORD also has taken away your sin; you shall not die. However, because by this deed you have given occasion to the enemies of the LORD to blaspheme, the child also that is born to you shall surely die"* (2 Sam 12:13–14).

What wonderful news, David was forgiven and would live, even though according to the Law of Moses, his sins were punishable by death. However, the good news was coupled with extremely sad news, especially for Bathsheba. Their newborn son would die. Why? The Scriptures let us know it was because of what David did. His sins gave opportunity for God's enemies to despise and curse the LORD's holy name.

Bathsheba's Son Dies

It seems so harsh, especially to a mother's ears, that such a pronouncement of death would come to their innocent infant who had done nothing wrong. However, the Lord uses this sorrowful situation to teach us all a truth and give us hope about the death of small children. David gave us this promise, as he answered the elders and servants of his household about the death of his son:

> 2 Samuel 12:22–23: *He said, "While the child was still alive, I fasted and wept; for I said, 'Who knows, the LORD may be gracious to me, that the child may live.' But now he has died; why should I fast? Can I bring him back again? I will go to him, but he will not return to me."*

This encouraging reality echoes throughout history and continues to comfort the hearts of millions of parents with the fact that we will one day see our children who have gone on before us. I think of my third baby that I miscarried and never knew. I genuinely believe that I will be rejoined with this child that I carried in my womb for such a short time and that one day we will rejoice in heaven together before the King of kings.

THE RESTORATION

David Finally Comforts Bathsheba

David must have had this same comfort from God because the next thing he did was truly remarkable. This was the first record of David reaching out to Bathsheba with comfort and love.

> 2 Samuel 12:24 (definition added): *Then David comforted his wife Bathsheba, and went in to her and lay with her; and she gave birth to a son, and he named him Solomon. Now the LORD loved him* (Solomon) *and sent word through Nathan the prophet, and he named him Jedidiah for the LORD's sake.*

How was David able to be a comforting husband instead of a lustful king who just wanted to possess her beautiful body? If we read what David wrote in both Psalm 51 and Psalm 32, we gain insight into his frame of mind both before and after he confessed his sins.

Teaching Sinners to Turn Back to God

In Psalm 32:1–2, David gave us the top two reasons that should give us cause to be happy in the midst of this evil generation.

> *How blessed is he whose transgression is forgiven, whose sin is covered! How blessed is the man to whom the LORD does not impute iniquity, and in whose spirit there is no deceit!*

Both verses have to do with the fact of our total forgiveness that we find in the Lord. As we accept God's provision for and acceptance of us, we will grow deeper in our understanding of how to find happiness by God's design. This teaching that poured out of David's contrite heart under the influence of the Holy Spirit would have been a comfort to Bathsheba, as well. This teaching would have restored her, healed her grieving heart, as she realized that she, too, was accepted and forgiven by her God. Instead of growing bitter and cynical, she would have been filled with God's lovingkindness and courage, enabled to raise her son Solomon, able to be affirming to David. If God could forgive and restore King David and Bathsheba, will He do any less for you?

Proverbs 6:16-19

We must pay close attention to what David was saying to us. He was speaking from his own personal experience, teaching us how we can discover God's ways for great happiness and blessing. David had completely blown it, destroying his reputation and impugning God's character in the process. He hit all the top seven sins that God hates. Proverbs 6:16–19 says,

> *There are six things which the LORD hates, yes, seven which are an abomination to Him: haughty eyes, a lying tongue, and hands that shed innocent blood, a heart that devises wicked plans, feet that run rapidly to evil, a false*

witness who utters lies, and one who spreads strife among brothers.

Haughty Eyes

David had haughty eyes, which is a synonym for pride. In 2 Samuel 11:1–4, David displayed his pride and egotism by deciding not to be with his soldiers. Instead of submitting to God and doing his job as king of Israel, he stayed behind and did what he desired to do. He used his position of power to seduce and overpower Bathsheba, to gratify his lustful desires and inflated ego. Doesn't this sound similar to the fall of Satan as it was described in Isaiah 14:12–14. Satan had the position of chief worship leader in Heaven but in his arrogance and pride, he desired to ascend above the throne of God. When David carried out his prideful actions, he was emulating the actions of the evil one.

A Lying Tongue

The next sin that God hates is a lying tongue. David was caught up in a quagmire of lies. He lied to Bathsheba, to Uriah, and to many in the palace. Again, David was following Satan, who is called the father of lies in John 8:44:

> *You are of your father the devil, and you want to do the desires of your father. He was a murderer from the beginning, and does not stand in the truth because there is no truth in him. Whenever he speaks a lie, he speaks from his own nature, for he is a liar and the father of lies.*

Shedding Innocent Blood

The third sin God hates is described with the phrase *"hands that shed innocent blood"* (Proverbs 6:17). David deliberately had Uriah murdered. I believe in a court of law it would be regarded as a premeditated crime. Here, once more, David is following in the footsteps of Satan who was a *"murderer from the beginning"* (John 8:44).

Devising Wicked Plans

"A heart that devises wicked plans" is the fourth sin mentioned in Proverbs. David used his military and executive skills to cook up evil and sinister ways to cover his many sins. In Ephesians 6:11 we are told that Satan is one who is scheming against us and against the plan of God and for this reason we are instructed to: *"Put on the full armor of God, so that you will be able to stand firm against the schemes of the devil."*

Running to Evil

The fifth sin listed in Proverbs 6 is *"feet that run rapidly to evil."* Instead of confessing his evil schemes and turning back to God, David ran away from God and continued to run headlong down an evil path while he kept silent about his deceitful deeds for almost a year.

Bearing False Witness and Spreading Strife

And the final two sins are listed as: *"False witness who utters lies"* and *"one who spreads strife among brothers"* (v. 19). Can you imagine the lying and strife that was happening in the palace while David kept silent about his sins?

We can see at a glance that David had really messed up and offended the LORD. But, as much as David sinned against God, the LORD cared enough about him to have Nathan the prophet confront him. And when David acknowledged his sins, the Lord forgave him and enabled him to be a source of comfort to Bathsheba and reign in Israel for another twenty years.

For deeper consideration, think of what David did that caused others to blaspheme the Holy One of Israel and grieve God's heart.

Take time to re-examine your own life and ask the LORD to reveal any secret sins in your life. As you consider how you may have sinned against the LORD, take time to confess them to the LORD and accept His total forgiveness. Meditate on

Psalm 32 and praise the LORD for His complete forgiveness in Messiah Yeshua and your acceptance into His family.

What Can Psalm 32 Mean for Your Life?

In traditional Judaism, Psalm 32 is read every year at the close of Yom Kippur—the Day of Atonement. When the Temple stood in Jerusalem, the Day of Atonement was the one time a year when the high priest of Israel entered the Holy of Holies to seek atonement for the whole congregation of Israel. One of the day's important traditions concerned two scapegoats. The high priest was instructed to take two goats and present them before the LORD. Then the high priest would cast lots for the two goats, one lot for the LORD and the other lot for the scapegoat. The goat that was for the LORD became a sin offering and the other goat was presented alive before the LORD so that the sins of the people could be confessed and placed on the scapegoat to make atonement for the nation. The scapegoat was then driven into the wilderness to a high, rocky precipice in the Judean desert never to be seen again, carrying away with it the sins of the people (Leviticus 16:7–10).

Verse One

This concept of having our sins removed and never to be brought up again is found in Psalm 32. The first verse reads:

> *How blessed (ashrei, happy) is he whose transgression is forgiven, whose sin is covered (Ps 32:1, definition added)!*

God cannot have sin in His presence. However, we are accepted because we are forgiven and our sins are covered (actually *removed* in the Hebrew). Forgiven (*nasa*) in Hebrew means to remove the burden of—this concept of the removal of the burden of sin is foreshadowed by the scapegoat at Yom Kippur. Just as the scapegoat was chosen to carry the sins of the people into the wilderness never to be seen again, so also, because of Yeshua's sacrifice, our sins are forever hidden from

God's sight. In other words, when God covers our sins, they are permanently removed.

The prophet Micah declares our sins are cast into the depths of the sea.

> Micah 7:18–19 (definition added): *Who is a God like You, who pardons iniquity and passes over the rebellious act of the remnant of His possession? He does not retain His anger forever, because He delights in unchanging love. He will again have compassion on us; He will tread our iniquities under foot. Yes, You will cast* (tashlich) *all their sins into the depths of the sea.*

We also see this idea of removal of our sins forever in David's Psalm 103.

> *For as high as the heavens are above the earth, so great is His lovingkindness toward those who fear Him. As far as the east is from the west, so far has He removed our transgressions from us. Just as a father has compassion on his children, so the LORD has compassion on those who fear Him* (Ps 103:11-13).

For us, Yeshua fulfilled this picture of the scapegoat and removal of sin by taking away our sins away permanently, even as John the Baptizer declared: *"Behold, the Lamb of God who takes away the sin of the world"* (John 1:29)! Yeshua also fulfilled this cleansing power every time we agree with God about our sins and confess them to Him. 1 John 1:9: *If we confess our sins, He is faithful and righteous to forgive us our sins and to cleanse us from all unrighteousness.*

Verse Two

But's that not all! The second verse of Psalm 32 declares,

> *How blessed* (happy) *is the person to whom the LORD does not impute iniquity, and in whose spirit there is no deceit!* (definition added).

Have you ever been in a drive-thru lane, say at Chick-fil-A, and when you tried to pay for your food, the server says, "Your bill has already been covered by the person in front of you. Your bill is paid in full. Have a great day!"? How did that make you feel when you found out your bill was covered?

The word impute (*chashav* in Hebrew) means to charge to your account. In Yeshua, all debts are cancelled because Yeshua paid your debt of sin on the cross. Your sin bill is PAID IN FULL by the blood of Yeshua. Therefore, we can conclude from what David is teaching us that this first aspect of being blessed, happy (*ashrei*) is essential for us to understand deep within our hearts and souls in order to live in light of what God has already done for us.

Totally Accepted

In a general sense, what does it mean to be accepted? Let's consider some synonyms which include involved, approved, and supported. The opposite of acceptance would be rejection, exclusion, left alone, disapproved, and unsupported.

Why do we check our phones fifty times a day? Why do we long to be in the most popular group—whether at school, at work, or even in the congregation? We long to be accepted, right? Well, here is the most extraordinary news flash—and spiritual truth for our hearts today—because of what Yeshua has done for you by removing your sins, God accepts you completely. You are clothed in Messiah's perfect righteousness and wrapped in His garments of salvation that don't wash off in the shower.

> Isaiah 61:10: *I will rejoice greatly in the LORD, my soul will exult in my God; for He has clothed me with garments of salvation, He has wrapped me with a robe of righteousness, as a bridegroom decks himself with a garland, and as a bride adorns herself with her jewels.*

Plus, God's acceptance of us has nothing to do with our own works. The Apostle Paul wrote this to the Corinthian congregation and to us as well:

> 2 Corinthians 5:21 (definitions added): *He* (the Father) *made Him* (Yeshua) *who knew no sin to be sin on our behalf, so that we might become the righteousness of God in Him.*

Paul, in his letter to the Congregation at Ephesus, explains what it means to be accepted in His beloved Son.

> Ephesians 1:3–6: *Blessed is the God and Father of our Lord Yeshua the Messiah, who did bless us in every spiritual blessing in the heavenly places in Messiah, according as He did choose us in him before the foundation of the world, for our being holy and unblemished before Him, in love, having foreordained us to the adoption of [daughters] through Yeshua the Messiah to Himself, according to the good pleasure of His will, to the praise of the glory of His grace, in which He did make us accepted in the beloved (YLT).*

What does it mean for you to be *accepted in the Beloved?* Can we agree that this acceptance by God, standing before Him in the righteous robes given to us by Yeshua, can be our starting point, our focus every morning, to be thankful and acknowledge who we are in Messiah? Every day you can begin anew by recognizing your identity in Him.

Verse Five: Selah! Stop and Think About It!

In Psalm 32:3–5, we have the description of what happened to David when he did not confess his sin to the LORD.

> *When I kept silent about my sin, my body wasted away Through my groaning all day long. ⁴ For day and night Your hand was heavy upon me; My vitality was drained away as with the fever heat of summer. Selah. ⁵ I*

acknowledged my sin to You, And my iniquity I did not hide; I said, "I will confess my transgressions to the LORD"; And You forgave the guilt of my sin. Selah.

I made reference to verses three and four in light of what it would have been like for Bathsheba to live with David during his time of estrangement from the LORD. Now let's look deeper into these verses, especially verse five.

The Hebrew word *selah* is found only in the poetical books of the Hebrew Scriptures and occurs seventy-one times in the Psalms and three times in Habakkuk. The exact meaning of the word is unknown, but it's believed by many scholars to be a musical term that means to pause or reflect. In modern parlance: Stop and think about what the writer is saying, because this is vitally important for you.

Note that David used *selah* after verses four and five as he first gave the condition of not confessing his sins and then the consequences of both acknowledging his sins and confessing his sins to the Lord. The word for confess is such an encouraging word picture in Hebrew. It is *yadah* from the root word for hand, which is *yad*. Do you feel guilty about something? Throw it to God, accept His forgiveness, and walk in His freedom. You are accepted in the Beloved of the Most High God. The Lord's Right Hand has done mighty things for you. You can absolutely throw your hand into His mighty hand and cast all your cares upon Him.

Verses Six and Seven

Therefore, let everyone who is godly pray to You in a time when You may be found; Surely in a flood of great waters they will not reach him. 7 You are my hiding place; You preserve me from trouble; You surround me with songs of deliverance. Selah (Psalm 32:6–7).

These verses contain beautiful promises to those of us who are His children. We are promised that when the troubles come like a great flood of waters, His protection will be there for us, surrounding us as we trust and hide in Him. As you read these verses, let them reaffirm God's care for you and His assurance to surround you with His songs of deliverance.

After this, we have another *selah*, to pause and reflect how the LORD is our place of refuge—He will preserve or guard us and He will protect us during trouble.

Verses Eight and Nine

I will instruct you and teach you in the way which you should go; I will counsel you with My eye upon you. ⁹ Do not be as the horse or as the mule which have no understanding, Whose trappings include bit and bridle to hold them in check, Otherwise they will not come near to you. ¹⁰ Many are the sorrows of the wicked, But he who trusts in the LORD, lovingkindness shall surround him.

Verses 8–9 promise us that God will teach us and show us His path for our lives. However, God also warns us not to be like a horse or mule which have no understanding but needs the restraints of the bit and bridle to guide them.

What can this say to us? When we submit to God's authority and guidance, we may not need to have those restraints put upon us. When we put our confidence in the LORD, His lovingkindness will surround us.

The Last Verse

The final verse of the psalm reiterates the fact that in our blessedness, or being happy, we have reason to be glad, to rejoice and shout for joy. We can end this section with the good news of forgiveness and acceptance found in Psalm 32. We can affirm along with Bathsheba and David: Psalm 32:11:

Be glad in the LORD and rejoice, you righteous ones; and shout for joy, all you who are upright in heart.

Redemption for Bathsheba

The comfort that David extended to Bathsheba came from his renewed understanding of God's forgiveness. David demonstrated that they could both live in light of the Lord's acceptance and forgiveness. The main reason that Bathsheba was so important to God's plan of redemption was that she gave birth to their second son, Solomon. He was indeed a great blessing and comfort to both Bathsheba and David—and he was the son included in the royal line of Messiah Yeshua.

The Scriptures do not give us a name for the first child of David and Bathsheba, the child who died on the seventh day. He died just before his circumcision on the eighth day, when he would have been named. Nevertheless, I believe that the LORD who formed this first child in Bathsheba's womb knows his name and that he is rejoicing in Heaven today.

Solomon Is Born

This second birth was quite a contrast to the first son who died. At the birth of Solomon, he was given two names:

> 2 Samuel 12:24b-25: *Now the LORD loved him and sent word through Nathan the prophet, and he named him Jedidiah for the LORD's sake.*

David calls him Solomon (*Shlomo*) which means "man of peace" and Nathan names him *Yedidiah* which means "beloved of God." The end of verse twenty-five says this name Yedidiah was for the LORD's sake, or on account of the LORD. What a wonderful God of love we serve, who reminded Solomon's parents of His love—every time they said the name Nathan gave him.

In fact, in 1 Chronicles 22:8, when David was giving instructions to Solomon about building the Temple, he also explained why God would not allow him to build it:

But the word of the LORD came to me, saying, "You have shed much blood and have waged great wars; you shall not build a house to My name, because you have shed so much blood on the earth before Me."

Amazingly, in verse nine David told of a promise God made to him about Solomon and his name:

"Behold, a son will be born to you, who shall be a man of rest; and I will give him rest from all his enemies on every side; for his name shall be Solomon, and I will give peace and quiet to Israel in his days" (2 Chron 22:9).

God's Answer to Solomon's Request

King Solomon was known for the wisdom that was given to him by God. 1 Kings 3:5 says,

In Gibeon the LORD appeared to Solomon in a dream at night; and God said, "Ask what you wish Me to give you."

Solomon asked the Lord for an understanding heart to know how to judge the people and have God's discernment in his decisions. The Lord was pleased to not only answer Solomon's request, but also bestow on Solomon unlimited riches and honor (see 1 Kings 3:6–15).

Solomon's wisdom, wealth, and writings originated from the blessing and provision of God. He gave Solomon all he needed to be the wisest king of Israel of all time. His crowning achievement was the building of the holy Temple in Jerusalem. In 1 Kings 10:23–24 we have a brief synopsis of his ongoing reign. Even though it was the desire of his father David's heart to build a temple for the Lord, God gave David the assurance that Solomon would be the one to build the temple. In 1 Chronicles 22:5, David said that his son Solomon—even though he was young and inexperienced— would build the Lord an *"exceedingly magnificent"* temple that would be *"famous and glorious throughout all the lands."*

Before his death, David made sure that Solomon had ample preparations in place to build this temple for the Lord.

> 1 Kings 10:23–24: *So King Solomon became greater than all the kings of the earth in riches and in wisdom. All the earth was seeking the presence of Solomon, to hear his wisdom which God had put in his heart.*

Nathan's Respect for Bathsheba

Even though there was turmoil, rebellion, and war during the last half of David's reign, we are given an example of how Bathsheba was involved with raising Solomon and was respected in matters of politics with her influence at court. This is clearly seen from the account of David's son, Adonijah, the son of Haggith, when Adonijah usurped the throne from Solomon and declared himself to be king of Israel (1 Kings 1:5–10).

When the Prophet Nathan heard of this, he appealed to Bathsheba to go to David. Instead of going directly to see King David, Nathan directs Bathsheba to talk to David about what Adonijah had just done to declare that he was king instead of Solomon, even though it was God who had promised that Solomon would be the next king. Nathan assured Bathsheba that he would be right behind her to confirm all that she was saying to David (see 1 Kings 1:11–31).

Why didn't Nathan go directly to David? I believe the answer lies in the fact that Bathsheba had proven to be a trustworthy and wise woman. Nathan wanted her to be involved in this crucial exchange about the promise that God made to David concerning the fact that, indeed, Solomon would be the next king. Nathan, as God's prophet, was there throughout all that had happened to Bathsheba. His request to her displayed his respect and esteem. He knew he could trust her, so he brought her into the situation and let her be a part of the solution.

Solomon's Esteem for His Mother

The Scriptures do not give us many details about Solomon's relationship with his mother; however, we can learn much from a public exchange when Solomon became king of Israel. Shortly after Solomon ascended to the throne and after the death of David (1 Kings 2:12), we have a glimpse of the respect that Solomon gave to his mother.

Solomon's esteem for his mother was revealed in 1 Kings 2:19:

> So Bathsheba went to King Solomon to speak to him for Adonijah. And the king arose to meet her, bowed before her, and sat on his throne; then he had a throne set for the king's mother, and she sat on his right.

Notice how Solomon greeted his mother and honored her before the entire court. He humbled himself as he bowed before her and then he had a throne placed on his right side for her to sit. This right side is always the place of honor. It confers equal honor and respect to the one who sits at the king's right hand. This indicated that Solomon not only loved his mother but also greatly respected her. Solomon would have learned through Nathan and his mother that she was the one who approached David about Adonijah usurping the throne to save his monarchy.

When Adonijah asked Bathsheba to speak to Solomon on his behalf, Bathsheba was displaying her heart of forgiveness and compassion for him. In light of how she and David had been forgiven, I think her character was proven in her willingness to ask Solomon to forgive Adonijah. Suffice to say that Solomon was able to discern Adonijah's evil intentions and ultimately had him executed. Nevertheless, this does not diminish the fact that Bathsheba was trying to be merciful toward Adonijah.

Solomon Foreshadows Yeshua

The Old Testament Scriptures declare Solomon to be *greater than all the kings of the earth in riches and in wisdom. All the earth was seeking the presence of Solomon, to hear his wisdom which God had put in his heart* (1 Kings 10:23–24).

However, when Yeshua was speaking to the crowds that were demanding He provide a sign from heaven to prove His authenticity, Yeshua said to them,

> *For just as Jonah became a sign to the Ninevites, so will the Son of Man be to this generation. The Queen of the South will rise up with the men of this generation at the judgment and condemn them, because she came from the ends of the earth to hear the wisdom of Solomon; and behold, something greater than Solomon is here"* (Luke 11:30–31).

When they demanded a sign, Yeshua told them there would be no more signs except the sign of Jonah the reluctant prophet. But why would Yeshua bring up the queen of Sheba as well? Well, she had traveled a great distance just to listen to Solomon in contradistinction to those who were asking for Yeshua to prove Himself to be the Messiah. These crowds with their questions and accusations did not have to travel from afar to hear Yeshua, but rather had seen His many miracles and heard His teachings in their hometowns.

The queen of Sheba recognized that what she had heard was true:

> 1 Kings 10:6-7: *Then she said to the king, "It was a true report which I heard in my own land about your words and your wisdom. Nevertheless I did not believe the reports, until I came and my eyes had seen it. And behold, the half was not told me. You exceed in wisdom and prosperity the report which I heard."*

The queen of Sheba went on to praise the Lord:

"Blessed be the LORD your God who delighted in you to set you on the throne of Israel; because the LORD loved Israel forever, therefore He made you king, to do justice and righteousness" (1 Kings 10:9).

Therefore, in Yeshua's rebuke of this crowd of Pharisees and blasphemers who had gathered to accuse Him, He told them that the queen of Sheba, a Gentile who became a follower of the God of Israel, would rise up and pass judgment on them. Why? Because Yeshua declared, speaking of Himself: *"Behold, something greater than Solomon is here"* (Luke 11:31).

Yeshua is Greater than Solomon

Revelation 19 is a description of Yeshua returning with us to judge all His enemies and establish righteousness for eternity.

> Revelation 19:16: And *on His robe and on His thigh He has a name written, "KING OF KINGS, AND LORD OF LORDS."*

Additionally, Yeshua, as your King, gives you every spiritual blessing in the heavenly places:

> Ephesians 1:3: *Blessed be the God and Father of our Lord Yeshua the Messiah, who has blessed us with every spiritual blessing in the heavenly places in Messiah.*

Yeshua lavished His wisdom on you according to the riches of His grace:

> Ephesians 1:7–8: *In Him we have redemption through His blood, the forgiveness of our trespasses, according to the riches of His grace, which He lavished on us. In all wisdom and insight … .*

You have continual, confident access into your King's presence:

Hebrews 4:14–16: *Therefore, since we have a great high priest who has passed through the heavens, Yeshua the Son of God, let us hold fast our confession. For we do not have a high priest who cannot sympathize with our weaknesses, but One who has been tempted in all things as we are, yet without sin. Therefore let us draw near with confidence to the throne of grace, so that we may receive mercy and find grace to help in time of need.*

Yeshua is the Living Word and you have the mind of Messiah your King:

1 Corinthians 2:16: *For who has known the mind of the Lord, that he will instruct Him? But we have the mind of Messiah.*

Yeshua is your Prince of Peace—Sar Shalom:

Isaiah 9:6 (definition added): *For a child will be born to us, a son will be given to us; and the government will rest on His shoulders; and His name will be called Wonderful Counselor, Mighty God, Eternal Father, Prince of Peace— Sar Shalom.*

John 16:33: *These things I have spoken to you, so that in Me you may have peace. In the world you have tribulation, but take courage; I have overcome the world.*

This is by no means an exhaustive list. It is just a glimpse to encourage you to see how Yeshua is greater than Solomon in every aspect. Yeshua, the Messiah of Israel, is your eternal King of kings and Lord of lords.

Bathsheba's Name Is Fulfilled in God's Promises to Her

Bathsheba's name means "Daughter of an oath" (*sheva*— to swear). As a forgiven daughter of the God of Israel, she experienced God's faithfulness and fulfillment in her life. Even though her first husband was killed in battle by David's command and her first son died at seven days old, God gave her Solomon. She was a woman of trustworthiness and influence as the queen mother of Israel. When you meet her in Heaven, what will be your first question for her?

One Last Word

Thank you for joining me on this journey! We began in Genesis to discover how God used women to accomplish His redemptive program for the world. In Genesis, the first promise of the coming Messiah through "her seed" encouraged our hearts. Then we met the Matriarchs of Israel, including Sarah, Rebekah, Leah, and Rachel. They were women in many ways just like you and me. We saw how God healed these ordinary women with His kindness and supernatural power. What made them unique is that they were chosen for God's purposes in His plan of redemption for Israel during the formation of His nation. That nation would go on to bless the world through their sons, and their grandsons, and their grandsons—culminating in the coming of Yeshua the Messiah.

We also met Miram, who was an important part of God's redemption of His people out of Egypt. Then Abigail stepped in to strategically prevent David from ruining his reputation as the anointed one while he was still on the run from King Saul.

Because God's plan of redemption climaxed in the coming of Yeshua the Messiah to accomplish our redemption, we also studied the lives of Tamar, Rahab, Ruth, and Bathsheba. I love to call these women God's "genealogy of grace," since they are specifically noted in the genealogy of Yeshua in Matthew chapter one. In 2018, I wrote a book entitled *Compassion and Redemption- Celebrating the Women in Messiah's Royal Line* and some of those studies I have incorporated into this book as they related directly to His genealogy of grace.

My prayer is that, like me, you are totally overwhelmed by God's love for you as a woman. Why does He use ordinary women like us? Because He is an extraordinary God who chooses to love us and pour out His lavish grace into our lives through our Beloved Messiah Yeshua.

And please be aware that there will be another book, *Messiah: The Healer of Women, Volume Two* to explore Yeshua's earthly ministry to women from the Gospel accounts!

About the Author

During my college years, as a very young believer, I was discipled by Arnold Fruchtenbaum. He a Jewish believer in Yeshua who founded Ariel Ministries. By God's grace, Arnold saw ministry potential in me—even though I was very immature and untaught in the Scriptures. He encouraged me in all aspects of the faith, including believing God to provide for my school bill as I worked my way through college, and imparting an understanding and love for the Jewish people. To help me grow in that understanding, he recommended that I write my papers for English and History on various aspects of Jewish life, especially the Holocaust. I became involved in Arnold's prayer group for Israel, and the Lord put a burden on my heart to reach out to Jewish people.

God gave me wonderful places for ministry during my college years. I spent four summers ministering in Brooklyn, New York, teaching Jewish children about the Messiah. For the rest of each summer I served as a camp counselor at Camp Sar Shalom for Jewish teens.

After graduating from Cedarville University with a degree in teaching, I knew that the Lord was calling me into Jewish ministry. For a short time, I taught in public school to pay off my college loans; then, with great joy and anticipation I moved to New York City, where I studied under Moishe Rosen, who worked for Chosen People Ministries and who would go on to found Jews for Jesus.

In New York City, I immersed myself in Jewish culture, learned the Hebrew language, and soaked up Israeli music. I began a small women's Bible study that met Friday evenings on the Upper West Side. After three years of ministry in the city, I had the opportunity to move to Jerusalem. There I studied at Hebrew University and attended an *ulpan,* which is an immersive Hebrew language program. That year in Israel turned out to be not merely a time to study but a time to minister. After that life-changing year in Israel, I returned to New York City for another year before the Lord led me to California to help start Jews for Jesus. I was a part of the newly formed musical outreach team called The Liberated Wailing Wall. It was there I met a new believer named Sam Nadler. The Lord brought us together in love and in ministry.

The first few years of our married lives we were on the road, crisscrossing the USA, doing concerts for both evangelistic outreach and deputation. When our touring days ended, Sam and I moved to New York City to open the New York branch of Jews for Jesus. I jumped right in, discipling women both individually and in small groups. Sam and I became increasingly convinced that discipling needed to be done in the context of a congregational community. In 1979, Sam accepted the position of Northeast Regional Director of Chosen People Ministries (CPM). There, together with the New York area staff, we started Messianic congregations in Westchester, Long Island, Connecticut, and New Jersey. We saw a number of people not only make decisions for the Lord but also be discipled and grow in their faith.

In 1989, we moved our two sons, Josh and Matt, to Charlotte, NC, where Sam led the ministry of CPM in their new headquarters for the next seven years. These were fruitful years as we saw the Lord open the doors to reach Russian Jews in the former Soviet Union. During these years, we helped plant congregations in the cities of Kiev, Ukraine and Berlin, Germany, to name a few. As Sam mentored and coached these new congregational leaders, I had the privilege of mentoring several of the leader's wives and also teaching Scriptures studies overseas.

Then, in 1997, Sam and I founded Word of Messiah Ministries to concentrate on planting and strengthening Messianic congregations by developing practical discipleship materials and implementing proven programs. I still consider the opportunity to disciple women and develop teaching materials a special calling of God and am thankful for ongoing opportunities to see the lives of women transformed by the Word of God.

We are very thankful for our sons who are married to wonderful women, and for our two grandsons who bring us much joy! In June of 2023, Sam and I celebrated our fiftieth wedding anniversary—our year of Jubilee to the praise of Yeshua's glory.

By His Grace,

Miriam

Listed here are the books I've written:

- *Compassion and Redemption: Celebrating the Women in Messiah's Royal Line*
- *Honoring God with My Life: Issues of Sense and Sensibility*
- *Eternally Desired: Living Out Your Value in Yeshua*
- *Abiding in Messiah: Bearing Fruit in Yeshua*

For more information, go to WordofMessiah.org. There you can read about the books and resources Sam and I have to offer.

Bibliography

- *Messianic Marriage Matters, Restored to Our Original Design*, Sam Nadler, Word of Messiah 2019
- *Honoring God with My Life*, Miriam Nadler, Word of Messiah, 2012
- *Compassion and Redemption,* Miriam Nadler, Word of Messiah 2018
- *Gleanings in Genesis*, Pink A. W., Moody Press 1976
- *Abiding in Messiah*, Miriam Nadler, Word of Messiah 2013
- *Eternally Desired*, Miriam Nadler, Word of Messiah 2014
- *Bible Exposition Commentary (BE Series) - Old Testament* - The Bible Exposition Commentary – History.
- *The Life and Times of Jesus the Messiah*, Edersheim, Alferd, MacDonald Publishing Company
- *Exposition of Isaiah,* Leupold, H.C., Baker Book House, 1981
- *Exploring Genesis,* John Phillips Commentary, Moody Press 1981

Made in the USA
Las Vegas, NV
18 December 2023

83000615R00184